Strategic Marketing

Strategic Marketing

In the Customer Driven Organization

Frank Bradley
University College Dublin

WILEY

Other Wiley Editorial Offices

John Wiley & Sons Inc., 111 River Street, Hoboken, NJ 07030, USA

Jossey-Bass, 989 Market Street, San Francisco, CA 94103-1741, USA

Wiley-VCH Verlag GmbH, Boschstr. 12, D-69469 Weinheim, Germany

John Wiley & Sons Australia Ltd, 33 Park Road, Milton, Queensland 4064, Australia

John Wiley & Sons (Asia) Pte Ltd, 2 Clementi Loop #02-01, Jin Xing Distripark, Singapore 129809

John Wiley & Sons Canada Ltd, 22 Worcester Road, Etobicoke, Ontario, Canada M9W 1L1

Wiley also publishes its books in a variety of electronic formats. Some content that appears in print may not be available in electronic books.

Library of Congress Cataloging-in-Publication Data

Bradley, Frank, 1942–
    Strategic marketing : in the customer driven organization / Frank Bradley.
        p. cm.
    Includes bibliographical references and index.
    ISBN 0-470-84985-1 (alk. paper)
     1. Marketing – Management. 2. Marketing. I. Title.

    HF5415.15.B66 2003
    658.8 – dc21   2003041121

British Library Cataloguing in Publication Data

A catalogue record for this book is available from the British Library

ISBN 0-470-84985-1

Typeset in 10/13pt Stone Serif by Laserwords Private Limited, Chennai, India
Printed and bound in Great Britain by Antony Rowe Ltd, Chippenham, Wiltshire
This book is printed on acid-free paper responsibly manufactured from sustainable forestry in which at least two trees are planted for each one used for paper production.

This book is dedicated to my wife and best friend, Breda, with love

Contents

Preface

Marketing is a philosophy that leads to the process by which organizations, groups and individuals obtain what they need and want by identifying and selecting value, providing it, communicating it and delivering it to others. Marketing is strategically concerned with the direction and scope of the long-term activities performed by the organization in obtaining competitive advantage to satisfy customers while meeting shareholder expectations.

This book places the focus on customers and how organizations identify and select the value desired by them; how to provide, communicate and deliver it. The focus is on providing satisfaction profitably. The book adopts an integrated strategic view within a customer orientation. In many organizations strategic thinking is reserved for the corporate level whereas the reality forces organizations to integrate decisions across hierarchies and functions. It is necessary to examine strategic marketing at the corporate level which is implemented at the product or brand level. Strategic marketing is, therefore, both a business philosophy and a process of implementation. Practitioners and academic writers frequently focus on the operational aspects of marketing – as a tool-kit – providing guidance on how to prepare sales presentations, brochures or a list of prospects for a direct marketing drive, instead of focusing on the real needs of customers and on providing value in an integrated way.

In contrast we adopt a customer focus in this book rather than the traditional mechanistic approach to marketing based on the four Ps which places an emphasis on the operational and functional role of marketing. A customer orientation allows for a wider scope for marketing to include all actors in the business system – customers, competitors, suppliers and partners in the provision, communication and delivery of value. The book is informed by the resource-based view of the organization in the context of obtaining a competitive advantage within a value-added business system. In doing so, exchanges occur and long-term relationships are developed that enhance customer value – the responsibility of everybody in the organization.

One of the distinctive features of the book is that it addresses strategic marketing perspectives for readers in the English-speaking world outside the United States. Furthermore, a global perspective is required, especially for readers for whom traditional marketing may still be a controversial management technique. In new emerging markets such as Eastern Europe, among other new entrants to the European Union and in many countries in the Far East, marketing processes and applications are highly culture bound. In these circumstances the role of marketing is challenged and strategic marketing needs to be explained as an important determinant of value creation leading to a higher standard of living.

The target audiences for this book are people who hold or expect to hold senior management positions in organizations. The book is relatively short but it contains the essentials for a complete understanding of strategic marketing. As marketing is a philosophy in the organization and central to its success, everybody in the organization needs marketing. I have noticed over the years that the needs of MBA students and managers on executive programmes have converged on the same strategic marketing issues. This book provides an integrated perspective on strategic marketing in the organization; unnecessary details have been avoided to ensure that busy students and managers obtain the guidance necessary to think strategically about marketing.

The book has benefited enormously from what I have learnt from my consulting work over many years. In particular I am indebted to the managers of the following organizations who helped in many ways:

- Alltech Inc
- Bord Failte – Irish Tourist Board
- Guinness Ireland
- Tipperary Cereals
- Electricity Supply Board
- Avonmore Foods
- Aer Rianta – Irish Airports Authority
- Chamber of Commerce, Valencia
- Petronas

- Siemens Ireland
- R. & A. Bailey and Co. Limited
- Enterprise Ireland
- ING Bank
- Greencore
- ICC Bank
- KPMG
- Ford Europe

The book is organized in 14 chapters. In the first, the scope of strategic marketing is outlined and discussed in its various dimensions. In Part I (Chapters 2–6) issues related to the identification and selection of customer value are examined. How this value is to be provided to customers is examined in Part II (Chapters 7–9), how it is to be communicated to them, in Part III (Chapters 10 and 11), and how it is to be delivered, in Part IV (Chapters 12 and 13). The final chapter examines the need to align marketing performance with marketing strategy.

I am grateful to Gao Yuhui who provided research assistance and helped to prepare the figures used in the book. Her dedication and continuous good humour are much appreciated. Thanks are also due to Roisín O'Loughlin who helped to prepare part of the manuscript. I also very much appreciate the assistance of Margaret O'Boyle, a practising manager and MBA graduate, who kindly reviewed the entire manuscript and provided many helpful suggestions. A very special thanks are due to Professor Lui Hon-Kwong, Lingnan University Hong Kong, Professor Douglas West, Westminster Business School, London, and Mr David Tonks, Lancaster University, who reviewed early drafts of the material and provided valuable guidance. I am most grateful to the graduate students and managers I have taught at the Smurfit Graduate School of Business, University College Dublin, ESC Paris, HEC Paris, University of Venice, University of Santiago de Compostella, University of Murcia, University des Saarlandes, Hong Kong Polytechnic University, and the University of California at Berkeley.

My deepest appreciation goes to my wife Breda and our children Jonathan, Siobhán, Simon and Maedhbh who provided me with the support, encouragement and inspiration to complete this book.

Frank Bradley
Michael Smurfit Graduate School of Business
University College Dublin
September 2002

About the author

Frank Bradley is the R.&A. Bailey Professor of International Marketing and Head, Department of Marketing at the Michael Smurfit Graduate School of Business and the Quinn School of Business at University College Dublin, where he teaches Marketing and International Marketing. Professor Bradley's research interests lie in the area of strategic marketing with special reference to international market entry and the impact of culture and values on the competitive positioning of the firm in international markets. He has also applied his marketing and entrepreneurial knowledge to programmes within the university by designing and implementing the very popular BComm (International) Degree and he was responsible for negotiating and implementing international exchange contracts with universities located in many countries. More recently he established a successful university joint venture in Spain. His management and marketing skills have also been applied during the periods he served as Director of the Master of Business Studies and the Master of Business Administration programmes at the university. He also served as Dean of the Faculty of Commerce during expansionary phases of the Quinn and Smurfit Schools of Business.

He has also served in an advisory capacity to a number of national and multinational companies including Alltech Inc., R.&A. Bailey and Company Ltd, Siemens Ireland Ltd, Guinness Ireland Ltd, Greencore, Flahavan, Tipperary Cereals, Bord Failte – the Irish Tourist Board, Enterprise Ireland, FAS – Irish Training Board.

The fourth edition of his book *International Marketing Strategy* (Prentice Hall 2002) has been adopted as a textbook by many universities and business schools in Europe, the Far East, Australia and the US. His book *Marketing Management: Providing, Communicating and Delivering Value* (Prentice Hall 1995), has also been adopted as a textbook in Australia, the UK, Ireland, Hong Kong, Singapore, Sweden, and the Netherlands. Frank Bradley's research has also been published widely in journals such as: *Journal of International Marketing, Journal of Business Research* (US), *Industrial Marketing Management* (US), *Management Decision* (UK), *Research in Marketing* (US), *Irish Marketing Review*, and the *Irish Journal of Management*.

Chapter 1

Scope of strategic marketing

Marketing is a philosophy that leads to the process by which organizations, groups and individuals obtain what they need and want by identifying value, providing it, communicating it and delivering it to others. The core concepts of marketing are customers' needs, wants and values; products, exchange, communications and relationships. Marketing is strategically concerned with the direction and scope of the long-term activities performed by the organization to obtain a competitive advantage. The organization applies its resources within a changing environment to satisfy customer needs while meeting stakeholder expectations.

Implied in this view of strategic marketing is the requirement to develop a strategy to cope with competitors, identify market opportunities, develop and commercialize new products and services, allocate resources among marketing activities and design an appropriate organizational structure to ensure the performance desired is achieved.

There is no unique strategy that succeeds for all organizations in all situations. In thinking strategically about marketing many factors must be considered: the extent of product diversity and geographic coverage in the organization; the number of market segments served, marketing channels used, the role of branding, the level of marketing effort, and the role of quality. It is also necessary to consider the organization's approach to new product development, in particular, its position as a technology leader or follower, the extent of innovation, the organization's cost position and pricing policy, and its relationship to customers, competitors, suppliers and partners.

The challenge of strategic marketing is, therefore, to manage marketing complexity, customer and stakeholder expectations and to reconcile the influences of a changing environment in the context of a set of resource capabilities. It is also necessary to create strategic opportunities and to manage the concomitant changes required within the organization. In this world of marketing, organizations seek to maximize returns to shareholders by creating a competitive advantage in identifying, providing, communicating and delivering value to customers, broadly defined, and in the process developing long-term mutually satisfying relationships with those customers.

Understanding marketing – antecedents

The fundamental management issue in marketing is to determine a superior value position from the customer's perspective and to ensure that, by developing a consensus throughout the organization, value is provided, communicated and delivered to the customer group. The core concepts of marketing are needs, wants and demands which directly affect the identification and selection of relevant customer values reflected in products, services and ideas that the organization provides, communicates and delivers in the form of exchanges to build long-term satisfactory relationships with customers (Figure 1.1). Needs are the internal influences which prompt behaviour, e.g. biological needs refer to a person's requirements for food, air and shelter while social needs refer to issues such as security, personal gratification and prestige. Wants are culture bound and may be satisfied using a number of technologies, e.g. a teenager may listen to music on one of the rock radio stations or on DVDs played on a computer. Demand refers to the ability and willingness of a customer to buy a particular product or service which satisfies the want and the more latent need. A student may want a BMW but can afford only a bicycle. The organization may set out from the start or be established with those objectives or, more likely, as a result of trial and error and experience, the organization evolves into a position over time of being the desired source of value. The core concepts of marketing may be decomposed into a number of basic components:

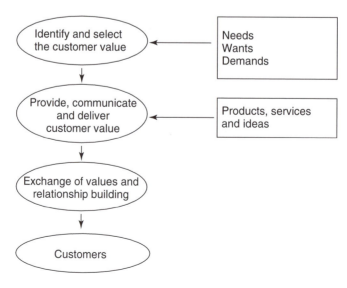

Figure [1.1]   Core concepts of marketing

- Provide the value
  - product planning
  - packaging
  - branding
  - pricing
- Communicate the value
  - advertising
  - personal selling
  - direct marketing
  - sales promotion
- Deliver the value
  - channels of distribution
  - logistics
  - servicing

Successful organizations recognize value positions and ensure that learning occurs throughout the organization as a result of discovering the value position. Choosing the value position is one of the most important strategic decisions facing the organization. Once chosen, it the task of management to ensure that everyone in the organization directly contributes to delivering the chosen value.

Marketing and sales orientations

A sales emphasis is very different from a marketing emphasis in the organization. Four important areas where they differ separate the two approaches: organizational objectives, orientation, attitudes to segmentation and the perceived task facing marketing in the organization (Kotler 2002). A sales emphasis results in objectives which are aimed at increasing current sales to meet quotas and to derive commissions and bonuses. Little discrimination is made between products or customers in terms of profits unless these differences are written into the incentives. In contrast, objectives with a marketing emphasis take profits into account. Marketing objectives include an explicit consideration of product mixes, customer groups and different communications and ways of reaching the market in attempting to achieve profitable sales and market shares at acceptable levels of risk.

The selling and marketing orientations produce very different emphases in the organization. A selling orientation predominantly reflects a production approach whereby something is produced and the task is to sell it thereby

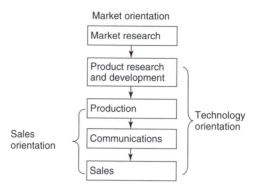

Figure [1.2]   Alternative business orientation of the firm

increasing consumption (Figure 1.2). A focus on sales means a focus on individual customers rather than market segments or market classes. Such organizations are very knowledgeable about individual accounts and the variables which influence specific sales transactions but they are less interested in developing an approach to an entire segment of similar needs and wants in the market. A technology orientation is similar to a sales orientation except that the organization also engages in product research and development (Figure 1.2).

A marketing approach attempts to determine ways of offering superior value to the more profitable segments without damaging individual customer relationships. A marketing approach reflects an integrated approach based on research and feedback. Customer needs are first evaluated through market research, an integrated marketing effort is developed to satisfy customers so that the organization achieves its goals, especially those affecting shareholders. This is a customer orientation and contrasts very bluntly with a narrow competitor orientation based on sales in which the organization by capitalizing on the weaknesses of vulnerable competitors or by removing its own competitive weaknesses attempts to obtain high sales and long-run profits (Figure 1.3).

In many situations marketing evaluates itself and presents its case to senior managers of the organization based on sales, efficiency or, worst of all, internal awards, not marketplace outcomes or financial success. Senior managers deal with issues that involve the allocation of resources and how such allocation affects the return on investment. These hurdle rates are calculated differently from one organization to another but they need to be understood for a marketing programme to be effective and accepted. In a business world dominated by financial considerations the ability of the organization to produce award-winning marketing programmes or attractive but fuzzy images in TV commercials is not of much value. Traditional marketing thinking assumes that the organization is in complete control of the marketplace, whereas interaction and market integration are required.

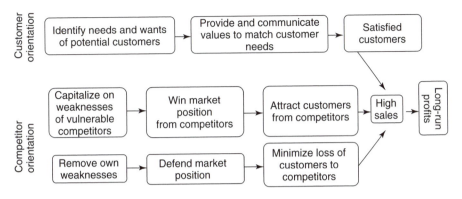

Source : Adapted from Alfred, R. Oxfenfeldt and William L. Moore (1983): 'Customer or competitor: which guideline for marketing?' in Stewart Henderson Britt, Harper W. Boyd, Robert T. Davis and Jean Claude Larreche (eds), *Marketing Management and Administrative Action*, New York: McGraw-Hill.

Figure [1.3]   Customer and competitor orientation in the organization

Strategic marketing concept

Marketing has been defined as the management function responsible for identifying, anticipating and satisfying customer requirements profitably. Marketing is, therefore, both a philosophy and a set of techniques which address such matters as research, product design and development, pricing, packaging, sales and sales promotion, advertising, public relations, distribution and after-sales service. These activities define the broad scope of marketing and their balanced integration within a marketing plan is known as the marketing mix. A modification of a definition of marketing by Doyle (2000) suggests that marketing is the management process that seeks to maximize returns to shareholders by creating a competitive advantage in providing, communicating and delivering value to customers thereby developing a long-term relationship with them. This definition clearly defines the objectives of marketing and how its performance should be evaluated. The specific contribution of marketing in the organization lies in the formulation of strategies to choose the right customer, build relationships of trust with them and create a competitive advantage (Doyle 2000, p. 235). A marketing strategy consists of an internally integrated but externally focused set of choices about how the organization addresses its customers in the context of a competitive environment. A strategy has five elements: it deals with where the organization plans to be active; how it will get there; how it will succeed in the marketplace; what the speed and sequence of moves will be; and how the organization will obtain profits (Hambrick and Fredrickson 2001, p. 50).

The organization must identify the problem that its customers use its products and services to solve. It is also necessary to identify the benefits customers seek from using a product or service available in the market. A market consists of all the potential customers who share a particular need or want who might be willing and able to engage in exchange to satisfy that need or want.

A marketing orientation helps to define the organization's business. Marketing is concerned with problem solving and customer benefits. The organization must be able to answer the following questions:

- What is the problem customers are trying to solve?

- What benefits do customers seek?

- How well does the organization's product solve this problem and provide these benefits?

A statement that the organization is in the movie business is not very useful. An organization is not in the movie business because that says nothing about customer needs. Some movie organizations assumed they were in the movie business when the entertainment business left them behind!

Marketing is a philosophy that encourages the organization to ensure that the needs and wants of customers in selected target markets are reflected in all its actions and activities while recognizing constraints imposed by society. This marketing concept first received formal recognition in 1952 by one of its leading exponents, the General Electric Organization – the marketing concept:

> ... introduces the marketing man at the beginning rather than at the end of the production cycle and integrates marketing into each phase of business. ... marketing establishes ... for the engineer, the design and manufacturing man, what the customer wants in a given product, what price he is willing to pay and where and when it will be wanted. Marketing will have authority in product planning, production scheduling and inventory control, as well as in sales distribution or servicing of the product (General Electric Organization, New York, 1952, *Annual Report*, p. 21).

Three aspects of this statement are interesting: the customer orientation; the profit orientation; and the emphasis on integrated organization effort. These three aspects are fundamental to the adoption of the marketing concept.

Marketing means, therefore, being oriented to the needs of customers rather than emphasizing what is convenient to produce. Effective marketing requires that the organization analyses the needs that its products are supposed to satisfy. Customers do not buy 'coffee'; they buy a warm stimulating drink or a unique café experience if it is Starbucks. Likewise, customers do not buy sisal; they buy a material to make baling rope to tie things together or fibre to serve as backing for a floor covering.

The organization should realize that many alternative products may satisfy the needs identified; there usually are many substitutes – for coffee include tea, cocoa, alcohol or soft drinks and for sisal include polypropylene fibre or polythene sheeting.

The real lesson of a marketing philosophy is that better performing organizations recognize the basic and enduring nature of the customer needs they are attempting to satisfy. It is the technology of want satisfaction which is transitory (Anderson 1982, p. 23). The products and services used to satisfy customer needs and wants change constantly.

The adoption of a marketing philosophy confers specific authority and responsibility within the organization in regard to the provision, communication and delivery of customer value. Marketing is concerned with all parts of the organization; it is more than a set of tools, it is an orientation which pervades the thinking of the organization as a whole.

Internal marketing

In addition to equipping the organization to cope with the outside world of customers and competitors, it is also necessary to train and motivate all staff within the organization to provide the appropriate level of service to customers. Internal marketing is very closely related to human resource management and the way in which the organization develops its own distinctive corporate culture. Internal marketing is the task of successfully hiring, training and motivating able employees who want to serve customers well. It is obvious that it is necessary to determine the organization's internal culture before venturing forth to serve customers in the external world. This internal market must be motivated to react in a certain desired way which is best described as marketing-like (Gronroos 1984, p. 3).

Internal marketing helps employees make a strong connection to the products and services sold by the organization. Without such a connection employees may unwittingly undermine expectations set by the organization's marketing communications. When people believe in what the organization does and stands for, they are motivated to work harder and their loyalty to the organization increases. According to Mitchell (2002), however, in most organizations internal marketing is done poorly, if at all, and few organizations understand the need to convince employees of the organization's mission and purpose; they take it for granted.

Since satisfying customers is central to the task of marketing, it is essential that everybody in the organization who deals with customers must be imbued with a sense of marketing which means internal marketing for some and external marketing for others. Customers exist, therefore, both within and outside the organization. By focusing on customers, in this way a different perspective of the organization is obtained. In traditional organizations the chief executive and senior manager appear at the top of the chart with sales and other front-office people at the bottom. In many such charts customers are not represented at all.

A contrary view, driven by a strong sense of marketing and especially internal marketing places the customer on top, the front-office people next, middle managers below that and finally senior managers (Figure 1.4). As the front-office people meet and serve customers, they should receive a lot of

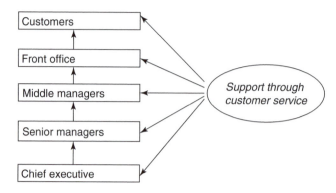

Figure [1.4]   Internal marketing and customer orientation

attention within the organization. Middle managers exist, in this view of the world, to support the layer of middle level operators. It is important to note that everybody is somebody else's customer. That is why the customer is placed on top and is so important to the survival and growth of the organization.

Responsibility in marketing

Marketing should distinguish between the individual customer's short-term needs and wants and the longer-term welfare of society. For example, large cars greatly contribute to the pollution and traffic congestion of cities and cigarettes cause major health problems, even death, for smokers and for those who inhale the smoke. It is necessary, therefore, to integrate profitability requirements with health, ecological and environmental constraints.

For many years writers on marketing have been at pains to point out that the principal function of marketing 'is not so much to be skilful in making the customer do what suits the interests of the business as to be skilled in conceiving and then making the business do what suits the interests of the customers' (McKittrick 1957, p. 78). In a present-day context, to be skilful in conceiving the real interests of customers, the organization must balance environmental considerations against profitability requirements; society's welfare against individual needs; and the long-term welfare of customers against their short-term wants. For these reasons, therefore, we must broaden the marketing concept to include wider dimensions.

The two major assumptions behind marketing are that consumers know what they want and are informed and highly rational in satisfying their wants, and that customer sovereignty prevails (Dickinson *et al.* 1986, p. 9). These authors argue that if the organization were right in assuming that customers know what they want, then the key issue would be to create the product, create awareness of it and make it available at an acceptable price.

The fact is that both goals and corresponding wants can be unstable, with wants being only vaguely articulated as consumers remain open to persuasion as to what might better serve their interests (Dickinson *et al.* 1986, p. 20). This is especially true in high technology markets where new product development is frequently technology driven.

The marketing concept also assumes that the customer is sovereign, i.e. organizations follow the dictates of the market in regard to exactly what should be provided. But customers do not always know exactly what they want and they may be unsure of their trade-offs among product or service attributes. Many organizations see no inconsistency in referring to marketing as the basis for management while at the same time accepting that customer perceptions are important and can be influenced.

Social and ethical constraints

Social responsibility in marketing means accounting for the relationship between marketing and the environment in which it operates. Social responsibility refers to the obligation of the organization, beyond the requirements of the law, to take into practical consideration in its decision making the social consequences of its decisions and actions, as well as profits. This view of social responsibility implies constraints on the organization more rigorous than arise if the organization attempted to fulfil its economic and legal requirements only. The reasons for a greater interest in social responsibility stem from the greater involvement of business with government and the influence of myriad stakeholders in the organization: shareholders, institutional investors, employees and other regulatory and environmental bodies. The more important dimensions of the environment which relate to an appropriate application of marketing are the social and moral environment, the business environment and the physical environment.

In recent years ethical issues, social and moral standards which are acceptable in a society, have become very important in marketing. Trust is a related issue which is an essential ingredient in building long-term relationships between organizations and their customers. Trust is well placed where ethical standards are upheld. It is misplaced where ethical standards are ignored or flaunted. Both trust and ethics are highly dependent on culture and vary according to the culture and background of customers. Organizations operating in many cultures have greater difficulty in coping with a heterogeneous set of customers, drawing on disparate cultures for their ethical standards.

One example will illustrate the issue. In a questionable practice, with strong implications for marketing responsibility, advertising agencies in the US have begun to assist pharmaceutical organizations to recruit patients for clinical trials. According to Thomas Harrison, the Omnicom Group, Inc., parent organization of advertising agency BBDO Worldwide, BBD Worldwide and TBWA Worldwide:

What you're seeing is an emergency convergence between clinical development and the commercialization of drugs. The ultimate goal is to make drug development more efficient. What we want to try to do is look at the molecule in the test tube as a brand. A lot of people don't think a brand is a brand until it has FDA (Food and Drug Administration) approval. But we are asking, 'What is the maximum commercial potential of this molecule? What will it be when it grows up? What is the message? How should the clinical trial be developed?' (*The Wall Street Journal Europe*, Friday, Saturday, Sunday 15–17 March 2002, p. A 10).

There is potentially a real ethical clash of science and business in such a development.

There are clear benefits for the advertising agency as becoming involved early in the process can be lucrative and can greatly increase the chance of acquiring the account if the product is ultimately launched. For the pharmaceutical organization the involvement of the agency can shorten the time and costly process of getting a drug from development to market. In these circumstances there could be a temptation for the agency to modify the test results or at least present them in such a way as to favour the pharmaceutical organization in anticipation of eventually being retained to produce the advertising campaign and thus obtain high advertising fees. This is a conflict of interest – a potentially controversial practice that directly raises ethical questions for marketing.

Environmental responsibility in marketing

The view that marketing has a special responsibility when discussing the natural environment is also well developed. By promoting product manufacture and usage, the organization may be encouraging resource depletion, pollution or other environmental deterioration. Most organizations believe that it is not sufficient to make profits and generate employment while ignoring an obligation to society regarding the preservation of the natural environment even though their behaviour is within the law. Some organizations, however, continue to ignore this implied obligation claiming that their behaviour is not illegal when they dump chemicals in watercourses, over-package products, or damage the atmosphere. Such organizations often cite a concern for the feasibility rather than the propriety of believing that they should not be expected to take action to protect the environment if their competitive position were to be jeopardized. In a general way, social responsibility is an investment in future profits which should be made even at the expense of short-term profits.

Providing customer value in marketing networks

Superior market positions depend on the organization's customer base, relations with suppliers and partners, relations with customers (e.g. brand equity), facilities and systems, and the organization's own endowment of technology and complementary property rights. These are the organization's assets or resource endowments which it has accumulated over time.

In addition, the organization possesses certain capabilities, the glue that binds the organization's assets together and enables them to be used to advantage (Day 1994, p. 38). Capabilities are so deeply embedded in the organization's routines and practices that they cannot easily be traded or imitated (Dierickx and Cool 1989). The organization's competitive advantages are derived, therefore, from the nature of the its products, markets, technological orientation, resources and knowledge.

Providing customer value means delivering on a whole range of promises to the customer. Products and services that customers perceive have a superior value compared to those of competitors are demanded while others are not, hence, the importance of the concept of 'value-added' defined as the component of customer value provided by an individual organization within the overall business system. Value is derived from the business system in which the organization operates.

Each organization leverages other participants in the system – customers, suppliers and particularly others who complement the organization in what it provides – in creating that value (Figure 1.5). The value-added chain runs from suppliers through the organization forward to the customer aided by partners in the context of a competitive environment influenced by economic, political, legal and cultural factors. At each stage of the value chain there exists an opportunity to contribute positively to the organization's competitive strategy, by performing some activity or process in a way that is better than one's competitors, and so providing some uniqueness or advantage. If an organization attains such a competitive advantage which is sustainable,

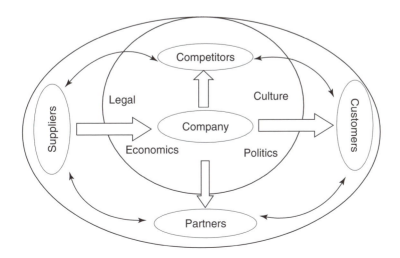

Figure [1.5]   Marketing system

defensible, profitable and valued by the market, then it may earn high rates of return even though the industry structure may be unfavourable and the average profitability of the industry modest.

A long-term marketing orientation draws together suppliers, customers, competitors and partners in the business system to create value in the marketing system. It is the business system as a whole that creates value. The marketing system consists of five major participant groups:

- customers

- competitors

- partners

- suppliers

- the organization itself.

Viewing the value in the business system as the result of a network of important relationships highlights two important factors. First, decisions made by one organization affect and are affected by decisions by other organizations. Second, organizations often make decisions that are normally associated with those of other actors in the system. Thus, the organization makes important decisions which affect suppliers, just as suppliers make important decisions which are normally thought of as in the purview of the organization. Because so many decisions are part of a network in which a decision in one organization directly or indirectly influences decisions in other organizations, major decisions must be consistent with the goals of the participants in the network and their products. Herein lies the importance of the contribution of the leading organization – the organization making the key contribution to the establishment and growth of the business system (Moore 1993). This key contributor of value or the business system leader emerges in the early stage of the evolution of the business system to begin the process of continuous improvement which draws the entire business system towards an improved future.

A fundamental service provided by the business system leader is to encourage and persuade other organizations in the business system to complete the full value mix for customers by attracting 'follower' or 'imitator' organizations and thereby prevent them from developing other emerging business systems. The multitude of decisions in the business system must complement each other to maximize their overall positive impact on value. Within this framework the organization must decide its overall product–market business system strategy which has two elements – decisions on product–market segments and decisions on positions to adopt within the business system itself

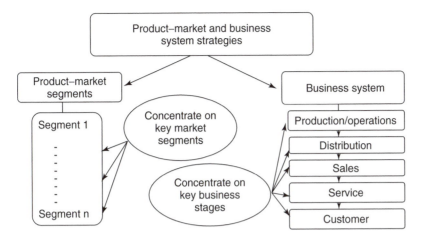

Figure [1.6]   Generic product–market and business system strategies

(Figure 1.6). The organization's resource base enables it to decide the appropriate positions on which to focus in the business system. Decisions regarding the relevant product–market segment to serve are discussed in Chapter 3 while decisions regarding the appropriate position in the business system to select are examined in Chapter 6.

Sources of marketing advantage

Sources of marketing advantage are reputation, brands, tangible assets, knowledge, customer service and people. To be worthwhile the marketing advantage must be sustainable. It must, therefore, be tangible, measurable and capable of providing competitive protection for some time. An illusory marketing advantage is one that is easily matched by competitors. The organization's marketing advantage depends on how well it chooses its strategy:

- Concentrating on selected market segments.

- Offering differentiated products.

- Using alternative distribution channels.

- Using different manufacturing processes to allow higher quality at lower prices.

Superior skills and resources, taken together, represent the ability of the organization to do more and better than its competitors. Superior skills are the distinctive capabilities of people in the organization that distinguish them from people in competing organizations, e.g. superior marketing skills that lead to fewer product failures in the marketplace or superior selling and distribution skills which lead to fewer returns of unwanted products and improved customer satisfaction.

Organizational resources and marketing capabilities

Organizations are endowed with different amounts and types of resources and capabilities, which allow them to compete in different ways. Organizations which are better endowed have lower average costs than competitors and can provide products and services at lower cost or provide greater customer value. These resources are difficult to transfer among organizations because of transaction costs and because the assets may contain tacit knowledge (Teece *et al.* 1996, p. 15). Such resources and core capabilities of the organization, particularly those which involve collective learning and are knowledge based, are enhanced as they are applied (Prahalad and Hamel 1990). Resources and capabilities which are distinctive and superior, relative to those of rivals, may become the basis for competitive advantage if they are matched appropriately to market opportunities (Thompson Jr. and Strickland 1996, pp. 94–5). These resources may, therefore, provide both the basis and direction for the growth of the organization itself, i.e. there may be a natural trajectory embedded in a organization's knowledge base (Peteraf 1993, p. 182). Hence, the importance of studying the organization itself when attempting to predict its likely performance.

Resources and capabilities determine the organization's long-run strategy and are the primary source of profit. In an environment which is changing rapidly and where consumer tastes and preferences are volatile and myriad, a definition of the business in terms of what the organization is capable of doing may offer a more durable basis for strategy than a traditional definition, based solely on needs and wants of consumers. Defining markets too broadly is of little help to the organization that cannot easily develop the capabilities to serve such a broad market.

The organization's ability to earn profits depends on two factors:

- the success of the organization in establishing competitive advantage over rivals; and
- the attractiveness of the industry in which the organization competes.

As was seen above, the two sources of competitive advantage are:

- the ability of the organization to reduce costs; and
- its ability to differentiate itself in ways that are important to customers.

The ability to establish a cost advantage requires the possession of scale-efficient plants, access to low-cost raw materials or labour and superior

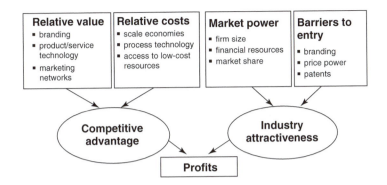

Figure [1.7]   Influence of resources on the profitability of the firm

process technology. Differentiation advantages derive from brand reputation, proprietary and patented technology and an extensive marketing network covering distribution, sales and services.

The attractiveness of an industry depends on the power the organization can exert over customers, rivals and others in the business system, which derives from the existence of market entry barriers. Market entry barriers are based on brands, patents, price and the power of competitive retaliation. These are resources which are accumulated slowly over time and a new entrant can only obtain at disproportionate expense (Grant 1991, p. 115). Other sources of market power such as price-setting abilities depend on market share which is a consequence of cost efficiency, organization size and financial resources. Grant (1991) has integrated these ideas in a way which serves as a very convenient summary of this discussion (Figure 1.7).

Strategic marketing effectiveness

Marketing's role in strategic planning for the organization means identifying the optimal long-term positions that will ensure customer satisfaction and support. These optimal positions are determined largely by fundamental changes in demographic, economic, social and political factors (Anderson 1982, p. 24). Thus, strategic positioning is more likely to be guided by long-term demographic and socioeconomic research than by surveys of consumer attitudes, the hallmark of the market-driven organization.

Value in marketing is a combination of product or service quality, reasonable or acceptable prices and responsive service. It is noteworthy that marketing value combines high quality with acceptable prices. It is not low quality products at low prices or high quality at high prices. Value in marketing means delivering on a whole range of promises to the customer.

Marketing effectiveness is not necessarily revealed by current marketing performance. Good results and growing sales may be due to the organization being in the right place at the right time rather than having effective marketing management. This is frequently the situation during the entrepreneurial phase of an organization's growth and development. The innovator frequently has considerable discretion in the market. At this stage the driving force is entrepreneurship rather than marketing. With acceptance of the product or service in the market and with the rise in competition which normally accompanies the acceptance of a new product or service, performance becomes more marketing-dependent.

In a competitive environment, especially where customers have learned how to respond to various offerings, the situation changes. Improvements in marketing in the organization might improve results while another organization might have poor results in spite of excellent marketing planning. It depends on how well the organization matches its own resources against those of the competition to attract and hold the loyalty of customers.

The marketing effectiveness of the organization in serving customers in the face of existing and potential competition is reflected in the degree to which it exhibits five major attributes of a marketing orientation:

- demonstrated customer philosophy

- integrated marketing orientation

- possesses adequate marketing information

- adopts a strategic orientation

- experiences a high level of operational efficiency.

The performance of the organization on these individual attributes may be used to indicate which elements of effective marketing action need most attention. It should be recognized, however, that this evaluation provides general information only but has the merit of obtaining an approximate measure of the orientation of the organization.

Key marketing success factors

The organization attempts to convert skills and resources into superior market positions and thereby meet performance objectives. A knowledge of the key marketing success factors is essential to enable the organization to invest in markets and marketing to ensure performance objectives are attained. By identifying the key success factors the organization can identify ways of obtaining the greatest improvement in performance for the least expenditure. The key success factors of any business are the skills and resources which exert the highest degree of leverage on market positions and future performance. Having identified them, the organization attempts to selectively allocate resources towards these sources of leverage. The drivers of market position advantage are the high leverage skills and resources that contribute most to lowering costs to or creating value for customers.

Marketing focus on customers

Marketing means identifying values desired by customers, providing them in some way, communicating these values to customer groups and delivering the value. Customer values refer to those benefits focused on solving customer problems and not merely on the products and services themselves. The focus is on the customer and on solving problems faced by the customer.

This is an integrated longer-term view of marketing (Figure 1.8). Seeking value from the customer's perspective means building a long-term mutually profitable relationship with customers instead of trying to maximize profits on each transaction. An emphasis on relationships rather than individual transactions focuses on the customer as the profit centre, not the product. It also means that attracting new customers is an intermediate objective in the process of maintaining and cultivating an existing customer base. This interactive approach views marketing as a continuous relationship with customers in contrast to the more traditional and almost adversarial view which is short term and focused on immediate sales.

The first sale to a customer is often very difficult, costs a lot and results in little or no profit. With a strong continuing relationship the customer becomes more profitable. Such long-term relationships are established through the exchange of information, products, services and social contacts. In this way the organization–customer relationship is commercialized.

The fundamental issue is to understand the customer's perception of value and to determine a superior value position from this perspective and to ensure

Figure [1.8] Integrated marketing orientation

that, by developing a consensus throughout the organization, that value is provided and communicated to the customer group in selected markets. The role of marketing in the business system is:

- To understand the customer's perception of value – identify the value the organization expects to provide.

- To determine a superior value position for the organization – provide the value expected.

- To determine the appropriate positioning and brand strategy – communicate the value.

- To distribute and price the product/service – deliver the value to the customer.

References

Anderson, Paul F. (1982), 'Marketing, strategic planning and the theory of the firm', *Journal of Marketing*, **46** (Spring), 15–26.

Day, George (1994), 'The capabilities of market-driven organizations', *Journal of Marketing*, **58** (October), 37–52.

Dickinson, Roger, Herbst, Anthony and O'Shaughnessy, John (1986), 'Marketing concept and consumer orientation', *European Journal of Marketing*, **20** (10), 18–23.

Dierickx, I. and Cool, K. (1989), 'Asset stock accumulation and sustainability of competitive advantage', *Management Science*, **35**, 1504–11.

Doyle, Peter (2000), 'Valuing marketing's contribution', *European Management Journal*, **18** (3), 233–45.

Grant, Robert M. (1991), 'The resource-based theory of competitive advantage: implications for strategy formulation', *California Management Review*, Spring, 118.

Gronroos, Christian (1984), 'Internal marketing – theory and practice', in *The American Marketing Association 3rd Conference on Services Marketing, Services Marketing in a Changing Environment Vol. III*. Chicago: American Marketing Association.

Hambrick, Donald C. and Fredrickson, James W. (2001), 'Are you sure you have a strategy?', *Academy of Management Executive*, **15** (4), 48–59.

Kotler, Philip (2002), *Marketing Management: Analysis Planning and Control* (8th edn). Englewood Cliffs, NJ: Prentice Hall.

McKittrick, J. B. (1957), 'What is the marketing management concept?', in *The Frontiers of Marketing Thought and Science*, Frank M. Bass, ed., Chicago: American Marketing Association.

Mitchell, Colin (2002), 'Selling the brand inside', *Harvard Business Review*, **80** (1), 99–105.

Moore, James F. (1993), 'Predators and prey', *Harvard Business Review* (May–June), 75–86.

Peteraf, M. A. (1993), 'The cornerstones of competitive advantage: a resource based view', *Strategic Management Journal*, **14**, 179–91.

Prahalad, C. K. and Hamel, G. (1990), 'The core competence of the corporation', *Harvard Business Review*, **68**, 79–91.

Teece, D. J., Pisano, G. and Shuen, A. (1996), *Dynamic Capabilities and Strategic Management*, Working Paper, 53. Berkeley, CA: University of California Press.

Thompson, Jr, A. A. and Strickland, A. J. III (1996), *Strategic Management* (9th edn). Chicago: Irwin.

PART I
Identifying and Selecting Customer Value

Chapter 2

Focus on the customer

In earlier years the dominant business paradigm was mass production in which firms produced as much as they could, depending on cost structures. In many situations the market was only partly satisfied. A mass production mentality encourages a strong pressure to move output down the distribution channel to where it can be consumed with an accompanying pressure on selling what has been produced. Selling is emphasized, not marketing.

> Marketing, being a more sophisticated and complex process, gets ignored. ... Selling focuses on the needs of the seller, marketing on the needs of the buyer. Selling is preoccupied with the seller's needs to convert his product into cash, marketing with the idea of satisfying the needs of the customer by means of the product and the whole cluster of things associated with creating, delivering, and finally consuming it (Levitt 1991, p. 10).

While a focus on mass production still exists in many organizations, the beliefs and assumptions held in common and taken for granted in successful organizations are a customer orientation where the focus is on satisfying customer needs and wants while providing a profit for shareholders. A focus on customers means addressing their needs in consumer and industrial markets and understanding their behaviour in all its aspects.

The wide selection of products available nowadays indicates that most of us find something that meets our requirements. Pleasing the customer is, therefore, not about producing more products and services but about producing the right products.

Relevance of a customer orientation

A customer orientation means focusing exclusively on customers as the way to achieve long-run profits. It means directly appealing to customers by offering a better match of products or services to customer needs. An unbalanced customer focus may arise, however, where the product category or brand manager devotes attention only to customers and pays less attention to other actors in the business system. Too great a focus on customers can lead to rapid pseudo-product innovation and differentiation, short product life cycles and emphasis on small-batch production of specialized products that may be a response to a wish list rather than to real needs.

Companies which treat every customer the same are following an approach based on mass production–mass marketing presuming that all customers have similar needs and wants and that the provision of value means satisfying customers with standard products, communicated in the same way throughout the market and delivered at the same price and through the same distribution channels. The mass market approach is appropriate when there is little variation in the needs of customers for a specific product. Apart from some commodities, it is extremely rare to find this condition in practice since people express wide-ranging preferences for the things they buy. The extensive range of product and service options available in retail outlets attests to the validity of this claim.

For this reason a customer orientation obliges the organization to examine customer expectations regarding the performance of a product or service purchased. The balance of expectations when measured against performance presents managers with a measure of customer satisfaction (Figure 2.1). Satisfied customers are presumed to manifest long-term loyalty which results in profits for the organization.

Consumer–organizational market continuum

A consumer market is defined as all the individuals and households who are actual and potential buyers of products and services for personal, family or household consumption. An organizational market contains all the organizations which buy products and services as components, raw materials or equipment to be used in the provision of other products and services. While these markets are often treated separately, they have much in common. Buying behaviours at both ends of the continuum from consumer to organizational markets are similar, only the emphasis is different. The actors and influencers are people motivated by similar factors but to different degrees.

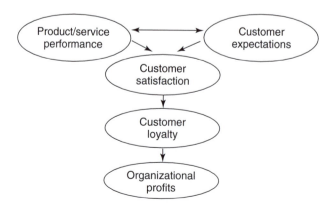

Figure [2.1] Expectations and performance determine organizational profits

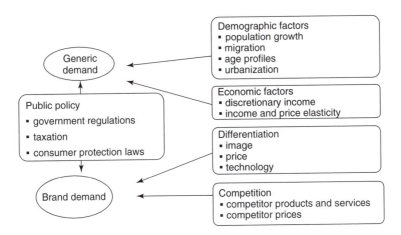

Figure [2.2]   Major influences on demand

It is a matter of examining a continuum of buying behaviour. In both consumer and industrial markets there are a number of identifiable influences on the demand for products and services. For both markets it is possible to distinguish between generic demand, which is influenced by demographic and economic factors, and brand demand, which is primarily influenced by the degree of the organization's product differentiation and the extent of competition (Figure 2.2).

Organizational markets tend to be far more complex than consumer markets because they involve a more intricate network of buying influences. The technical nature of many of the products purchased adds to the complexity of industrial marketing. Generally, the size of the purchase in money terms is greater and the buying relationship is more complex and long term. In the marketing of industrial products, technology is a more pervasive element which frequently produces a technologically driven production orientation rather than a marketing orientation.

It is possible to distinguish organizational markets from consumer markets in three respects:

- market structure

- buying decisions

- how companies reach their customers.

In regard to structure, a small number of users in organizational markets usually account for a very high proportion of total sales in that market. In addition, many industrial products sold, e.g. equipment and machinery, usually have a high unit value and are not purchased frequently. The purchasing decision for capital products can usually be postponed, something which can be difficult for many consumer products.

Buyers in industrial markets are thought to be more rational than buyers in consumer markets. A degree of rationality enters into all purchases but it is necessary to recognize that buying motivations in organizational markets are also influenced by psychological and political factors in addition to the more rational economic factors that are often stated as the only basis for industrial purchases.

Buying decisions in organizational markets are also influenced by the derived demand for the products and services their products serve as inputs. Demand in organizational markets depends on the demand for other industrial or consumer products. In this sense the demand for the output of industrial markets is derived from the demand arising in other markets.

In organizational markets there is usually greater emphasis on direct selling to the final user. Products have to be demonstrated, technical issues must be exploited, and special before- and after-sales services provided. If distributors are involved in the process, they are usually customers and may be regarded as final users by the manufacturer. In such circumstances the manufacturer must consider providing customer satisfaction to distributors and final users.

Exchange relationships in marketing

Most marketing exchanges between the organization and its customers are characterized by transactions involving a product or service being sold for money where the latent reasons for the transaction are economic, social and psychological in nature. Based on this latent structure, marketing exchanges may be economic, symbolic or some combination of the two. Marketing exchange as economic is built on the concept of economic man which assumes that people:

- are rational in behaviour;

- attempt to maximize satisfaction through exchange;

- possess complete information on alternatives available to them; and that

- exchanges are reasonably free from outside influences.

Symbolic exchange, in contrast, refers to the mutual transfer of psychological, social or other intangible benefits associated with products and services. 'People buy things not only for what they can do, but also for what they mean' (Levy 1959, p. 118). But experience demonstrates that marketing exchanges involve economic and symbolic dimensions which are often quite difficult to separate. Successful transactions depend on deriving an appropriate mix of the two. Customers seek economic and symbolic rewards in their purchases and relationships with organizations which leads to the suggestion of the existence of a marketing person (Bagozzi 1975, p. 37) who:

- is sometimes rational, sometimes irrational;

- is motivated by tangible and intangible rewards;

- engages in economic and symbolic exchanges;

- faces incomplete information;

- strives to maximize benefits but settles for less than optimum gains in exchanges;

- is constrained by individual and social factors.

Transactions and relationships

A fallacy that is perpetuated among business commentators and readily believed by chief executive officers of many organizations is that customer relationship management (CRM), requiring large sophisticated databases of customer information, is the panacea for establishing customer loyalty. Without an emphasis on technology or software, CRM aligns business processes with customer strategies to build customer loyalty and increase profits over time.

Customer relationship management is not a software tool that manages customer relationships but is rather the bundling of customer strategies and processes, supported by relevant software, for the purpose of improving customer loyalty and eventually profits in the organization. Effective customer relationship management is based on segmentation analysis and an appropriate customer strategy for each segment. According to Rigby *et al.* (2002, p. 109) 'successful CRM depends more on strategy than on the amount spent on technology. ... The only way you can make CRM work is by taking the time to calculate your customer strategy, which helps employees understand where they are going and why, and to align your business processes before implementing technology.' These authors provide a framework to ensure an appropriate alignment of CRM strategy with technology. Five steps lead to the successful retention of customers (Figure 2.3). First, it is necessary to acquire the right customer, which depends on selecting an appropriate strategy supported by suitable technology. During the next stage the organization develops the right value proposition after which it establishes the best processes. It is then necessary to involve employees in the task of retaining customers.

Customer relationship management, loyalty programmes, relationship marketing, life-time customer value are, therefore, fashionable terms used by commentators and managers who ignore the importance of the sale – the transaction – as the primary purpose of multiple communications with customers. A focus on the transaction provides immediate feed-back on the effectiveness of marketing activities. It also serves to prequalify customers

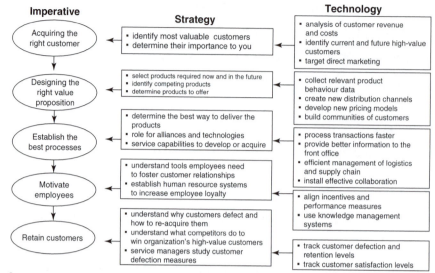

Figure [2.3]   Customer relationship management strategy and technology

and measure their potential value before the organization invests in building a relationship with them. Relationship marketing aims to create a customer relationship from the start of the sales cycle and satisfy and retain existing customers whereas the goal of transactional marketing is to make the sale and locate new customers.

Advocates of relationship marketing or customer relationship management believe that the approach delivers accurate data to the organization to assist in making decisions but in fact these data are unfiltered because they are not calibrated against any benchmarks or standards. There is, however, a clear relationship between the transactional activities of an organization and resulting revenues. Observing customer behaviour rather than basing decisions on attitudes seems the better option.

Transactional marketing techniques should be used as a precursor to relationship building efforts as retaining customers ultimately is more profitable than searching for new ones. In this regard the ability of transactional marketing to prequalify customers is the approach favoured.

Customer loyalty and profitability

The relationship between customer loyalty and profitability is much weaker and more subtle than proponents of loyalty programmes claim. Loyalty programmes are based on three assumptions: that it costs less to serve loyal customers; that loyal customers pay higher prices for the same bundle of goods; and that loyal customers through good word-of-mouth communication, promote the organization (Reinartz and Kumar 2002). In regard to the first assumption, many advocates of loyalty programmes claim that loyal customers are profitable because the initial costs of recruiting them are amortized over a larger number of transactions. This assumes that these transactions are profitable. It is necessary to test for a direct link between loyalty and costs. No doubt there are circumstances where such links exist but the organization should determine the circumstances in which loyalty programmes are profitable.

The second assumption depends on high switching costs among some customer groups whereby they are willing to pay higher prices to avoid making the switch. In practice, loyalty is rewarded with discounts so just because a customer is willing to pay a relatively high price does not mean that the organization will benefit from this loyalty.

Under the third assumption loyal customers should promote the organization. The idea that more frequent customers are also the strongest advocates for the organization holds a great attraction for managers. Many organizations justify their investments in loyalty programmes by seeking profits not so much from the loyal customers as from the new customers the loyal ones attract. Furthermore, loyal customers may have formed a positive attitude toward the organization which they pass along to new customers. As noted previously, however, the organization must study customer behaviour, not just attitudes to determine the effectiveness of loyalty programmes.

Understanding consumer buyer behaviour

Approaches based on understanding consumer buyer behaviour draw heavily on the other social sciences. Four groups of factors underlie buying behaviour in consumer markets: external factors, e.g. competitive substitutes; individual factors, e.g. the customer's family needs, budget constraints and social concerns; buying processes; and a product or service or something of value provided by the organization which stimulates the consumer into a buying routine (Figure 2.4).

The external factors which influence consumer buying behaviour are culture, ethics, legal restrictions, social class, interhousehold communications and other influence processes. The internal factors refer to the individual's own cognitive world which determines the individual's reaction to stimuli. The individual's cognitive world is influenced by needs, past experience, personality, learning and attitudes.

The organization also has a strong role to play in designing and providing appropriate stimulation to the purchase decisions. The organization modifies its marketing mix to accommodate the demands and subjective expected

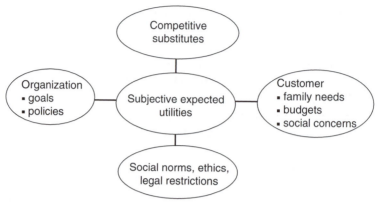

Source: Adapted from Richard P. Bagozzi (1974): "Marketing as Organised Behavioral System of Exchange", *Journal of Marketing*, 38, 4, pp.79 and 81

Figure [2.4]   Influences in the customer–organization interaction

utilities expressed by consumers. It is believed that to the extent that it is successful in matching its marketing mix with expressed and latent demands in the market, the greater is the possibility that consumers will patronize the organization's products now and in the future.

Stimulating buying behaviour

An element in understanding consumer behaviour refers to the relationship between a stimulus of some kind created by the organization, such as a new product, the way information about the innovation is processed by the consumer and the response the consumer makes having evaluated the alternatives. The stimulus is captured by the range of elements in the marketing mix which the company manipulates to achieve its corporate objectives. These stimuli derive from the product or service itself or from other elements of the marketing mix developed by the company to support its products and services.

Process refers to the sequence of stages used in the internal processing of these influences by the consumer which highlights the cause and effect relationships in making decisions. These processes include the perceptual, physiological and inner feelings and dispositions of consumers toward the product or service being evaluated. These internal processes characterize the buyer's state of mind and the disposition to respond in a particular way.

The third component refers to the consumer's response in terms of changes in behaviour, awareness and attention, brand comprehension, attitudes, intentions and actual purchase. This response may indicate a change in the consumer's psychological reaction to the product or service. As a result of some change in a stimulus, the consumer may be better disposed to the product, have formed a better attitude toward it or believe it can solve a particular consumption problem. Alternatively, the response may be in the form of an actual change in purchasing activity. The consumer may switch from one brand to another or from one product category to another. Consumer responses may also take the form of a change in consumption practices whereby the pattern of consumer behaviour is changed.

Cultural values and social influences

Individual and family decisions are affected by individual and social values. Values are centrally held enduring beliefs which guide actions and judgements in specific situations and in more general circumstances as people orient themselves in their environment (Rokeach 1973, p. 160). There are many types of values; people possess moral values, express political values and satisfy utility values which are often mixed together. The significance of values is determined by their function in understanding how the individual, groups and organizations in society adapt and behave.

Values in society are beliefs about desirable behaviours that transcend specific situations to guide behaviour and are ranked by their relative importance (Schwartz and Bilsky 1987). Values are also drawn into use when interaction between the individual and the group arises. These are the formal characteristics of values and their meaningful content may be defined as the cognitive representation of universal human requirements (Grunert and Juhl 1991). These requirements refer to biological needs and wants such as food and shelter, personal interactions in families and groups, esteem and social or institutional requirements, welfare and survival of the group (Maslow 1959; Rokeach 1973).

Culture influences buying behaviour in a number of ways. Culture is a complex mixture of ideas, attitudes and images created by people in society to shape human behaviour. Culture comprises numerous elements which affect marketing and consumer buying behaviour: language, education, religion, values and attitudes, organization, technology and material culture and the political and legal environment. Social characteristics involving group norms and role behaviour, reference groups, social class and the family are important considerations in this respect. The norms of a society influence the type of products and services members of that society purchase. Role behaviour in society depends on social norms which regulate relations among individuals and so provide a guide to social behaviour; compliance with norms is rewarded while non-compliance is punished.

Seemingly a powerful social influence is the reference group; real or imagined people with whom individuals compare themselves or to whom they ascribe a set of standards for the purpose of modelling their own behaviour. The degree of reference group influence tends to vary by product and service type. Reference groups consist of people with whom the individual compares his or her own behaviour. Stereotyping and image are usually involved. Reference group influence is thought to vary by product and by brand and to be stronger for some products and brands than others.

Perhaps the strongest social influence on individual buying behaviour is the role of the family. In examining this influence from the point of view of buying behaviour, it is necessary to decide who influences the buying decision, who makes it, who purchases and who uses it. The family is considered as a major source of influence in the buying process. Adults and children display varying degrees of influence in household purchases. Shared and joint decisions are now more common for a greater range of products and services than was the case traditionally. With increased informality in lifestyles the source and importance of the influence vary.

Path from beliefs to preferences

Beliefs and attitudes are personal influences which affect buying behaviour. Beliefs may be based on direct use of the product or brand or what has been gleaned about it from advertising and word of mouth. Attitudes, on the other hand, are feelings of like or dislike towards a product or service. Beliefs are thought to help form attitudes. The combination of beliefs and attitudes towards a product or service determines the extent to which buyers like the product or service as a whole.

Perception is the process by which people receive, interpret and recall information from the world about them. Perceptions are most powerful influencing factors in buying behaviour as they are shaped by the physical characteristics of the stimuli, the relation of the stimuli to their surroundings and condition within the individual. The scope for advertising, product and package design in this context is obvious.

Perceptions are thought to influence behaviour, especially preferences. While perceptions refer to an individual's judgements concerning the similarities and differences among a set of products or brands, preferences refer to a ranking of these products or brands regarding the extent to which they meet customer requirements as indicated by distance from some ideal preference point.

So far we have discussed buyer dispositions. Preferences, for example, must be converted into behaviour such as a purchase. This involves motivation. A motive is a stimulated need which an individual seeks to satisfy, e.g. hunger, thirst, security or esteem. A need must be aroused before it can serve as a motive. It is possible to have latent needs which do not influence behaviour until they become stimulated. The source of this stimulation may be from within the individual, e.g. hunger, or external, e.g. an advertisement for a Big Mac meal. Satisfaction of basic needs permits higher level needs to emerge. Needs which dominate at any time are dependent on the extent of satisfaction achieved for the more basic needs. In countries suffering chronic food shortages and hunger, higher level needs may be sacrificed. In more affluent societies the needs for affiliation, prestige and self-fulfilment tend to dominate buyer behaviour.

Involvement in buying behaviour

For most customers, many fast-moving consumer products are 'trivial' and uninvolving both in terms of the amount of decision making they require, and in terms of their personal relevance to the customer (McWilliam 1992). Consequently, customer behaviour may be viewed as a two-fold dichotomy: low-involvement behaviour and high-involvement behaviour (Engel *et al.* 1993). Inherent in the concept of involvement is a recognition that certain product classes may be more or less central to life, attitudes about the self or sense of identity, and relationship with the rest of the world (Traylor 1981). Involvement is frequently measured by the degree of importance the product has to the buyer:

- perceived importance of the product;

- perceived risk associated with its use;

- symbolic value of the product;

- hedonic value of the product.

Perceived risk refers to the perceived importance of negative consequences in the case of poor choice. Symbolism refers to the value attributed by the consumer to the product, its purchase or its consumption that differentiates products in terms of psycho-social risk. The hedonic value of the product refers to its emotional appeal, its ability to provide pleasure and affect.

Most buying behaviour is low involvement. Low-involvement purchasing assumes that the major goal in repetitive and relatively unimportant decisions is not to make an 'optimal' choice but, rather, to make a satisfactory choice while minimizing cognitive effort. Such buying decisions are unimportant, decisions are routine, and the buyer faces time constraints.

Generally marketing practitioners would appear to be at odds with this concept of low involvement, especially in regard to routine purchases in which buyers do not buy on the basis of any long-term or deeper-rooted, exclusive loyalty to the organization or the brand. If the concept of low involvement has validity, particularly among fast-moving consumer goods, there would seem to be no economic justification for either manufacturers or retailers to engage in expensive branding activities except to trigger a response within a low-involvement category to select a familiar brand.

High-involvement conditions are believed to exist for the many types of products or brands including lifestyle products, special interest products, hedonic products and differentiated brands. Products which are 'lifestyle products', or used as ways of self-expression or self-concept enhancement are considered to be high-involvement products as are special-interest products, purchased as a hobby, or related to the consumer's role or occupation. Products and brands which provide 'pleasure' or fit the hedonism criterion are also considered to be high-involvement purchases. Where there exists a high degree of brand differentiation based on the product's attributes, there is usually a high degree of involvement in the purchase due to the element of risk involved.

Hedonic consumption and impulse purchases

Of particular interest when considering involvement in the purchase of brands is their hedonic role in consumer behaviour. Also important is the extent to which consumers engage in planned, unplanned and impulse purchasing.

When the motivation for purchase is hedonic, high-involvement conditions obtain. Hedonic consumption is described as 'those facets of consumer behaviour that relate to the multisensory, fantasy and emotive aspects of one's experience with products' (Hirschman and Holbrook 1982, p. 92). Tastes, smells, sounds, looks and tactile preferences are largely idiosyncratic and often used by people to define themselves (e.g. 'I'm a sweet-toothed person'). Some brand and product choices may be seen, therefore, as highly involving, since they reaffirm these idiosyncrasies. In addition, some of these sensory sensations can be used to evoke memories or even dreams or desires, thus certain brands of foods such as chocolate, e.g. the 'secret self-indulgence' of Cadbury's Flake or perfume, evoking romantic scenes as well as actual remembered occasions, are good examples of hedonic purchases.

It is of course difficult to know whether it is the physical product which is the source of the hedonism or the brand name, as we do not know whether hedonism is experienced differently with different brands that are physically indistinguishable.

Impulse purchasing is related to hedonic impulses and hedonic consumption. Impulse buying has been defined as the kind of buying which 'often occurs when a consumer experiences a sudden, often powerful and persistent urge to buy something immediately. The impulse to buy is hedonically complex and may stimulate emotional conflict. Impulse buying is prone to occur with diminished regard for its consequences' (Rook 1987, p. 191). A buyer's impulse or urge toward immediate action may discourage consideration of the consequence of that behaviour. For some consumers the urge proves irresistible, despite an awareness of potentially negative consequences. These negative consequences include financial problems, disappointment with the purchase, guilt feelings, disapproval by others, and spoiled non-financial plans, a diet, for example. Impulse buying, therefore, represents a distinctive type of consumer behaviour.

Unplanned purchasing is distinguished from impulse buying because it includes items for which the purchasing decision was made at the point of sale and not beforehand. Thus, all impulse buying is unplanned, but all unplanned purchases are not necessarily impulse. Reasons cited by buyers for their unplanned purchases demonstrate that purchases are partially planned or that the customer saw the item merchandised in some way, for example. In such cases recognition of a need is probably triggered by point-of-sale cues including price, quality and sales promotion.

Nature of organizational buying

An organizational market, located at the opposite end of the consumer organization buyer spectrum, consists of all individuals and organizations that acquire products which are used in the manufacture of other products – a demand derived from the demand for the finished products the organization produces. In broad terms organizational buying is influenced by factors in the environment, by the nature and structure of the organization itself and by the way the buying centre in the organization operates.

Complexity in organizational buying

The complexity of the market for a product and the difficulties of marketing it should not be confused with the complexity or high technical content of the product itself. To be useful from a marketing viewpoint the classification of industrial products should be on the basis of the ways the products are bought and serviced rather than on technical specifications. Determining the marketing complexity of the product forces the firm to adopt a marketing rather than a purely technical orientation when attempting to understand industrial buyer behaviour.

Marketing complexity may be measured as the extent of interaction which must exist between the seller and buyer to bring about a successful exchange. In many cases the interaction can be extensive. Six major areas may be identified where interaction can be high (Figure 2.5). The more extensive the interaction required, the greater the marketing complexity involved. Understanding the technical dimensions of the product is essential but so also is understanding the buying process, the communication needs of buyers and the negotiation positions to adopt at the various stages of the buying process.

Product complexity and commercial uncertainty

The buying responsibility in organizational markets is largely determined by product complexity and commercial uncertainty. Product complexity refers

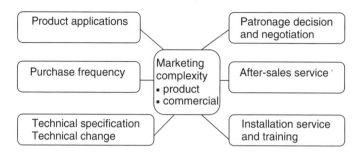

Source: Adapted from Roy W. Hill (1973) *Marketing Technological Products to Industry*, Oxford: Pergamon Press, p. 34

Figure [2.5] Marketing complexity in industrial markets

to the relationship of product technology and the extent of the customer's technical knowledge. It refers to issues such as product standardization, technical complexity, product-in-use experience, newness of application, ease of installation and the extent of after-sales service required.

Commercial uncertainty refers to business risk and its impact on future company profits. It refers to the level of the investment, order size, length of commitment, adjustments required elsewhere in the company, the effect on profitability and the ease with which the effect can be forecasted.

Where product complexity and commercial risk are low, the buyer usually carries out all the buying functions, while at the other extreme many people may be involved at different levels in the organization (Figure 2.6). When product complexity is high and commercial uncertainty is low, the technical staff tend to dominate the buying decision. When the commercial risk is high and the product complexity is low, the buying decision becomes the responsibility of specialist buyers supported by the finance department.

	Product complexity	
	Low	**High**
High Commercial uncertainty	Directors, senior managers	All levels in the organization
Low	Purchasing department	Design engineers, manufacturing operations

Source: Adapted from L. Fisher (1969) "Understand industrial markets", Chapter 2 in *Industrial Marketing*, London: Business Books, pp. 11–27

Figure [2.6] Patterns of industrial buying influence

Buying process framework

Although buying decisions in some circumstances can be quite complex, a simple stage model provides a useful framework for analysing buying behaviour in consumer and organizational markets and the marketing actions that are likely to be successful (Figure 2.7). One complexity is faced by the customer – that of identifying a suitable product and seller simultaneously.

The individual buying process starts when customers recognize that a need exists; they are aware of a need. The customer then proceeds through an additional three stages before arriving at a decision or outcome of the buying process. In the next stage the customer attempts to identify the products that satisfy the need. During the following stage the customer may wish to seek alternatives which could satisfy the need and may search for information about the alternatives available. A suitable product readily available may satisfy the potential customer who is not curious about alternatives. If the buyer decides to search for information, the organization takes an interest in the information sources used. Simultaneously, the customer attempts to identify relevant sellers of the product of interest. Information about sellers is collected and they are evaluated before a seller is chosen.

The following stage involves an evaluation of the alternatives available or shortlisted; the chosen seller's product is evaluated. In this regard buyers differ in their approach to evaluation but a number of aspects are common. Products or services are viewed by individuals as bundles of attributes. Cars are seen as transport, safety, prestige, speed, carrying capacity. Some attributes are more important than others so customers allocate importance weights to each

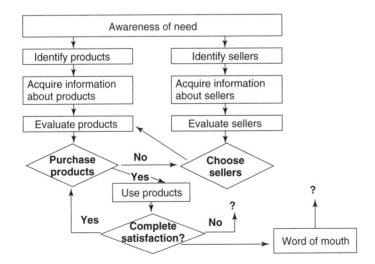

Figure [2.7] The buying decision process

attribute identified. The organization can divide the market into segments according to the attributes which are important to different groups.

After making a purchase, the product is used and if the customer is completely satisfied, additional products are purchased from the same seller after an appropriate interval. Presumably the customer provides good word-of-mouth promotion for the product in question. If the customer is not satisfied, new sellers may be evaluated and chosen.

In each organization a number of buying roles may be identified which may be taken by one individual or shared by many in the group. The customer buying process is characterized by a number of distinct roles played by the same individual in a sequence or by a number of different people in a complementary fashion (Figure 2.8).

The initiator is the person who first suggests the purchase of a particular item, the person who is first aware of a particular need. The influencer is the person who carries implicit or explicit influence in the final decision. The decider is an individual or group involved in the decision-making process who share common purchasing objectives and share the risks and rewards which may arise from the decision. This person may decide whether to buy, what to buy, how to buy, when to buy or where to buy. Gatekeepers, important in both consumer and organizational markets, have a strong information role in their relationship with influencers and deciders. The buyer is the person who makes the actual purchase. This may be an administrative role but is likely to be more centrally involved in setting the contract terms or in the actual purchase. The user is the person who consumes or uses the product. Feedback loops exist among these roles, providing an opportunity for interaction and integration of the buying activity.

The buying process for industrial products is often conceptualized similarly as a sequential process. Industrial buying processes begin when a need for

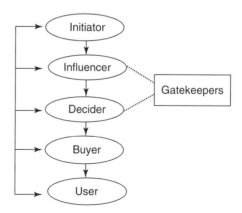

Figure [2.8] Customer buying roles

a product or service is recognized. This step can occur in many different ways. At one extreme, need recognition is routine, such as for straight rebuy decisions. At the other extreme, a need for a product can arise because of events which happen in specific situations. For instance, the buying approach is different for the organization that decides to install a power generating system to reduce its energy costs than it is for the purchase of a new computer system to process sales orders.

Having recognized a product need, members of the buying centre in the organization specify performance factors and other benefits important to the user of the products as well as non-product criteria important to the buying organization. New task and modified rebuy decisions require that information to evaluate alternative products and suppliers be obtained.

The organization attempts to encourage repeat purchases and loyalty among customers. Traditional economic variables such as price, quality and delivery; the buyer's previous experience with suppliers; the organizational structure of the buying firm; and factors which simplify buyers' work each strengthen source loyalty.

The performance of the organization's product or service from the customer's point of view is evaluated and a level of satisfaction determined. The greater the level of customer satisfaction, the more customers are expected to reward the company with their long-term loyalty which should result in healthy profits over the life cycle of the product or service. By following the analytical approach suggested here the organization may be able to form a strategic view of its customers. Such a view should take account of customer profitability and vulnerability to poaching by competitors (Figure 2.9). Highly profitable customers who are vulnerable to competitors should receive improved service levels and improved products while the organization might reduce the service level and remove non-essential product attributes for customers who provide meagre profits and are not likely to switch to competitors.

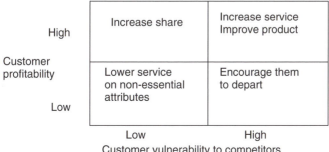

Figure [2.9] Strategic view of customers

References

Bagozzi, Richard (1975), 'Marketing as exchange', *Journal of Marketing*, **39** (4), 32–9.

Bagozzi, Richard (1994), 'Marketing as organized behavioral system of exchange', *Journal of Marketing*, **38** (4), 77–81.

Engel, James F., Blackwell, Roger D. and Miniard, Paul W. (1993), *Consumer Behaviour* (7th edn). Forth Worth, TX: Dryden.

Grunert, Suzanne C. and Juhl, Hans Jørn (1991), *Values, Environmental Attitudes and Buying Behaviour of Organic Foods: Their Relationships in a Sample of Danish Teachers*. Aarhus: Institute for Informationsbehandling, University of Aarhus.

Hirschman, Elizabeth C. and Holbrook, Morris B. (1982), 'Hedonic consumption: emerging concepts, methods and propositions', *Journal of Marketing*, **46** (Summer), 92–101.

Levitt, Theodore (1991), 'Marketing myopia', in *Marketing Classics*, Ben M. Enis and Keith K. Cox, eds. Boston: Allyn and Bacon.

Levy, Sidney J. (1959), 'Symbols for sale', *Harvard Business Review*, **37** (4), 117–24.

Maslow, Abraham H. (1959), *New Knowledge in Human Values*. New York: Harper.

McWilliam, Gil (1992), 'Consumer involvement in brands and product categories', in *Perspectives on Marketing Management*, M. J. Baker, ed., Chichester: Wiley.

Reinartz, Werner and Kumar, V. (2002), 'The mismanagement of customer loyalty', *Harvard Business Review*, **80** (7), 86–94.

Rigby, Darrell K., Reichheld, Frederick F. and Schefter, Phil (2002), 'Avoid the four perils of CRM', *Harvard Business Review*, **80** (2), 101–9.

Rokeach, Milton (1973), *The Nature of Human Values*. New York: The Free Press.

Rook, Dennis W. (1987), 'The buying impulse', *Journal of Consumer Research*, **14** (September), 189–99.

Schwartz, Shalom H. and Bilsky, Wolfgang (1987), 'Toward a universal psychological structure of human values', *Journal of Personality and Social Psychology*, **53** (3), 550–62.

Traylor, Mark B. (1981), 'Product involvement and brand commitment', *Journal of Advertising Research*, **21** (6), 51–6.

Chapter 3

Market segmentation and positioning

Very few organizations are single-product or single-service organizations. Most provide a range of products and services. Competitors similarly provide a range of products and services. These products and services may be relatively new in the market, growing rapidly or in decline. The portfolio of products and markets is necessary to ensure that a relevant match between products offered and the needs of segments of customers who share similar needs or segments is addressed. Furthermore, it is necessary to position these products in the minds of buyers in such a way as to ensure that they are differentiated from competing products to accurately meet customer needs.

Because products have life cycles, they have a differential impact on organization performance depending on whether they are new or growing or mature or coming to the end of their life. Using life cycle and portfolio frameworks helps the organization to ensure that the short- and long-term contributions of diverse products and businesses are balanced to achieve corporate goals. The strategies emerging from a product portfolio analysis emphasize a balance between cash flows, ensuring that there are products in the mature stage to supply cash to sustain growth of needy products in earlier stages of the life cycle. In this way too, the organization is in a better position to allocate resources to products in need of marketing support throughout their life cycles.

Portfolio analysis of product markets

A portfolio analysis of the organization's markets provides guidance in deciding how to compete in the market. The organization first performs a analysis of its customers and the general environment. It is also necessary to examine the activities of competitors. Finally, it must examine its own resource base. This chapter examines alternative business systems and the resulting life cycle, segmentation and positioning implications for the organization's marketing strategy (Figure 3.1).

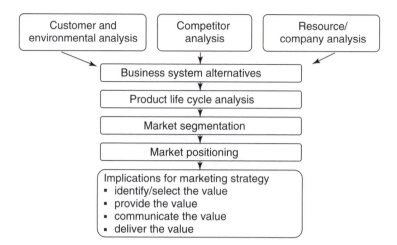

Figure [3.1]   Deciding how to compete

Competitive business position of the organization

A portfolio analysis of the organization's products involves classifying them on two dimensions: one internal, the organization's competitive position, and the other external, the attractiveness of markets. The competitive position of each business may be measured by determining the organization's ability to match competitors on:

- cost

- product quality

- ability to compete on price

- knowledge of customers and markets

- technological capability

- ability and skills of people

- fit of these factors with requirements for success.

Internal factors relate to the capability of the organization or its overall competitive business position in regard to its products. The organization's competitive position is influenced by its position in the market, its economic and technological position and its resource capability. Market position is usually gauged by reference to market share, the degree of product differentiation, the product mix and the image the organization and its products have in the market. Its economic and technological position depend on the cost structure, capacity and patents, trademarks and other secrets. The resource capability refers to its management and marketing strengths, its power in the channel of distribution and its relationship with workers and trades unions, government and other public bodies.

The organization's competitive position may be assessed by obtaining measures of the production and process technology which identify its position regarding current product quality and new technology. In addition, it is necessary to obtain measures of manufacturing efficiency and skills. Regarding marketing, it is necessary to measure the organization's market share, the cost of distribution and the extent of distribution attained.

Attractiveness of markets

Many of the factors that influence the organization's competitive position also influence the attractiveness of markets. Long-term product market attractiveness is measured by:

- market size and growth
- industry profitability
- market structure and competitive intensity
- scale economies
- technology and capital requirements
- cyclical and seasonal factors
- regulatory, environmental and social influences.

Market attractiveness stems from market, economic, technological, competitive and environmental factors. Market factors to be assessed include the size, growth and customer bargaining power existing in the market. Economic and technological factors refer to the nature and intensity of investment in the industry, the technology used and the industry entry or exit barriers that may exist. Competitive factors include the structure of competition, the number and range of substitutes available and the perceived product differentiation present. Environmental factors include matters collectively subsumed under culture, social norms, government and legal regulations. Market attractiveness may be gauged by obtaining a measure of the total size of the market, growth of sales volumes, and profitability. It is also necessary to obtain measures of long-term trends in the market and of any opportunity to segment the market.

Market investment opportunities

By classifying market investment opportunities in terms of the attractiveness of the market and the organization's business capability, it is possible to derive a two-way classification of opportunities (Figure 3.2). Market opportunities

Attractiveness of markets

		High	Medium	Low
	High	Invest to expand		Maintain investment
Organization's business capabilities	Medium		Indifferent market opportunities	
	Low	Questionable investments		Limit investment

Attractive markets

Unattractive markets

Figure [3.2]   Identifying market investment opportunities

which are highly attractive refer to circumstances where the market is very attractive and the organization's competitive position is strong. Opportunities classified as unattractive refer to the situation where the market is unattractive or the organization's competitive position is weak. Organizations are presumed to prefer the former to the latter and invest accordingly.

This analysis helps to identify a number of development alternatives or investment opportunities for the organization. Opportunities in highly attractive markets in which the organization has a strong competitive position should be developed. The obvious decision in these circumstances would be to invest for growth. Opportunities which arise in unattractive markets in which the organization is weak should be ignored. The interesting opportunities are those that fall in the middle. Some of these are questionable while others may prove worthwhile. These are investments which the organization might wish to develop opportunistically. If the organization does not possess the skills or knowledge to develop such markets, it might be possible to acquire them. The other situation arises where the market is not very attractive but the organization is very strong there. There may be no good reason to abandon such markets just because they do not fit the attractiveness and competitive position criteria. The organization is likely to be dominant or nearly so in such markets.

In general, the organization manages a portfolio of products which reflect different markets and resource circumstances (Figure 3.3). Positions of products in this capability–attractiveness matrix determine whether the organization has a balanced portfolio of products. Note that some of these products

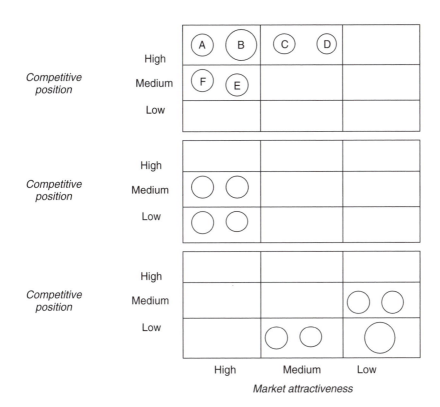

Figure [3.3]   Viability of product portfolios

are important in terms of sales; measured by the relative size of the circles. These are the products which produce surplus cash to ensure that other products, represented by the smaller size of the circles, become stars and avoid becoming marginal products to be removed. Many organizations seek to support a balanced portfolio such as that illustrated.

Seeking balance in the product portfolio is crucial in terms of the allocation of scarce marketing resources. It is important that the organization has a range of products at different stages of development. A range of products in the top section of Figure 3.3 is a very attractive portfolio.

Most managers report that it is difficult, if not impossible, to develop and maintain a perfectly balanced portfolio. It is important to note, however, that some portfolios are viable while others are not. The portfolio of products shown at the top of Figure 3.3 is attractive provided Products A and B in the mature stage of the life cycle continue to produce cash to support the doubtful products E and F, and the markets for C and D improve. Rapidly changing and shorter life cycles especially in high technology businesses could make the portfolio difficult to manage successfully. In contrast, lack of internal resources would make it very difficult for any organization to support the portfolio illustrated in the centre of the figure while the portfolio shown at the bottom of the figure suggests an early exit from the market and possible demise of the organization or its acquisition by another.

The benefits of the portfolio concept in strategic marketing planning for the organization are that:

- It provides a uniform measurement system to evaluate all product lines.

- It assists in identifying key issues and needs, for individual products and for the organization.

- It classifies product lines in terms of invest to grow, invest to maintain, or limit investment or divestment categories.

- It evaluates the portfolio of current products and businesses in terms of these classifications.

- It identifies the need for new products and businesses.

- It focuses marketing planning and operations on key issues and suggests how resources might be allocated.

Market segmentation

Market segmentation – theory and experience

Successful market segmentation comes from a combination of theory and experience. Usually market segments are easily identified by managers who know their customers well. From the theoretical point of view there are a number of methods of market segmentation. The more traditional approaches include the use of buyer demographics or socioeconomic factors, size of purchase, motivation for buying and the manner of buying as ways of segmenting the market. Other methods include the use of life cycles, family cycles and product innovation cycles.

Customer and organization benefits of segmentation

A market segment is a customer group whose expected reactions are similar for a given marketing mix. A segment seeks a unique set of benefits from the product or service purchased. In this sense a person who orders a beer usually seeks a different set of product benefits than the person who orders a gin and tonic, however, both are in the market for beverages. An original equipment manufacturer in the car industry seeks different performance standards, delivery and price terms than a buyer who serves the replacement market. Both may be in the car business but seek different product benefits. Market segmentation means dividing the market into customer groups who merit separate marketing mixes reflecting different product benefits. Market segmentation is based on identifying buyer characteristics that are correlated with the probable purchase of the organization's products, services or ideas.

Customers wish to buy things that exactly meet their needs as opposed to things that are merely acceptable but do not precisely address needs. Customers are usually willing to pay more for things that exactly meet their needs and respond more positively to marketing communications directed at them in specific ways.

A market segment has been defined as 'a group of customers with some common characteristic relevant in explaining their response to a supplier's marketing stimuli' (Wind and Cardozo 1974, p. 154). The organization recognizes the role of segmentation when it begins to focus on customer needs and interests rather than on the product itself and its physical dimensions.

Marketing segmentation refers to the activity of identifying and profiling distinct groups of buyers who might require separate products, communicated and delivered differently. For Kotler (2002, p. 279) a 'market segment consists of a group of customers who share a similar set of wants'. Alternatively, segmentation may be viewed as the strategic marketing process of 'dividing a potential market into distinct sub-sets of consumers and selecting one or more segments as a market target to be reached with a distinct marketing mix' (Shiffman and Kanuk 1978). A market segment is, therefore, a customer group, the expected reactions of which are similar for a given marketing mix.

By simultaneously considering the technology of want satisfaction and customer function with segmentation analysis it is possible to define the business in three dimensions (Figure 3.4). In this hypothetical market for bicycles the customer function is transport or recreation, the technology used in the bicycle frame is steel or aluminium/titanium and the customer segment is students or middle management executives.

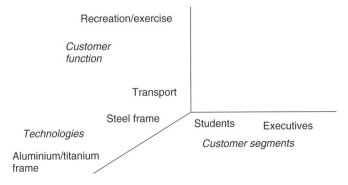

Figure [3.4] Technology, function and market segments define the business

The customer function dimension in Figure 3.4 refers to the question 'what need is being satisfied?'. Sometimes products are multifunctional and serve clusters of related needs while in other situations the organization serves multiple customer functions with separate products or services. The organization provides a mix of benefits sought by customers to solve problems. These benefits include the product itself, supporting services and other enhancements. The pattern of benefits sought is dictated by the application contemplated by customers. The technological dimension refers to the question 'How are customers being satisfied?'. The technologies refer to the alternative ways a particular function can be performed. Frequently the organization has a choice of several different technologies to satisfy the same desire. In this case it might choose between a relatively inexpensive steel frame and a much more costly but lighter weight titanium frame.

Refining the product–market dimension in this manner recognizes the interaction of product technology with manufacturing and the need to co-ordinate marketing and product design issues (Abell 1980). Market segments are thus identified for which the organization might differentiate its products and services. This approach to market segmentation also highlights potential problems. A broad definition of the business along the customer segment dimensions may achieve manufacturing cost advantages but it can fragment sales, distribution and service activities while a broad definition along the customer function dimension, by serving myriad related functions, runs the risk of uneconomic dispersion of scarce technological and manufacturing resources (Day 1981). At the same time too narrow a business definition may endanger the organization. A relatively broad definition may be necessary to allow change to occur and thereby the continued survival of the organization.

Process of market segmentation

There are many techniques which may be used in segmenting markets. Most depend on understanding underlying needs and wants and quantifying the buying responses of different customer groups. Market segmentation is the process by which an organization divides its market into smaller sections in such a way that the response to marketing variables varies greatly among segments but little within segments. Segmentation may also be thought of as a process of aggregation, starting with a segment of one customer. In selecting market segments for separate marketing mixes, the organization considers factors such as:

- market size
- competition
- effective demand in the segment
- compatibility of products and services with the needs of the segment.

Irrespective of the approach used, it must be possible to obtain information on the buyer characteristics used as a basis for segmentation. Customers in each segment should be identifiable in terms of measurable characteristics. Measurability is, therefore, the first criterion. It must be possible for the organization to focus its marketing efforts on the segments identified. Specialized advertising and promotions should be available so that the segments identified can be reached efficiently. If the segments identified are not accessible, they are of little practical value to the organization. Segment accessibility is the second criterion. Third, the segments identified must be large enough and sufficiently profitable to justify a separate marketing mix. Finally, each segment identified should manifest a different type of response to the marketing effort. In the example above it would be expected that the bicycle market could be effectively segmented into a student segment and a segment focused on wealthier executives with different needs.

Generic market segmentation

Generic market segmentation strategies may be undifferentiated, differentiated or niche. Organizations sometimes make no effort to segment the market; they do not recognize that the market is capable of being segmented. An organization following an undifferentiated strategy does not recognize market segments but rather focuses on what is common to all customers in the market. By following an undifferentiated segmentation strategy organizations design products and services to suit the broadest possible customer appeals. Such a strategy minimizes certain costs and may help concentrate the attention of competitors in one or two areas of the market, assuming that competitors do not attack across a broad front but select points where they are strong and the organization is vulnerable. In certain circumstances it is inappropriate to attempt to segment the market (Young *et al.* 1978). Market segmentation is unlikely to provide any benefits when:

- The market is so small that marketing to a portion of it is not profitable.

- Heavy users constitute such a large proportion of sales volume that they are the only relevant target.

- The brand is the dominant brand in the market.

In some product categories the frequency of use is so low that the market can only sustain one brand. Because this brand must appeal to all market segments, decisions on product positioning, advertising, distribution and pricing must meet the requirements of the entire market. When heavy users dominate the market for a product, conventional market segmentation is meaningless since most of the marketing effort will be directed at that group. If the heavy user group itself is large, other segmentation criteria may, however, be applied. When the brand is dominant, it draws its customers from all segments. In such circumstances targeting a selection of segments may reduce instead of increase sales.

Success with an undifferentiated mass market strategy depends on there being large numbers of customers with more or less common needs and a product with sufficient features and benefits to provide all of the required product benefits, e.g. Coca-Cola produces nearly the same product for each market worldwide and promotes it in the same way.

A differentiated strategy means operating in two or more segments using separate marketing strategies in each segment. A differentiated approach can have the effect of enlarging the size of the total market, but costs are increased.

By following a niche strategy the organization selects a single segment in the market which represents the best opportunity for the organization to serve customers well and builds a defensible competitive position against new entrants. Organizations following such a strategy often seek dominance through specialization. The key advantage of a niche strategy is that the organization may be able to obtain specialization economies. Niche markets are typified by specialist needs among small groups of customers served by few competitors. To be successful in a market niche the organization must understand the needs of its customers thoroughly. Niche customers are usually very loyal and pay a premium for the attention they receive.

Macro segmentation criteria

Cultural and geographic segmentation

One of the simpler management approaches to market segmentation is to treat different cultural and geographic regions or countries as different market segments. This approach is very common in large market areas like the US or Europe. At a very general level European markets are often treated as similar based on language, geographic proximity and level of development.

The value of this approach depends on the existence of regional disparities in tastes or usage or some other important criterion. Usually there is a market variation in consumption patterns but this is not always the case. In some markets, mass media, transportation and multiple production locations have substantially eroded many of these differences based on geographic factors. Many differences still remain, however, and the emergence of local differences based on ethnic, cultural and regional factors suggests the possibility of successful geographic segmentation. In Europe many geographic and regional differences continue to exist in major markets. The same is true in the US though until recently this was ignored by many large organizations.

Demographic and related characteristics

Demographic features are also used to segment markets. For some products consumption is positively related to age. Clothing, holiday centres and confectionery snack products are examples; older customers tend to buy more than younger people. Product consumption can similarly be related to a person's gender. Men and women buy different products and have different needs. The family life cycle may also be relevant to the purchase of consumer durables. Family size can yield different consumption patterns, as may educational attainment. Families with adult children and older people also have different needs and expenditure patterns.

Social class and income have been used extensively as segmentation variables as they are thought to influence consumer behaviour. Using social class as a segmentation variable means classifying customers into groups which manifest different buying behaviour. Classification has traditionally been determined by the world of work which has changed dramatically in recent years. But classifications based on occupation are beginning to lose their appeal because of the increasing complexity of occupations and the unsubstantiated presumptions about the composition of households.

Micro segmentation criteria

Segmentation on the basis of usage

Selection of important market segments may be discovered by studying several product dimensions:

- usage of the category

- frequency of use – heavy, moderate and light users

- brand use and brand share

- product attitudes.

Segmenting markets on the basis of usage is very popular. Many markets can be segmented into non-users, previous users, potential users, first-time users and regular users of a product or service. Organizations with high market share frequently attempt to convert potential users into actual users while smaller organizations try to encourage users of competing brands to switch to their brand. Potential users and regular users require different marketing approaches. Segmenting the market on the basis of usage is a strategy often used by large organizations with resources to develop numerous brands aimed at different market segments. Bacardi launched five specific brands of rum, each aimed at a different segment of the market for alcoholic spirits:

- 'Silver Rum' to compete with vodka and gin

- 'Amber Rum' to compete with American whiskey

- 'Gold Reserve' to compete with brandies

- '983' to compete with Scotch whisky

- '151 Proof Rum' to compete in the mixed drinks and cooking segments.

Behavioural and psychographic segmentation

A person's interest in various products and services is influenced by lifestyle factors and in many cases the products people use reflect their individual lifestyles. There is an increasing tendency among product and brand manufacturers to segment their markets based on consumer lifestyle or psychographic considerations.

Lifestyle and psychographic segmentation means classifying people into different groups characterized by their opinions, activities, lifestyles, interests and personalities. These bases for segmentation begin with people, their lifestyles and motivations, and then determine how various marketing factors fit into their living. Lifestyle has been used as the suggested basis for segmentation in a number of studies but measurement and accessibility may raise difficulties in using this approach.

Benefit segmentation

People also buy products for their perceived benefits. The benefits demanded by customers vary by market segment. Many organizations attempt to provide differentiated products and services for different market segments, each with its own distinctive or unique customer benefit.

By analysing customer needs and wants in each market segment and by determining the organization's capacity to serve these needs and wants, the manager is in a better position to decide which market segments should be selected for separate marketing mixes. This process is referred to as targeting markets to be served. Benefit segmentation focuses on the benefits sought by customers.

Cohort segmentation

An alternative way of segmenting consumer markets is to group buyers into cohorts – groups of individuals who are born during the same time period and go through life together and experience similar external events such as economic changes, wars, technological innovations, social upheavals and political ideologies, during their lifetime. These events, referred to as defining moments, shape an individual's values, attitudes, beliefs and behaviours such that these shared experiences distinguish one cohort from another. In a detailed review of the literature Schewe and Noble (2000) illustrate the utility and validity of using a cohort perspective to investigate shared experiences and consumption trends and conclude that segmenting consumers by cohorts may be a more effective technique than those in current use. It is, however, a very broad-based approach but is used extensively in the music industry with the launch of compilations of music popular in previous decades e.g. the 'baby-boomers' of the 1960s and 'Generation X'.

Segmenting organizational markets

Organizational markets are highly heterogeneous, complex and often hard to reach because of the multitude of products and uses as well as a great diversity among customers. Failure to properly segment an industrial market can result in missed opportunities, surprise competition and even business failures (Hlavacek and Reddy 1986). Universal needs and similarities in buying processes are, however, far more evident in industrial markets than in consumer markets (Day *et al.* 1988).

The organization has a choice of market segmentation approaches suitable for industrial markets. A staged approach using macro variables such as type of industry, size of customer and product usage may be used. Then these segments are subdivided on the basis of micro variables such as the characteristics of the decision-making unit.

Segmentation approaches used in consumer markets can equally be applied in industrial markets (Wind 1978, p. 318). The complexity found in industrial markets, however, demands a different emphasis. 'The choice of segmentation strategy for industrial goods and services is predicated on the same assumptions and criteria as segmentation for consumer goods. The only differences between consumer and industrial market segmentation involve the specific bases used for segmentation' (Wind and Cardozo 1974, p. 154). In industrial markets the benefits sought are derived from the benefits of the product in use. Industrial buyers need different products for different purposes. Product benefits are relevant in segmenting industrial markets.

Market segmentation is appropriate in industrial markets under three sets of circumstances (Johnson and Flodhammer 1980, p. 203), when:

- products and services are heterogeneous

- products are used in a variety of industries

- heterogeneous customers have different profitability requirements, buying structures and supplier requirements.

Many products and services purchased in industrial markets are technically complex and require highly technical sales, research and other support. Other products are less complex and less expensive and can be sold on a more conventional basis as might be found in consumer markets. In regard to the second point, because of the variety, a wide range of segmentation variables are used in segmenting markets. Similarly, myriad customer requirements necessitate a complex set of variables to be considered in deciding appropriate approaches to segmentation.

When these circumstances are present it is necessary to decide on the approach to segmentation. Focusing on this objective (Hlavacek and Reddy 1986) propose a four-step method:

- identifying segments

- qualifying customers in these segments

- assessing the attractiveness of the market segment

- monitoring each segment in regard to competitive activity and technological change.

The identification phase involves classifying the particular product and segmenting the market for it on the basis of typical end uses employing industry classification codes such as the SITC or BTN. Once a segment is selected, there is continuous monitoring of both competitive and technological changes which could dramatically change the boundaries and attractiveness of segments (Figure 3.5). Within each segment it is necessary to qualify customers in regard to their needs, capabilities and readiness to accept the organization's products and services.

Selecting a target segment

In selecting a target market the organization uses the broad criterion of market attractiveness compared to the organization's capabilities relative to the competition. Factors such as segment size, growth in the segment, profitability, and the behaviour of competitors are evaluated. Most importantly the organization judges how well the requirement of serving the proposed segment are matched by its resources and capabilities. The market attractiveness–organization capability matrix discussed above may be used in this

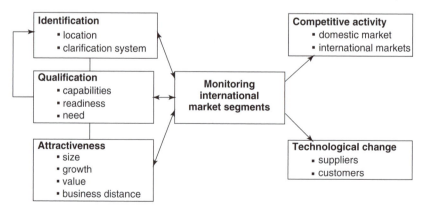

Source: Hlavacek, J. and Reddy, N.M. (1986) "Identifying and qualifying industrial market segments", *European Journal of Marketing*, **20** (2), 8–21.

Figure [3.5] Process of monitoring market segments

Influencing factors	Attractiveness of market segment	Organization's business capability
Market factors	Size and growth Diversity/cyclical nature Sensitivity to marketing mix	Customer/market knowledge Product capacity, product quality Flexibility
	Market structure/supplier power Channel power End-user power	Push/pull orientation Ability/skills of staff Advertising and promotion
Competitors	Number and types Degree of concentration Barriers to entry/exit Knowledge	Relative positioning Ability to 'buy share'; compete on price Depth of resources Knowledge
Technology	Necessary technologies Maturity and volatility Potential for innovation Competitors' patents and copyrights	Organization's current technologies Speed of R & D Quality of R & D Patents and copyrights
Financial factors	Economies of scale	Access to capital

Figure [3.6] Evaluating segment attractiveness and organization business capability

analysis (Figure 3.2). It is necessary, therefore, to determine the attractiveness of the segment and the organization's business capabilities under a number of headings (Figure 3.6).

In choosing the target segment, successful organizations are always cognizant of the possibility of using it as a base from which to launch sequential entries to other contiguous market segments. The encroachment of a sequence of segments in this fashion may eventually lead to complete control of the market.

Applying and extending segmentation analysis

Segmentation analysis may be used to identify products and customers that are attractive to the organization in varying degrees. Many organizations seek to concentrate their endeavours into profitable product–market segments. A reduction of product–market variety may be a desirable strategy in particular circumstances:

- resource constraints

- organization size

- strategic focus.

In these situations the organization may seek to manage product and market variety by reducing the number of products in the portfolio and reducing the number of customers served.

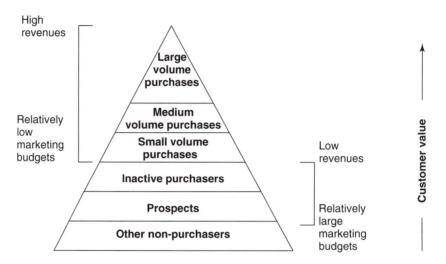

Figure [3.7]   Customer value analysis

Segmentation analysis can help in these decisions by identifying the more profitable and attractive customers and products. By classifying products into core, stars and marginals, the organization is building and improving upon traditional segmentation in that profitability tiers are established reflecting current and future profitability of the segments to the organization. A customer value analysis allows it to classify customers according to their value (Figure 3.7). Most organizations serve customers who are large volume purchasers of their products and provide high revenues, the market minority, while requiring relatively low marketing support. At the other extreme inactive purchasers, prospects and other non-purchasers, the market majority, produce low revenues but require relatively large marketing expenditures. Using a customer value analysis it is possible to identify 'Core', 'Star', and 'Marginal' product markets.

Core products might include all those products in the organization's portfolio that have a high turnover, high material value, are responsible for up to 80 per cent of sales and/or profits but only about 20 per cent of products by number. 'Stars' are products with high promise, likely to achieve 'Core' product status in the near future. 'Marginal' products are low cost, low turnover products with a questionable future. These are unlikely ever to grow to 'Star' status. Similarly, 'Core' customers are indispensable to the organization and very profitable. Customers classified as 'Stars' are likely to contribute large profits in the future while 'Marginal' customers are never likely to be important. The organization seeks to maintain and strengthen its core product markets while cultivating its star product markets and divesting from its marginal product markets (Figure 3.8). It, therefore, should treat 'Core' products and customers with great respect and care and similarly cultivate

Products	Core			
	Star			
	Marginal			
		Core	Star	Marginal

Markets

Figure [3.8]   Classification of products and customers

'Star' products and customers. 'Marginals' should be discarded or in some way offered to competitors as they are a drain on resources.

Separating customers into core, stars and marginals goes beyond usage segmentation because it measures costs and revenues for groups of customers, thereby capturing their financial worth to the organization. Using a classification similar to this one (Zeithaml *et al.* 2001) place customers into four categories ranging from very profitable down to loss makers where the most profitable are heavy users of the product and are not very price sensitive while customers at the bottom of the pyramid cost the organization money. The organization, according to these authors, should pamper the highly profitable customers, cultivate some and get rid of others 'if they cannot be made profitable'.

Process of market positioning

To simplify the buying process customers position organizations and services in their minds. A position is a complex set of perceptions, impressions and feelings and it is important to note that customers position the organizations's value offering with or without its help. It would seem good advice that organizations should not leave positioning to chance. It can strengthen its current position, search for a new unoccupied position valued by customers and focus on commanding that position or it may attempt to reposition competitors' brands to its advantage. Positioning may be decided on the basis of product attributes, benefits offered, usage occasions ('Have a break – have a Kit-Kat'), users, personalities, country of origin, societal or environmental concerns.

Market positioning means understanding customer buying criteria and recognizing the performance of each competitor on each of the evaluative criteria identified. There are two aspects to positioning. The first deals with the customer and the second deals with competitors. In positioning a product relative to customer needs and wants, concern rests with introducing products and services to fill identified gaps in the market, altering product and service positions already in the market and altering buyer perceptions of the benefits sought. This means focusing on changing the importance customers accord to the benefits and identifying or emphasizing benefits previously not recognized.

Most organizations can refer to an actual or inferred positioning statement that describes the value proposition of the product for the target market segment – for whom (the target market); reasons for buying (points of difference); comparison with other products (frame of reference). Positioning is accomplished by using all the elements of the marketing mix with a focus on a few key benefits, often referred to as the unique selling proposition or value proposition, sometimes modified to emotional selling proposition for particular types of luxury brands. It is essential, however, that the organization chooses a position it can defend.

Positioning involves making a clear choice of the target segment to be served, the points of difference compared to competitors and the frame of reference for customers. Every successful product offers more than a single benefit and appeals to more than one segment of the market. It is important, therefore, to choose the key benefit carefully and to identify for whom it has greatest appeal. Positioning also allows the organization to choose with whom it competes. A hypothetical example based on Nikon's 'Coolpix 5000' digital camera as an example illustrates how the framework can be applied:

- Possible target segments

  - home photography

  - professional photographers

  - architects, engineers

- Potential points of difference

  - ease of use

  - ease of editing

- Corresponding frames of reference

  - regular 35 mm SLR cameras

  - Polaroid cameras

  - direct competitors, e.g. Olympus.

Market positions may need to be changed from time to time to accommodate changes in the target market. Customer perceptions of available choices
may change and the organization may have to adapt its positioning strategy.
Frequently, customers change in regard to their wants. Competitors rarely
remain inactive – the organization must take account of changes competitors
introduce in their strategy. A simple example illustrates the point. At one
stage the R. & A. Bailey and Co. Ltd dominated the cream liqueur category
with its brand 'Baileys Original Irish Cream' by serving an older, more conservative market segment. After a number of years dominating this segment
the organization believed the Baileys brand was strong enough to withstand
the competitive pressures of the mainstream spirits market. To move to
the younger mainstream market Bailey's introduced its 'Bailey on Ice' campaign – drinks on ice being favoured by this large growing segment compared
to the Bailey's in a small glass favoured by the declining older segment.

In some sense brands, products or other marketing stimuli are represented
as a set of positions in multidimensional space. The axes of this space measure
the perceived attributes that characterize the product or brand. A multidimensional scaling of perceptions of middle managers of Irish and Scotch whiskies
indicates that the two most important dimensions for this group were image
and roughness (Figure 3.9). As may be seen, the management group in the
study perceive Jameson, Crested Ten and Famous Grouse to be rough but
with a modern image. The distance among these brands is a measure of the
perceived similarities of the brands for the market segment concerned. These
three brands are perceived to be relatively similar but very different from Black
& White, Haig, Bells and Paddy. The Irish whiskey brand, Powers, is perceived
to be rough and old-fashioned and holds a unique position at a distance from
the remaining brands. With this procedure the individual consumer's ideal
or preference point can also be identified. While this was not part of the

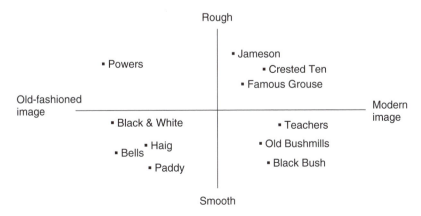

Figure [3.9] Positioning of Irish and Scottish whiskey brands

research study, it can be concluded that the distance between the ideal point, wherever it might be in the two-dimensional space, and the various brands can be interpreted as a measure of preference. Brands or products perceived as being closer to the ideal point are preferred.

To illustrate the concept of positioning in detail, assume that after carrying out the study mentioned above the whiskey market can be represented by the two dimensions: image and roughness. The three aspects of positioning for customers are shown in Figure 3.10. In Part A the organization introduces a new whiskey 'X' to fill an identified gap in the market. In Part B the organization alters the brand's position, Brand Y, from being old-fashioned and smooth to modern and smooth as this market segment is known to be large and growing. Part C illustrates the situation where the organization attempts to change one of the evaluative criteria used by customers – from rough–smooth to premium–economy.

In general the organization may use a variety of ways of changing customer evaluations (Figure 3.11). Positioning strategy must also account for what competitors are doing. It is essential that the organization knows who its current competitors are and who new entrants to the market might be.

The process of positioning therefore, involves two interrelated sets of activities. First, it requires the organization to analyse the market, to segment it and to select segments to serve. Second, it requires the organization to perform an analysis of competitors, to differentiate its products and services, to select a package of customer benefits to promote. These two sets of activities converge to position the organization's products which has implications for marketing strategy including the marketing mix (Figure 3.12). In selecting the

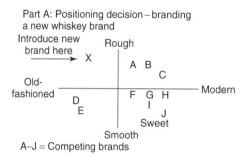

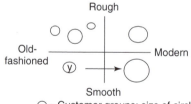

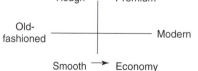

Figure [3.10] Brand positioning decisions

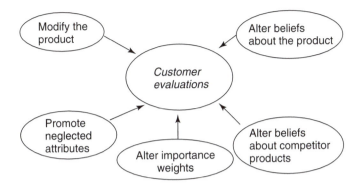

Figure [3.11]   Changing customer evaluations

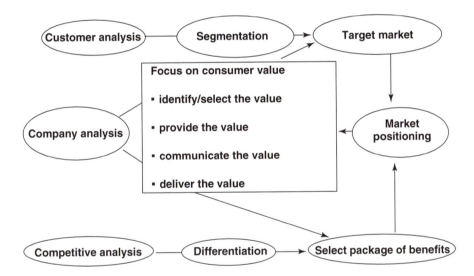

Figure [3.12]   Process of positioning

target markets to serve and the package of customer benefits to promote, the organization refers to an internal corporate resource analysis.

References

Abell, Derek F. (1980), *Defining the Business: The Starting Point of Strategic Planning*. Englewood Cliffs, NJ: Prentice Hall.

Day, Ellen, Fox, Richard J. and Huszagh, Sandra M. (1988), 'Segmenting the global market for industrial goods', *International Marketing Review*, **5** (3), 14–27.

Day, George S. (1981), 'Analytical approaches to strategic market planning', in *Review of Marketing 1981*, M. Enis Ben and Kenneth J. Roering, eds, Chicago: American Marketing Association.

Hlavacek, James D. and Reddy, N. Moham (1986), 'Identifying and qualifying industrial market segments', *European Journal of Marketing*, **20** (2), 8–21.

Johnson, Hal G. and Flodhammer, Åke (1980), 'Some factors in industrial market segmentation', *Industrial Marketing Management*, **9**, 201–5.

Kotler, Philip (2002), *Marketing Management: Analysis Planning and Control* (11th edn). Englewood Cliffs, NJ: Prentice Hall.

Schewe, Charles D. and Noble, Stephanie M. (2000), 'Market segmentation by cohorts: the value and validity of cohorts in America and abroad', *Journal of Marketing Management*, **16**, 129–42.

Shiffman, Leon G. and Kanuk, Leslie (1978), *Consumer Behaviour*. Englewood Cliffs, NJ: Prentice Hall.

Wind, Yoram (1978), 'Issues and advances in segmentation research', *Journal of Marketing Research*, **15**, 317–37.

Wind, Yoram and Cardozo, Richard (1974), 'Industrial market segmentation', *Industrial Marketing Management*, **3**, 153–6.

Young, Shirley, Ott, Leland and Feigin, Barbara (1978), 'Some practical considerations in market segmentation', *Journal of Marketing Research*, **15**, 405–12.

Zeithaml, Valerie A., Rust, Ronald T. and Lemon, Katherine N. (2001), 'The customer pyramid: creating and serving profitable customers', *California Management Review*, **43** (4), 118–42.

Chapter 4

Strategic market planning

Marketing planning is a process by which the organization attempts to understand the marketing environment, and the needs and wants of customers while recognizing that competing organizations also serve the market. It also means recognizing the organization's strengths and weaknesses in serving customers. Organizations attempt to develop strategies to build on their strengths while coping with their weaknesses. The marketing planning process consists of a number of stages including an assessment of existing product markets, preparing a detailed financial statement, reviewing the market situation, obtaining and analysing the relevant data, developing appropriate marketing objectives, sequencing and timing marketing activities to implement marketing strategies and preparing and controlling a detailed operational marketing plan.

Managerial framework for market planning

An organization may be conceived as being represented by three perspectives: an investment perspective, a financial perspective and a market perspective (Figure 4.1). Profit and shareholder value are central to all three perspectives. The market perspective is concerned with demand and supply as affecting the market for the value under consideration. The organization engages in a series of marketing activities leading to a set of receipts and costs. A trade-off between these gives rise to profit. In the financial perspective of the business, profit contributes to the organization's dividends and retained earnings which indirectly contributes to the funds available for investment.

The investment perspective considers the allocation of resources among various uses such as physical plant and equipment, research and development and investment in markets. Market investment and research and development investment influence demand, an element central to the market perspective of the organization. Investment in physical facilities and research and development contribute to supply, the second major element in the market perspective of the organization.

The three perspectives are intimately linked: market-based activities drive profit which in turn drives the organization's financial performance which

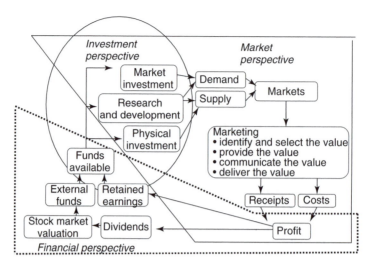

Figure [4.1]   Perspectives of the firm

then supports investment. Investment expenditures directly influence the market. The three perspectives of the organization represent an interlocking management system related to various markets.

Marketing in the organization is engaged in a competitive cycle emanating from the interaction of the three perspectives outlined above. Investment funds are central to the success of the venture. Investment in markets and marketing allows innovative products and services to be developed (Figure 4.2). These funds allow investment in new, more efficient manufacturing processes and equipment which lowers costs. The experience effect allows the organization to obtain a larger market share which in turn generates extra profits. These profits provide the excess funds for the next round of competition.

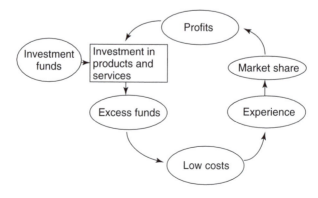

Figure [4.2]   Competitive cycle in marketing

Strategic differentiation in the organization

Successful companies invest in the market but they also invest in people to ensure that they are capable of managing in different cultures and under different political regimes. They must also invest heavily in adapting their existing products and services and in developing new products and services specifically for new and challenging markets; this means seeking to differentiate themselves strategically from competitors (Figure 4.3). Strategic differentiation means providing new customer benefits and focusing on customer value in selected markets.

Important sources of differentiation include knowledge of the market, the product and customers and the relationships within the organization and with suppliers. By differentiating the product or service, the company increases the value of its operations and, hence, improves performance which in turn leads to greater investment in the company, thereby allowing further differentiation.

Stages in marketing planning

Marketing planning involves five stages corresponding to the need for analysis, forecasting and making assumptions, resolving strategic issues, developing market strategies and organizing for marketing (Day 1984). The analysis stage involves a detailed examination of the marketing environment, customers, competitors and an internal analysis of the organization itself (Figure 4.4). In regard to forecasting and assumptions the organization must attempt to forecast or assume likely changes in the environment among its customers and competitors and determine how its own resource base is likely to develop during the planning period.

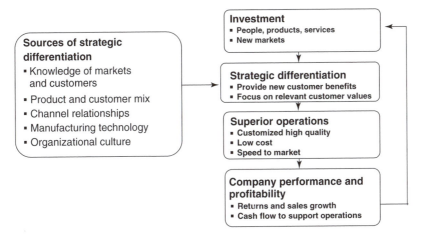

Figure [4.3]   Strategic differentiation and marketing performance

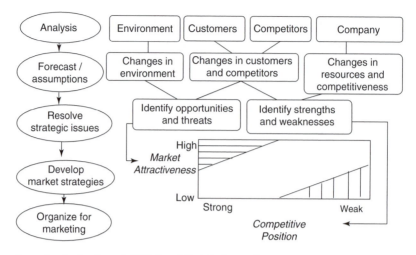

Source: Based on Day, George S. (1984) *Strategic Marketing Planning.* St Paul, MN: West Publishing.

Figure [4.4]   Stages in marketing planning

During the third stage the organization attempts to resolve strategic issues which arise which means carrying out a SWOT analysis. The identification of the strengths and weaknesses derives from a simultaneous analysis of customers, competitors and the organization itself and allows the organization to state its competitive position which may be strong or weak or somewhere in between. The identification of opportunities and threats derives from a simultaneous analysis of the environment, customers and competitors and allows the organization to determine the attractiveness of its various markets. Now it becomes possible for the organization to develop a set of appropriate market strategies. The last stage is to organize the marketing endeavour to implement the strategies decided.

Marketing objectives and performance

Marketing analysis is usually based on qualitative judgements supported by research and analysis. There is a series of questions managers must answer before developing a detailed marketing plan:

- how the environment will change
- how financial performance will be affected
- how costs will change
- how product technology will change
- how process technology will change

- how the character of competition will change

- how competitors are likely to redefine their activities

- how competitors are likely to change their investment and functional strategies

- how customer behaviour is likely to change

- how market segmentation may be influenced.

To make legitimate assumptions about changes in the marketing environment, the organization must analyse macro trends in politics, economics, technology and society and micro trends at the level of the industry and customer including market size, customer behaviour and changes in segments and channels of distribution. The more important dimensions of environmental uncertainty are changes in the macro environment – whether they are rapid or slow; the degree of homogeneity in the market and the complexity of product technology (Figure 4.5). Resource assumptions are based on an evaluation of the organization and its competitiveness: its ability to conceive and design, produce, market, finance and manage competitive projects. Competitive assumptions are based on an analysis of competitors: existing and potential, substitute products and any integration activity being followed by suppliers and customers.

There are six steps in the preparation of a marketing plan. First, it is necessary to have an assessment of the organization's marketing performance to date and a statement of its financial objectives. Second, it is necessary to review existing market conditions. Third, the organization will have to obtain and evaluate relevant industry and market data. During the fourth stage the organization must specify its marketing objectives. In the fifth stage activities, budgets and schedules are identified and determined. Finally, it is necessary to implement and control the marketing effort. The marketing planning process is summarized in Figure 4.6.

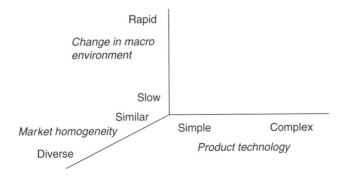

Figure [4.5]   Dimensions of perceived environmental uncertainty

Marketing performance and financial objectives	
Risk assessment	Qualification verification

Market review and situation analysis			
Products	Markets and customers	Company resources	Competitors

Obtaining relevant data		
Company	Customers	Competitors

Deciding marketing objectives			
Market penetration	Strategies and operations	Product development	Product-market diversification

Market development		
Strategy	Time plan	Resources
• Products • Distribution • Price • Advertising	• Time needs • Deadlines • Sequence	• Manpower • Manufacturing capacity • Budget

Controlling the marketing effort
Results vs targets Causes of differences Responsibility

Figure [4.6] The marketing planning process

Marketing performance and financial objectives

The starting point for any marketing plan is usually a corporate financial requirement by which the organization must meet a financial objective, e.g. 20 per cent ROI or similar objective. It then becomes the function of the marketing area to attempt to meet that requirement through its marketing and sales activities. In situations where the financial requirement is greater than the current long-run sales forecast, there is a gap which must somehow be filled. There are two generic approaches to improving marketing performance. One is to increase sales volume in some way. The second is to improve profitability in the organization.

Improving marketing performance

Improved performance means finding ways of achieving improved sales, or improved profits or a combination of both (Figure 4.7). Four distinct ways of obtaining sales growth may be identified: penetrating the market; new product development; new market development; forward integration in the market through investment and acquisition. Market penetration means selling more products to existing customers in the domestic market. This may be difficult where the firm is already strong, the market is saturated, or where there are entrenched competitors with very large market shares. An aggressive strategy would be to take market share from competitors by attracting their more profitable customers. The nature of the business system may make it difficult for the firm to discourage competitors by raising the stakes. Big-brand companies frequently raise advertising stakes or use preemptive pricing and announcements of capacity additions to discourage competitors. With regard to new product development a firm might use its own people or consultants. Alternatively, it could license or joint venture from other organizations where appropriate. Many firms start out as single-product firms and soon realize that it is necessary to possess a portfolio of products in order to serve chosen markets. It is likely, therefore, that a new product development strategy would be part of the firm's marketing strategy.

Developing new markets means identifying markets abroad not yet properly served. It could also mean using new distribution channels or information sources such as the Internet. Market integration would probably mean establishing marketing agreements, taking over distributors or retail outlets, which may or may not be feasible. Very often successful firms start by selling locally to give the firm a strong competitive presence in the market. Firms sometimes also integrate forward into the market by acquiring manufacturers who would assemble or produce locally.

The second way of improving marketing performance is to improve profitability, which means increasing yield, reducing costs, integrating suppliers, or focusing on key segments (Figure 4.7). Yield increases may come about through an improvement in the sales mix, e.g. promoting high-margin lines, increasing price or reducing margins in key markets. This approach may not be possible for smaller, weaker firms in highly competitive and fragmented markets. Many firms, even smaller enterprises, would, however, have room for manoeuvre with regard to the mix of products they sell. At the other extreme the firm may decide to rationalize its product line and to rationalize segments of the market served or distribution. Marketing audits of successful firms often indicate that they obtain all their sales with fewer products sold to fewer customers than weaker firms. Hence, a rationalization of the number of products and customers may improve performance in some companies. Selective distribution and a clear customer focus may be an attractive option for some firms.

Clearly, the firm may pursue a number of the strategies outlined. In deciding the best way forward, however, the firm is constrained by the needs of customers in the market, by growth in the market and by its competitors.

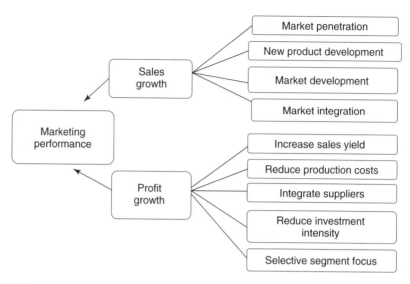

Figure [4.7] Improving marketing performance

Marketing planning questions

In analysing the present market situation it is necessary to ask the right questions so that the answers can be useful in marketing planning. In *The Elephant's Child* Rudyard Kipling identifies the kind of questions which are very useful in obtaining marketing information. He refers to these questions as his 'six honest serving-men':

> I keep six honest serving-men
> (They taught me all I knew);
> Their names are *What* and *Why* and *When*
> And *How* and *Where* and *Who*
> I send them over land and sea,
> I send them east and west;
> But after they have worked for me
> I give them all a rest.

Kipling's serving-men help to decide which customer segments should be served depending on the fit or match with the organization's resources. The question 'Who buys?' indicates the precise market. The question 'What do the customers buy?' specifies the benefits associated with the product or service.

The question 'How do customers decide?' helps identify approaches to pricing, selling and advertising. The question 'When do they buy?' assists with distribution decisions and pricing decisions. The question 'Where do customers buy?' focuses attention on the issue of distribution channels and the kind of outlets which are appropriate. The question 'Why do they buy?'

captures the impact of the entire marketing mix. The 'why' focuses on all reasons and conditions associated with buying; it covers functional and psychological reasons. Salesman Elmer Wheeler's famous dictum 'sell the sizzle, not the sausage' should be modified to allow the 'why' question to focus on 'the sizzle *and* the sausage'! The 'what', 'how' and 'why' questions together help to define the business.

Fact finding for market planning involves obtaining detailed information on the market itself, customers, competitors, the product desired and the channels of distribution:

- Market
  - size of total market and trends
  - shares held by competing brands/manufacturers
  - seasonal and regional variation

- Customers and users
  - customer identity (nature, type and demographics)
  - purchase timing, location and frequency
  - product in use and reason for purchase
  - perceived quality and benefits
  - brand and advertising recall

- Competitors
  - identity and products/services
  - areas of strength – quality, design, price, distribution, etc.
  - new product launches
  - innovation

- Distribution channels
  - types of intermediaries and their relative importance
  - turnover and stock levels in different types of outlet
  - frequency of 'stock-outs'
  - power of distributors and retailers
  - transport, storage facilities and cost

The customer segment dimension refers to the question 'Who buys or who is being served?'. Several alternative classifications based on geography, usage, industry, demography, buying behaviour and other segmentation methods may be appropriate.

Preparing the marketing plan

There are many ways to prepare a marketing plan. All of them have a number of features in common. Marketing plans should be modular; each module based on a preceding module. This means that objectives are based upon and related to market facts previously established and analysed. The plans or activities proposed are similarly chosen to meet the objectives established. There is a logical relationship between facts, objectives and activity.

Successful marketing plans are based principally on facts and not on opinion. Each item of information must therefore be checked and verified. Opinions may have a part to play in a marketing plan but they should be stated as such. Different objectives must be related to each other and should not conflict; each must be given weight according to their importance. A marketing plan also depends on activities adequate to meet objectives. In situations where this is not the case, it may be necessary to scale down the objectives to achievable levels or to use a different strategy which, of course, would have implications for resources.

Planning is concerned with selecting marketing activities, timing and resource allocation. In selecting marketing activities the organization is concerned with identifying those activities which are most likely to allow the attainment of the objectives. This means deciding the appropriate marketing mix or marketing programme. Sometimes organizations focus on one element of the marketing mix when developing a marketing strategy. Usually, however, it is a combination which works. In deciding the marketing mix, individual products, pricing, advertising and distribution strategies within an overall marketing operations framework are agreed.

In preparing the marketing plan it is also important to decide on timing and sequencing of events. Here it is necessary to establish a time schedule which can be incorporated into the operational plan. It is also necessary to identify the resources needed which means dealing with manpower, manufacturing materials and financial support. At this stage it may be necessary to specify roles for people in different parts of the organization and the organization's expectations of outside agencies and intermediaries such as banks, advertising agencies, distributors, and transport organizations. Finally, the organization is concerned with determining how the objectives will be attained. The basic principle to be applied in deciding the appropriate marketing activity is that the objective should govern the means, i.e. no activity should be justified unless it is clearly related to the accomplishment of an objective.

At the same time it is necessary to prepare a budget in sufficient detail so that all expenditures necessary to implement the plan are identified and can be provided. There are several methods to determine a marketing budget. A number of rules apply in preparing a budget. All expenditure items should be referenced to specific objectives. The associated marketing activity should be specified in detail so that everybody knows how it was derived and as much cost detail as possible provided. A spending plan should also be provided to show where the money is to be spent and the interrelationships involved in the overall plan.

Timescale of marketing planning

Marketing managers are concerned with different time frames – the short term, the medium term and the long term are commonly used phrases. By the short term is usually meant using existing assets as efficiently as possible and attempting to cut costs. By the medium term is meant the possibility of replacing labour and other scarce resources with equipment. Medium-term management decisions require the availability of capital and a willingness to take significant financial risks. In the long term, in contrast, the organization can develop new products and processes which introduces the possibility of new markets or the restructuring of old ones. Success in the long term demands imagination and a considerable amount of innovation.

Organizations which respond only to pressures of the short term 'simply delude themselves into believing that consumer surveys, techniques and product portfolio procedures automatically confer a marketing orientation on their adopters' (Anderson 1982, p. 23). The role of marketing is to manage the organization's customer relationships by:

- Identifying the optional long-term position that will ensure customer satisfaction and support.

- Developing strategies designed to capture the organization's preferred positions.

- Negotiating with senior managers in the organization and other functional areas to implement chosen strategies. (Anderson 1982, p. 24)

In regard to the first activity the optimal position reflects the organization's perception of what its customers' needs and wants are likely to be over the organization's strategic time horizon. Optimal long-term positions, according to Anderson (1982), are likely to be determined by fundamental changes in social, demographic, political and economic factors. In this regard strategic positioning will be guided by research in these areas and by research aimed at discovering the latent preferences of customers that reflect their value systems.

Behind the second activity is an attempt to gain a competitive advantage over organizations pursuing similar positioning strategies. This is likely to be incremental. Specific strategies focus on shorter time periods and are designed to move the organization toward a particular position without severely disrupting the organization itself or the market. Activity at this stage combines assessment of current performances of consumers with demographic and socioeconomic research to produce viable intermediate strategies.

The third activity listed suggests that marketing adopts an active and assertive role in promoting its strategic view. It can do so by demonstrating to other functional areas and to senior management the questionable survival value of a short-term consumer orientation.

Short-term marketing objectives are usually specified in annual budgets and are included with other objectives such as those related to profits, sales volume and market share. Short-term objectives are measurable and provide forecasts and targets for different activities within the organization. The most important short-term objectives in regard to marketing tend to refer to profits, sales volumes or market shares. Short-term operational marketing objectives assist the organization with its management control.

Setting strategic marketing objectives means devoting time to determining long-term levels for the various marketing variables at the organization's disposal. It implies thinking through the pricing, distribution and promotional strategies for the various stages of the product life cycle. In this instance marketing variables are not conceived of merely as tactical variables to be used to gain short-term advantage in the market. The myopia of ignoring the longer-term marketing objectives may be seen in the case of a organization installing a new plant and failing to accurately forecast the demand for the product.

Failure to adequately consider long-term strategic marketing issues influences all aspects of the business; financial performance, e.g. a combination of a known pattern of high fixed costs with an undesirable pattern of product prices, products and even variability.

References

Anderson, Paul F. (1982), 'Marketing, strategic planning and the theory of the firm', *Journal of Marketing*, **46** (Spring), 15–26.

Day, George S. (1984), *Strategic Marketing Planning*. St Paul, MN: West Publishing Co.

Chapter 5

Obtaining customer information

Marketing decision makers have selective needs for information. Marketing decision makers are usually faced with a time constraint and must make decisions rather quickly so both the timelines and accuracy of information are important. As marketing activities become increasingly complex and broader in scope, the nature of the marketing information required also changes. Marketing information must be comprehensive, sophisticated and have a wide angle of focus. At the same time organizations face a data explosion which requires the manager to screen data for effective and efficient generation of useful information. Organizations are concerned with the management of the process of informing marketing decisions but may not be directly involved in the actual research process, normally the responsibility of specialists in the organization or professional research organizations. The marketing manager must be able to recognize the need for marketing research in the organization and how best to carry out a marketing research study.

Strategic and operational marketing information

Senior managers in the organization require information to be collected from time to time on an *ad hoc* basis to help them take highly unstructured decisions whereas operational managers require prespecified information to take highly structured decisions. It is possible to envisage a continuum of information needs and decisions for different levels of management:

The nature of the information needed may be separated, therefore, into descriptive information about the market itself, strategic marketing information and information concerning operational issues. Regarding descriptive information about the market itself, the organization may be interested in knowing which markets hold the greatest promise and within these markets which segments are likely to be more lucrative than others. It is also necessary to determine risk levels in the market.

Information for strategic marketing decisions might include, for example, information on the competitive position to adopt and the entry mode most appropriate for a new product market. Similarly, the sequence of subsequent markets to enter and the timing of market entry require information of a strategic nature. In general terms strategic marketing information is required to help the organization discover the sales potential for a particular product or service. In specific terms marketing information provides answers to the following issues:

- Identity and description of the market segments offering greatest sales potential.

- Attributes of the product most in demand and any adaptation needed.

- Expected sales revenues at different prices.

- Alternative marketing options for the product.

- Costs of achieving marketing objectives.

Operational decisions for which information is required refer to issues arising in implementing the marketing programme. Here the organization is concerned about the relative emphasis to place on the elements of the marketing mix. It is also necessary to have operational marketing information when the product has been in the market for some time and it becomes necessary to fine tune or calibrate levels of the elements of the marketing mix.

Information on latent customer needs

A customer orientation means directly appealing to customers by offering a better match of products or services to customer needs. A customer orientation views the organization as identifying the needs and wants of potential customers and then designing, providing and communicating values to match customer requirements. As a result, the organization serves satisfied customers who produce high levels of sales and long-term profits. It is assumed that customers carry out intensive searches to find the product or service which meets their needs and that, once found, loyal patronage follows. A successful customer orientation suggests that the organization must:

- Identify customer needs and wants with great accuracy.

- Determine how much customers value the different things they want.

- Design and provide products and services to meet customer requirements and communicate these values to customers.

It has been argued, however, that a customer orientation is based on four questionable assumptions: that customers know what they want; that marketing research can ascertain what potential customers want; that satisfied customers will reward the organization with repeat purchases and loyalty; and that the competitive offers are significant enough to be important to customers (Oxenfeldt and Moore 1978, p. 44). These authors cite a number of situations where the above assumptions may not hold.

If customers do not know or cannot articulate what they want, the organization may be forced to guess. If customers cannot identify significant differences among products and the purchase is not very important, brand choice will not be based on a search of all brands in the category but on a brand that satisfied in the past, on recall of advertising or on a sales promotion. When such product parity occurs, organizations sometimes attempt to introduce significant product or service improvements or emphasize small differences through advertising, allowing greater retail margins to encourage them to promote the organization's brand. None of these approaches need be in the customer's best interests but they are commonly used by many organizations.

Too great a focus on customers can lead to rapid and illusory product innovation and differentiation, short product life cycles, and an emphasis on small batch production of specialized products and services. This is especially true in affluent markets when incomes are rising. In such circumstances it is especially important to take account of trends in the environment and the activities of competitors.

A special case is that of high technology products; customers only know what they have experienced; they cannot imagine what they do not know about emergent technologies and new materials, for example. They do, however, understand outcomes – what a new product or service should do for them. By focusing on the benefits a new product might provide customers, Ulwick (2002) suggests that data may be used to formulate a completely new product strategy that addresses important unsatisfied needs.

Immediacy of information requirements

There are a number of circumstances when the need for marketing information is greater. Rapid changes in the environment generally increase the need for marketing information. New government initiatives to regulate industry or to protect the environment have the same effect. Artificial barriers in the availability of resources similarly affect the need for information. For example, wars and strife in the Middle East usually result in the disruption in the supply of oil and its price tends to increase which affects organizations adversely.

Because of the pressure to respond quickly to changes in the environment, the time available for marketing decisions has shortened considerably which places added pressure on the need for speedy access to precise and accurate marketing information.

A second set of circumstances involves the cost of new ventures, the rate of technological change and its adoption by customers. Rapidly falling prices for mobile telephones, for example, reduce costs but because consumers are slow to adopt some of the new technologies, many organizations in the industry have seen a decline in their fortunes. In this case the organization must attempt to predict technology changes and the rate of adoption of innovations.

Converting data into knowledge

Good decisions are based on knowledge that derives from information and information, as seen above, is based on data. Data refers to raw, unsorted unstructured sets of numbers and observations. These data are obtained from within the organization, through market observations and from market research, which contribute to the body of theoretical and conceptual marketing knowledge and organizations use this knowledge in designing marketing research studies to collect data. Data, especially that available from published sources, is abundant and relatively cheap. They are considered to be 'noisy', unorganized and frequently irrelevant. There are many concerns with databases available to the organization. For the present it is sufficient to refer to the matter of accuracy and relevance of data. Published data are generally not well organized and sometimes irrelevant and available only sporadically.

By imposing a structure and a purpose in the search through data the organization develops information to help make decisions. Marketing information focuses on solving marketing problems and its relevance and value are easy to judge. Many organizations, however, gather so much data that they are overwhelmed by it. These organizations have yet to develop the very capability that prompted them to gather it in the first place – the capability to aggregate, analyse and use data to make informed decisions that lead to action and generate real business value (Davenport *et al.* 2001b).

Information made available to the organization is internalized and absorbed by managers into individual decision-making systems. Information which has been processed in this way is knowledge and it refers to how the manager reacts to the information provided. To convert information into knowledge it is necessary to have an analytical framework or model as an information processor, hence the discussion in Chapter 3 on portfolio models, segmentation and positioning.

A marketing information system which provides answers to the above questions when applied to a specific marketing research question contains

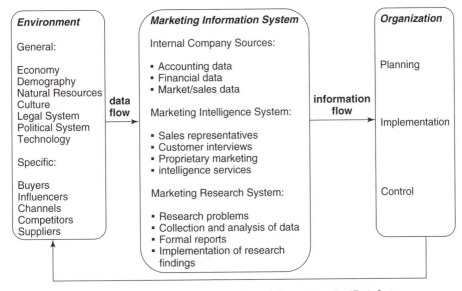

Environment	Marketing Information System	Organization
General: Economy Demography Natural Resources Culture Legal System Political System Technology Specific: Buyers Influencers Channels Competitors Suppliers	Internal Company Sources: • Accounting data • Financial data • Market/sales data Marketing Intelligence System: • Sales representatives • Customer interviews • Proprietary marketing • intelligence services Marketing Research System: • Research problems • Collection and analysis of data • Formal reports • Implementation of research findings	Planning Implementation Control

data flow → **information flow** →

Source: Frank M. Bradley and J. J. Ward (1983) *Export Marketing Research*, Geneva: International Trade Centre, (UNCTAD/GATT)

Figure [5.1]   A marketing information system

three components (Figure 5.1). Environmental issues refer at the general level to the macro marketing environment and to specific matters dealing with customers. The marketing information system itself refers to internal sources of information, marketing intelligence and marketing research. Finally, the information flows to the organization to assist in decision making.

Information on market potential

The benefits of a functioning marketing information system are obvious to the user. A well-designed practical marketing information system controls the distortion and loss of information in data and provides faster, more complete and less expensive information extraction to serve management decisions. A good system allows the organization to simultaneously monitor a variety of activities in the marketplace. Four sets of factors influence market potential and the organization requires information on each: market access; market size and growth; the price structure; and competitive environments (Figure 5.2).

Under market size and sales growth concern rests in establishing levels and trends in consumption, geographic patterns and the impact of segmentation. For industrial products it is also necessary to measure the extent of derived demand for the product or service as trends in final markets dictate demand in industrial markets. Under this heading the organization will also need to quantify other broader factors which affect demand. Among the more import-ant of these factors are social and cultural trends, economic development and

Figure [5.2]   Factors influencing market potential

the physical environment. Under market size and growth it is necessary to have information on:

- Demand influences – economic, geographic, climatic.

- Imports – volume, value, sources, trends.

- Consumption – volume and growth, segmentation, derived demand.

Access through distribution channels to potential customers must be determined. Blocked channels may make it virtually impossible to reach customers thereby forcing the organization to seek an alternative channel or even developing its own independent channel. Understanding the key dimensions of market access involves compiling information on:

- currency and tax regulations

- licensing requirements

- health and safety regulations

- tariffs and quotas

- currency restrictions

- political, social and cultural issues.

The third set of factors to be examined is the competitive structure of the market. In evaluating competition it is necessary to examine production levels, volume and growth trends. Examining market structures means identifying major competitors, estimating their market shares, knowing where their plants are located and their capacity. If possible, information on future plans especially regarding capacity additions and technology changes should be obtained. The organization must also attempt to measure the strength of competitors which means obtaining information on their size and other special advantages such as the possession of valuable patents and trademarks. There may be other factors which determine success levels among competitors that should be identified such as the marketing knowledge and skills of the competitor's staff. During this analysis the organization also has an opportunity to identify gaps in product lines. Evaluating the competitive environment requires information on:

- Production – volume and growth.

- Structure – market share, location, capacity.

- Strength – size, technology, product lines, trademarks and patents.

Related to the above factors but requiring separate treatment is the price structure in the market. The organization should determine the prices to end users and, if it is a consumer product or service, the price points involved. Other factors influencing prices and costs should also be evaluated such as ex-factory prices, trade mark-ups, and transport costs, if the organization is considering exporting. A number of aspects of the price structure must be examined:

- customer prices

- trade mark-ups

- transport costs

- price ex-premises.

Regulations, which include health and safety regulations and those designed to protect the environment, must also be considered. In recent years the growth of regulations on packaging, advertising and ingredients, in food and beverages especially, has given organizations great cause for concern. These are regulations which change periodically and keeping abreast of them requires considerable attention on the part of the organization.

Information on product and services

In determining product information requirements, four sets of factors dominate the consideration: the core product itself; its transport and storage; associated information; and promotion (Figure 5.3). Regarding the product itself, issues such as colour, taste, size, design and styling and materials used must be considered. Other product factors include the performance characteristics of the product, technical specifications and advertising and

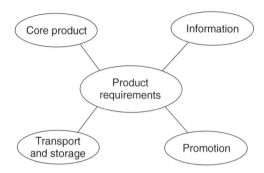

Figure [5.3]   Factors influencing market requirement

promotion as a persuasive justification for use and methods and conditions of use.

Packaging has two aspects, the physical aspect which serves the protective functions of packaging and the promotion and information functions which can be very effective especially for consumer products sold into mass distribution. To design packaging with protection as an objective, concern rests with knowing the transport methods to be used, handling methods and equipment used, storage conditions and any marketing requirements which may exist. Food products often have to be packed in a certain way to allow easy access and to facilitate merchandising in certain kinds of retail outlets.

Consumer products generally have some additional requirements too. It is necessary for the organization to recognize that special merchandising requirements may attach to the successful sale of some consumer products. These may be legal requirements regarding labelling, weights and measures. In some markets it is necessary to be specific in listing ingredients and materials used. Consumer packaging usually carries other types of information also. Instructions on assembly or preparation and use are common. Increasingly these must be prepared in numerous languages.

For industrial products it is also necessary to pay special attention to storage conditions. Materials which are dangerous or can contaminate others or are otherwise at risk or are themselves risky in some way require special storage conditions. Industrial products usually require detailed identification marks and codes. It may also be necessary to design the packaging in such a way that the contents can easily be removed and the packaging returned for further use.

Consumer packaging also offers the organization great opportunities for product and brand promotion. The design of consumer packaging from a promotional perspective is an important consideration for the organization not wishing to lose an opportunity to advertise its products. The design, use of colour, shape and size of the package all lead to an influence on consumer choice especially in the fast-moving consumer products market.

Information on marketing practices

Current marketing practices have the virtue that no matter how inefficient they may be, users have demonstrated that they know how to use them. For this reason the organization needs to understand how products and services are advertised and promoted in the market, the physical distribution system in operation, the channels used, pricing policies and customer service practices. If the organization is new to the market, it will collect this information for the first time whereas if it already operates in the market it will need to monitor changes which occur from time to time in the way the system operates and also in the costs involved. There are five sets of marketing practice the organization must understand: channels of distribution; market logistics; price levels; service levels; and advertising and sales promotion (Figure 5.4).

Advertising and promotion are among the first elements of the marketing mix the organization is likely to examine. Of concern here is the amount of money being used to advertise competing products. Very large advertising support for competing products is in itself a barrier to market entry which is difficult for the under-resourced organization to overcome. At the same time it may be necessary to match or surpass competitors to hold or increase market share or to gain a foothold in the market if the organization is considering a new entry.

During the review the organization also examines the advertising media and techniques used and the level of expenditure on each. Of greater importance is information concerning competitor products that may be obtained from a study of the content of the advertising. The sales messages and the positioning intended may be obtained from a close study of advertising content.

Figure [5.4] Factors influencing marketing practices

Sometimes organizations allocate part of their advertising and promotional budget to distributors and retailers in their efforts to push their products down the channel of distribution. It is a question of balancing how much to spend on consumer or ultimate user advertising and how much to spend on inter-mediaries. In recent years the power of retailers in many traditional branded product markets has forced manufacturers to spend a greater proportion of their advertising budget on retailer-controlled promotions. It may also be necessary to determine the timing sequence and geographic spread of the budget for advertising and promotion. A greater relative expenditure in one area of the country or at a particular time may indicate a competitor strength there or the onset of some new marketing activity.

Organizations need to know and monitor the major distributors for their products. In this regard it is necessary to monitor changes occurring in the nor-mal channels used and to determine the advantages of alternative channels. The services provided by distributors and retailers in breaking bulk, repack-aging, stocking and merchandising support are factors closely monitored by marketing organizations. The services expected by these intermediaries also need to be understood. Intermediaries have delivery time requirements, expected mark-ups and discounts, credit expectations and terms of sale. Organizations long active in a market understand these conditions and expec-tations but since they change from time to time it is necessary to monitor them. Organizations new to the market have to learn about them for the first time.

Related to the channel of distribution is physical distribution or market logistics; the methods by which products are moved from the point of pro-duction to the point of consumption. Two broad options are available to the organization; provide its own physical distribution system or use commercial fleets and storage organizations. The advantages and disadvantages of each must be understood. Factors which influence the decision are the amount and type of product being moved, the distance involved and any special conditions which attach to its physical distribution. Fresh food requires a cold chain all the way from the point of production to the retail outlet. Frozen goods have more special requirements. The delivery of bulk chemicals to factories requires special containers and tanks. A furniture manufacturer needs large storage space and large carrying capacity since the product is bulky. Other products which require special equipment and care in physi-cally moving from place to place are flammable products, compressed gases, corrosive, oxidizing and irritant materials, acids and poisons, explosives and radioactive materials.

Other physical distribution factors which must be considered are speed and frequency requirements, reliability, packaging requirements and the risks involved. Having taken each of these into consideration, the organization must also examine the costs of each alternative.

The practice of marketing also involves setting and changing prices. The level of competition in the market may determine the level and flexibility of prices. The organization needs to know the prices of competing products at any time and the likely reaction of competitors to the change in price. In this regard it is also necessary to understand the role of premium pricing in a market and the practice of discounting. Sometimes organizations new to the market develop relatively low prices as a market entry strategy. In consumer markets many products are sold at price points. The organization has some flexibility below the price point but cannot stray above it since the market expects the product to be available at that price point.

Many organizations compete by providing an excellent customer service. In some markets a certain level of customer service is expected. Customer service varies depending on the technical advice given, the policy on replacing defective products, guarantees, repair and maintenance. These service features apply in industrial and consumer markets. Training may also be a feature of consumer service in industrial markets.

Information on customers

Having accurate and reliable information on customers is an essential ingredient in strategic marketing. Many marketing organizations, however, claim that they know who their customers are and a methodical approach to collecting information on customers is unnecessary. The problem is that organizations may know who their customers are but the important thing is to know who they are likely to be in the future. In claiming that they know who their customers are, organizations are stating that they know which organizations or customers are most likely to buy their products and services in the following three to six months. This is usually a relatively easy matter since under normal circumstances signed contracts will account for most of the short-term revenues.

With the aid of modern technology and appropriate software, organizations can develop a customer information file which is easily accessible and designed to aid decision making. A customer information file for a commercial bank would draw upon computer-based data systems (Figure 5.5). For organizations like banks, online customer information is a common feature. Periodic marketing efforts directed at customers are also quite common. The benefits of the information technology revolution and its implications for the collection and analysis of customer data may prove illusory. Davenport *et al.* (2001a) argue that:

> Companies are rushing to invest in technologies that enable them to track patterns of customer transactions. Yet ... most firms have a larger data warehouse but very few additional insights into their customers. In other words, they may know more about their customers, but they don't know the customers themselves or how to attract new ones.

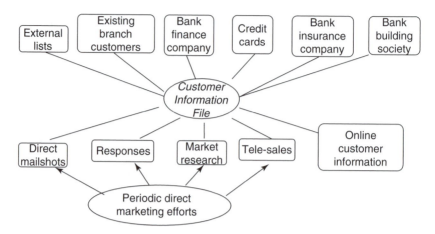

Figure [5.5] Sources of customer information in commercial banking

More traditional ways of collecting data which may be converted into information include a range of field research techniques:

- Personal interviews
  - most reliable method
  - depth and accuracy assured for wide range of questions
  - researcher controls the interview
  - product samples, videos, literature can be shown to respondent
  - respondents can be persuaded to co-operate
  - non-response is lower than with other techniques
- Telephone interviews
  - low-cost technique
  - used to pretest personal interview questionnaires
  - effective for short factual problems
  - polling audiences in response to television advertising
  - making initial contact
- Postal surveys
  - low-cost method but unreliable
  - effective in conjunction with other methods
  - can cover wide geographic area and many respondents
  - low response rates

- Exhibitions
  - in-store study of: prices, shelf space, packaging, merchandising and sales promotions
  - shopping traffic patterns

There are other ways of collecting actionable information about customers, some of them innovative. One of the innovative ways organizations like Procter & Gamble use to obtain information about customers is to build detailed mental maps that capture customers' thinking about products. These mental maps are based on extended discussions with typical customers and the input of Procter & Gamble marketing people who walk the supermarket floor with shoppers, noting their behaviour and their observations. To evaluate products Procter & Gamble uses mental maps and focus groups calibrated by statistical data from point-of-sale transactions collected electronically.

Wealth effect in emerging markets

One easy mistake for organizations to make when examining different country markets, especially developing country markets, is to compare average incomes. Comparing average incomes hides a lot of economic power elsewhere in the country.

The pattern of demand for any consumer good looks very much the same. Few households with incomes below a certain level buy certain consumer durables, e.g. CD players, cars etc. But large numbers of households suddenly enter the market for these products when their incomes surpass that level (Figure 5.6). Because incomes are unequally distributed, between regions and between households, a relatively small increase in average per capita income can lead to a much larger increase in the number of households in specific locations with incomes above the threshold for buying the product in question.

The wealth effect operates as follows: the total income of the people who can afford a particular consumer durable in Year $X + n$ is much higher that the total income of the same group in Year X. The threshold income which allows people to buy a durable good such as a refrigerator or a car is assumed to remain the same in the two periods but since the total income of the relevant segment increases dramatically between the two periods, the purchase impact is very significant. As incomes rise, the wealth effect can be an important driver of consumer goods expenditures throughout the world but particularly in developing countries.

Sales forecasting

Behind the need to understand how the market reacts to a particular product or service is the objective of providing sales forecasts. Organizations attempt

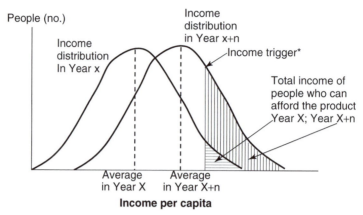

* Threshold income to afford the consumer durable.

Figure [5.6]   Impact of wealth effect on sales of consumer durables

to establish estimates of the value of a market to them by forecasting sales. Organization demand is related in some way to market demand. By forecasting market size and configuration it is possible to subsequently obtain an estimate of future sales. There is a wide range of sales forecasting techniques available. Some are valuable while others are quite complicated and the added value in complying with their rigid assumptions may not warrant their use by many organizations, especially smaller organizations or organizations operating in a very turbulent environment. To help choose a particular approach, the organization focuses on the accuracy of the forecasts, the time period to which they apply and the data requirements. Previous experience with a particular approach may be the overriding consideration in choosing the forecasting method.

Methods of forecasting sales

Five approaches which find favour among organizations are extrapolation of past sales, sales correlations, sales force opinions, buyer interviews and test marketing. Simple extrapolation techniques present as a sales forecast for one time period the sales actually achieved in the previous time period. Alternatively, forecasts based on extrapolation techniques focus on the change which has occurred between previous time periods. If seasonal factors are not very pronounced, extrapolation may give an acceptable estimate for monthly or weekly sales forecasts. By extending this technique to include the moving averages of a previous set of time periods, a greater historical weighting is applied which removes the seasonal element. Exponential smoothing may be applied to the procedure by which greater importance is attached to recent sales in the time series when making the forecast.

The use of correlation techniques depends on the assumption that the historical relationship between two variables, one which is independent or exogenous to the product market under examination, will continue into the future. Consequently, given a forecast of the independent variable, it is possible to derive a forecast of the sales of the product of interest. Independent variables include macro-economic and financial variables for which public institutions regularly provide forecasts. These variables become the independent variable in correlation analysis.

A valuable source of information about the market is the sales force. Therefore organizations frequently use the opinions of the sales force to build a market forecast. Each sales territory is treated separately and the separate set of opinions regarding likely future sales are aggregated to provide a composite forecast for the entire product market.

Sometimes customers are able to provide valuable opinions on their own future buying intentions. Surveys of buyer intentions are quite common especially in consumer durables and investment goods. Such surveys are often used in the motor industry when manufacturers attempt to gauge existing customers' likelihood of changing to a new model.

For new products the organization may have to carry out a test market to derive a forecast for the entire market. Test marketing is in effect a mini-market launch of a new product into an environment which simulates the ultimate market for which it is designed. Test marketing is used where the commercial and market risks associated with the demand of the new product are high. Where a large investment is at stake a test market is advised.

Evaluation of different methods

The first two approaches, extrapolation and correlation, are historical and depend on the assumption that what has happened in the past will continue into the future. For some product markets this may be a realistic assumption. For new product markets which have no history, these approaches have no value. Historical analyses reflect what people have done in the past which may or may not be repeated in the future.

There are weaknesses with the sales force opinion and buyer intentions approaches. Objections to sales force opinions reflect the subjectivity of the approach. Sales force opinions are conditioned by a host of factors besides an objective evaluation of the product market. Sales forces condition their opinions by referring to competitive marketing programmes in operation in the market and likely changes in these programmes. There is considerable doubt too regarding the validity of buyer intention surveys. Many changes in the environment can occur between stating an intention and making a purchase. The old adage may be relevant here 'there is many a slip between the cup and the lip'. These two approaches depend on what people say they will do or will happen. The strong element of opinion and subjectivity reduces their value to the organization.

Test marketing is designed for new product markets. It is of little value in established or mature markets. A new product introduced into a mature market is unlikely to make a change in overall market sales sufficiently significant to be detected in a test market. Another weakness of test marketing is that their results are highly susceptible to interference by competitor activity in the test area during the test. Competitors frequently attempt to spoil test markets by introducing temporary deals, price discounts or other tactical changes in their marketing mixes with the objective of confusing the testing organization's research results.

Quality and cost of information

The quality of the information available to the organization may be evaluated on the basis of:

- relevance

- accuracy

- timeliness

- compatibility

- cost.

Secondary sources of data usually provide information which is of limited value since it is collected and prepared for a wide audience with wide needs. Such data may be irrelevant to the task. There may also be a statutory reason for collecting it in the first place making it unlikely that the results would have specific and precise commercial value. Before engaging in a detailed search of such sources, the organization should determine the potential usefulness of the data.

Accuracy is an issue which arises in connection with sampling and methods of collection. Incorrect sampling procedures tend to generate the wrong type of data. Defective administration of the data collection task can also reduce accuracy. It is also necessary to judge the objectivity of the supplier of the data. Timeliness refers to the currency of the data used. Large changes in the environment between the collection time and use mean that the data are unlikely to be timely.

Generally the organization is interested in making comparisons of one period with another, a product with that of a competitor, one market with another. The issue of compatibility frequently arises especially when dealing with secondary sources of data. Statistics collected in different years may not be comparable because different categories are involved or definitions change.

Each of these factors gives rise to compatibility problems. Furthermore, the data required are frequently not available.

The organization faces the cost of data collection, analysis, storage and interpretation. Frequently, there is a significant cost of organizing the data so that it can be used. Updating the data, adding names and pieces of data and discarding old data also costs money which must be borne by the organization. This is the context in which the organization must evaluate the relevance of the information available.

References

Davenport, Thomas H., Harris, Jeanne G. and Kohli, Ajay K. (2001a), 'How do they know their customers so well?', *Sloan Management Review*, **42** (2), 63–73.

Davenport, Thomas H., Harris, Jeanne G., De Long, David W. and Jacobson, Alvin L. (2001b), 'Data to knowledge to results: building analytic capability', *California Management Review*, **43** (2), 117–38.

Oxenfeldt, Alfred R. and Moore, William L. (1978), 'Customer or competitor: which guideline for marketing?', *Management Review* (August), 43–8.

Ulwick, Anthony W. (2002), 'Turn customer input into innovation', *Harvard Business Review*, **80** (1), 91–7.

Chapter 6

Competition in the business system

A competitor orientation in the business system views customers as the ultimate prize to be won at the expense of rivals. A competitor orientation implies that the organization attempts to capitalize on the weaknesses of vulnerable competitors to win market position and customers from them, which in turn produces a high level of sales and long-run profits. At the same time, the organization attempts to remove its own weaknesses to defend market position and to minimize the loss of customers to competitors. The organization attempts to seek those activities in which its performance is superior to that of its competitors.

In this context it is necessary to determine the various positions competitors hold in the market. For each competitor it is necessary to understand what customer segments they focus on and what distinctive product or service benefits they offer. An understanding of their customer focus and strengths show the areas of the market that will be most difficult to penetrate and also the areas of the market that are not being serviced adequately. How competitors typically respond to changes in the market is something most companies attempt to glean from observation and other sources. Competition in the business system has been defined as 'the constant struggle among firms for comparative advantages in resources that will yield marketplace positions of competitive advantage for some market segment(s) and, thereby superior financial performance' (Hunt 2000). Many companies have predictable management styles which influence or even determine how they react in a particular situation. Elements of predictable management styles include the competitor's record on innovation and imitation. Some competitors match innovations very quickly through innovations of their own or imitate the success of others. Other competitors may be classified as price leaders or price followers. Understanding these patterns of competitive behaviour helps the organization to formulate a marketing strategy.

Marketing in the business system – customer acquisition and retention

Traditionally, competition for customers is defined as arising from other firms in the industry, which make products or provide services similar to those of the company. This industry perspective is irrelevant when the company's focus is on solving customer problems. Customers are interested in what they buy, not whether the buyer belongs to a particular industry. Competitors should be identified, therefore, from the customer's viewpoint. In this view of the business system, banks and software companies, though from separate traditional industries, could be competitors in supplying customers with added-value products and services like e-money and smart cards. Similarly, banks and insurance companies provide competing financial services. From an industrial economics viewpoint, neither would consider the other as competitors. Increasing industry convergence and the breakdown of traditional industry boundaries mean that the traditional view of competition is becoming less relevant (Hamel and Prahalad 1994, p. 45).

A similar situation arises on the supply side; firms compete with the company in attracting the resources of suppliers. Competition for suppliers frequently crosses traditional industry and international boundaries. Listening to and working with suppliers are just as important as listening to customers (Brandenburger and Nalebuff 1996). Many companies now recognize the importance of working with suppliers, acknowledging that they are equal partners in the creation of value within the business system. In this view of the business system, supplier relations are just as important as customer relations. Both share the common goal of increasing wealth. Both create value and provide access to markets, technology and information. In the traditional view of the business system the company serves customers and depends on suppliers for essential raw materials and other inputs.

As we move further into the knowledge-based economy, such complementary relationships on the supply side are likely to become standard practice. This is especially true where there is a large initial investment and where the variable costs are relatively modest. Practically all costs in designing computer software, for example, are fixed, so the larger the market, the greater the leverage and the more development costs can be spread.

Positioning in the business system

The objective of the organization is to manage the business system to achieve an increase in the level of perceived value added or a reduction in the price charged. In that way the total perceived value to the customer exceeds the collective cost to the organization of performing the value activities embodied in the final product. Positioning for competitive advantage in this sense is based on the organization's ability to manage the business system to provide the final customer with the desired perceived value at the lowest delivered cost which requires superior performance in at least one of the business system activities (Bradley and O'Reagáin 2002; Gilbert and Strebel 1988). Only by adding more value in this way can the organization develop a competitive advantage and thereby survive in a particular business system.

Obtaining competitive advantage by positioning the organization in the business system means identifying ways of sourcing manufactured components and launching products included in the organization's portfolio. The core of the business system positioning concept is the recognition that the organization competes within a business system, not an industry (Brandenburger and Nalebuff 1996; Lanning and Michaels 1988). A productive activity is viewed as a chain of many parts ranging from design to use by the final customer. The various parts of this chain can be ordered, therefore, in terms of stages of perceived value added.

Competition among organizations takes place at the product level but increasingly at the capability level. Successful marketing strategies take advantage of the organization's capabilities but recognize that no capability gives a permanent advantage. For example, Honda is known for its capability in engines which it applies in cars, lawn mowers and motorcycles. Canon has a known capability in optical imaging and scanning which it applies with great success in copiers, fax machines and cameras. Casio applies its capabilities in component miniaturization in calculators, watches, small TVs and hand-held personal computers.

A traditional view of the value chain stems from the idea of value being added progressively to a product as it passes through stages: inbound logistics, operations, outbound logistics, marketing, sales and service (Porter 1985). The Porter framework of value creation is, however, essentially production driven with an emphasis on the margin accruing to the organization. It does not adequately consider marketing activities in the process of adding value in the business system. This limitation is removed by viewing the marketing value system as consisting of all the activities and organizations that create and deliver value to customers (Figure 6.1). This figure is a modification and extension of Figure 1.6. Here concern rests with the four columns under the business system sub-heading. The business functions column is a traditional Porter value system that is linked to the three major dynamic activities of marketing – product development, customer acquisition and customer retention, represented by the column to the left while the following column describes information flows required in the fulfilment of marketing and business tasks – research and development, market and customer research. The left-most column represents integrated marketing communications activities. Also apparent in Figure 6.1, indicated by arrows, is the large number of interfaces critical to marketing, always considered a boundary spanning process function in the organization (Carson *et al.* 1999, p. 116).

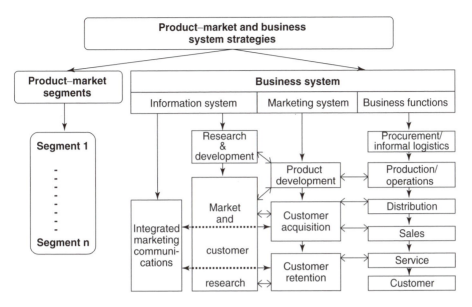

Figure [6.1]   Generic product–market and business system strategies

Each solid arrow represents an exchange of product, resources, information and effort that is governed by power relationships among parties to a specific exchange.

In this view of the marketing system some activities are internal to the organization while partners perform others. It is the system that delivers value. The cost of each activity is, however, borne by a organization individually. Similarly, though value is derived from the total margin produced by the system, the power of the other participants determines how this total margin is divided among the various participants.

It is misleading to think, however, that only the marketing function in the organization affects marketing outcomes. Value emanates from the business system in which the organization operates and it may leverage other firms and individuals in the system – customers, suppliers and particularly those who complement the organization in what it provides – in creating that value.

Marketing perspective of value added

A marketing viewpoint focuses on the customer and attempts to determine value from the customer's perspective. An emphasis on customer satisfaction means determining the values required now and in the future by customers, as well as the amount required, how it should be delivered and when it should be provided. Customer satisfaction also stems from attention to raw materials, engineering quality, design and innovation. The purpose of the organization in this added-value view is a never-ending search for continuous improvement in the cost base, through value analysis and value engineering. Most organizations recognize that in a competitive world, it is difficult to create added value.

Usually, added value arises by making better products, using resources more efficiently, listening to customers to determine how to make more attractive products and working with suppliers to discover more efficient ways of running the organization's business, while being more effective for them. Organizations that cannot produce an added value in the business system are not able to sustain a premium over cost, i.e. the organization makes very little money. Collaboration is, therefore, frequently required among organizations to provide this value and ensure customer satisfaction. Of course, adversarial competitive relationships also exist, but an emphasis on customer satisfaction in a redefined value chain introduces a balance between the concepts of collaboration and competition.

Value of an organization's resources

The value of an organization's resources and capabilities depends on a number of factors. Drawing on the work of Prahalad and Hamel (1990) and Barney (2002), the four criteria that seem most important to the present discussion are the value of the resources and capabilities, the appropriability of the value these resources and capabilities create, their rarity or uniqueness and the ability of competitors to imitate them (Figure 6.2).

Applying the value criterion

For a organization's resources and capabilities to be valuable, considered as strengths as opposed to weaknesses, they must enable the organization to exploit opportunities and avoid or neutralize threats. An organization's resources and capabilities are valuable if, and only if, they reduce the

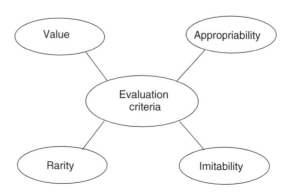

Figure [6.2]   Value of an organization's resources

organization's net costs or increase its revenues compared to what would have been the case if the organization did not possess those resources.

Changes in customer tastes, the business system structure or technology, however, can render an organization's resources and capabilities less valuable. The durability of the value, therefore, becomes an issue. Durability refers to the speed with which the resource depreciates. Most resources have a limited life span and earn only temporary profits; hence the benefits of speed to market and pioneering. Durability relates to issues of the life cycle. A temporary gain in sales or market share resulting from an illusory innovation or a spurt of heavy advertising will ultimately fail the durability test.

An organization that no longer possesses valuable resources and capabilities has two fundamental choices. It can develop new and valuable resources and capabilities or apply traditional strengths in new ways. For example, the invention and diffusion of portable bottle gas canisters, like those manufactured by CampingGas, significantly reduced the value of the skills used in the manufacture of paraffin oil lamps and heaters in the Tilley Lamp Company, a traditional oil lamp manufacturer.

Applying the appropriability criterion

This resource value criterion also concerns the issue of the appropriability of the value and attempts to discover who captures the value that the resource creates. The value of the resource is subject to bargaining among customers, suppliers, distributors and employees. In many situations the firm that owns the resource does not capture the full value of the resource; the value dissipates to other firms in the business system. This is a matter of concern in the new market entry decision whereby some distribution channels may favour the appropriation of value to the firm while others do not.

Applying the rarity criterion

If an organization's resource or capability is controlled by numerous competing organizations then that resource is unlikely to be a source of competitive advantage for any of them. Instead, valuable but common resources and capabilities are sources of competitive parity. This is a matter of rarity in the resources and capabilities. How rare a valuable resource and capability must be in order to be considered competitively advantageous depends on the circumstances. If the organization's valuable resources are absolutely unique among a set of competitors, they can provide a competitive advantage. It may be possible for a small number of organizations to possess a particular valuable resource and still obtain a competitive advantage provided there are many others who do not have the advantage.

While common resources and capabilities cannot generate a competitive advantage, they can help to ensure an organization's survival when they are exploited to create competitive parity. Under parity conditions no one organization gains a competitive advantage, but organizations increase their chances of survival.

Applying the imitability criterion

The most common competitor-centred approach, based on different forms of differentiation, refers to distinctive competences that are based on skills and resources used by the organization in ways not easily imitated by competitors (Hofer and Schendel 1978). The protection provided by the resource imitation test may be undermined if duplication or substitution is possible. Suppose an organization possesses a competitive advantage because of its research and development or marketing capabilities, then a competitor can attempt to develop its own research and development and marketing competences. If the cost of duplicating an organization's capabilities is greater than the cost of developing these resources and capabilities for the organization with the competitive advantage, then this may be a sustainable competitive advantage. If the cost of duplication is no more costly than the original development of these resources and capabilities, then any competitive advantage will be only temporary.

Imitating organizations may also attempt to substitute other resources for a costly-to-imitate resource possessed by an organization with a competitive advantage. If one organization, for example, has a competitive advantage because of its direct marketing skills, a competing organization may try to substitute a sophisticated CRM system. If the effects of direct marketing skills and CRM systems are the same, then these resources may be thought of as substitutes. If a substitute resource exists, and if imitating organizations do not face a cost disadvantage in obtaining them, then the competitive advantage of other organizations will only be temporary. If these resources, however, have no substitutes or if the cost of acquiring them is greater than the cost of the original resource, the competitive advantage can be sustained.

Competing organizations face a cost disadvantage in imitating another's resources and capabilities but there are circumstances where the imitability test can be met. To meet the criterion the resources must have a physical uniqueness which may be patented or are unique in some way and accumulated over time, e.g. brand loyalty. It also means that it should be impossible for outsiders to disentangle what the resource is or how to create it. Such causal ambiguity is often associated with organizational capabilities. To protect a resource, firms often engage in a strategy of economic deterrence whereby they make large investments in the asset relative to its current market share; hence the large advertising expenditures by big-brand organizations.

Strategic response to competition

In carrying out a competitive analysis most companies start by attempting to define their business. In defining a business, factors such as products, markets, segments, technologies and competitors are identified. The choice of business definition depends on the personality, leadership qualities and vision of senior managers. In circumstances where the company is changing its competitive focus, the business definition itself may be the most important element of the business strategy.

Generic strategies

Competition is limited by the threat of substitute products and services and the new entrants (Porter 1980). These external threats pose the greatest difficulty to incumbents attempting to respond. It is rare that dominant incumbent firms can survive the onslaught of continuous threat from substitute products and services (Cooper and Schendel 1976). For this reason, many companies succumb to new competition from manufacturers using alternative materials and technologies and to imports from low-cost countries. According to Porter (1980) there are three ways a company can succeed, by attempting to be:

- a low-cost provider of products and services
- a high-cost, differentiated provider
- a focused provider of unique products and services in a niche market.

In Spain Banco Popular has successfully served a large number of small and medium-sized companies that form the backbone of the Spanish economy by following a market niche strategy. Unlike other Spanish banks Banco Popular did not acquire banks in Latin America nor merge with other financial institutions nor amass a large industrial portfolio or invest in dot.com projects. More than half its business is with small enterprises. Lending to small companies remains a risky business, however, so Banco Popular invested heavily in a risk management platform that strengthens its early warning systems and also allowed the bank to identify cross-selling opportunities. The bank believes that it places an average of seven financial packages with each customer – more than double that of its competitors. According to Angel Ron, Banco Popular's CEO, 'servicing small companies requires a large bank network and a lot of personal attention but it is also more profitable than the mass retail market' (*The Financial Times*, 7 August 2002, p. 24).

Business strategies

A precursor to deciding appropriate business strategies for the organization is to carry out a SWOT analysis. While there are many specific activities

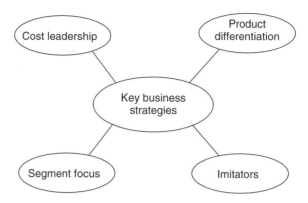

Figure [6.3]   Key business strategies

that organizations can engage in to exploit opportunities and strengths while neutralizing threats and avoiding or correcting weaknesses, the more important business strategies with a marketing focus include cost leadership, product differentiation, segment focus and imitation (Figure 6.3).

Cost leadership strategies

An organization that chooses to compete on cost focuses on gaining advantages by reducing its costs below all of its competitors. This does not mean that the organization abandons other business strategies, merely that much of its endeavours are devoted to lowering costs. A single-minded focus on just reducing costs may result in low-cost products that no customer wants. Cost leadership arises for a number of reasons. By investing in larger-scale modern equipment some manufacturing firms are able to reduce costs and thereby obtain economies of scale in manufacturing. Overall cost leadership involves generating higher margins relative to competitors by achieving lower relative manufacturing and distribution costs. Higher margins reinvested in new manufacturing equipment help to maintain cost leadership. The globalization of business also helps; companies marketing global brands may obtain marketing and distribution-scale economies unavailable to companies that permit regional autonomy. Global manufacturing decisions allow firms to concentrate production in larger factories in low labour cost countries. Low cost also derives from labour effectiveness as a result of flexible co-operation and commitment of workers. To achieve cost leadership a company must focus on controlling costs.

Cost leadership should not be confused with low prices. Low costs allow companies to lower prices if they choose to penetrate markets but they can also be used to produce profit which in turn is used for investment purposes that contributes to maintaining market dominance. Low-cost airlines offer low fares by aggressively controlling costs. They cut out the 'frills' – in-flight meals and allocated seating and they promote Internet reservations and payments. Typically they fly from secondary, lower cost airports distant from main centres of population. Two low-cost airlines dominate the European market – easyJet (1.1 million passengers) and Ryanair (1.5 million passengers). Ryanair continues to use secondary airports while easyJet has moved to primary airports such as Gatwick in the UK. Low-cost airlines fly their aircraft for more hours than traditional carriers. Using daily use as a measure, easyJet and Ryanair both obtain about twice the productivity of the larger, more traditional airlines such as British Airways or Aer Lingus, their principal national full-service competitors.

The rapid expansion of this low-cost sector to challenge established airlines has given rise to concerns that success is achieved at the expense of customer satisfaction and even safety. Critics point to the poor punctuality of the low-cost airlines, poor luggage handling systems leading to much lost luggage and rostering systems that do not work. These airlines strongly deny any safety problems and point to their market growth as an indication that customer behaviour belies the charge of poor customer satisfaction.

Product differentiation strategies

In contrast the organization that bases its competitive strategy on differentiation attempts to offer products and services which are unique or superior to those of competitors. Product differentiation is a business strategy whereby organizations attempt to gain competitive advantage by increasing the perceived value of their products relative to those of rival companies or providers of substitutes. BMW, for example attempts to differentiate its cars from Nissan's cars through sophisticated engineering and performance. McDonald's attempts to differentiate its food service from the fast food sold by locally owned, single-outlet fast-food stores by selling the same food, at the same quality, at the same prices and in the same way in all of its outlets throughout the world. Differentiation by added value insulates a firm from competitive rivalry by creating customer loyalty, lowering customer sensitivity to price, and protecting the business from other competitive forces that reduce price–cost margins (Porter 1980, pp. 26–46). Differentiation is a strategy favoured during the emergence of a product life cycle when innovation attracts customers whose present value of having new products and services outweighs the cost of waiting. Differentiation also works in mature markets as market growth may be rejuvenated when new technology replaces old technology in well-known standardized products.

Competitive strategies based on differentiation require an innovative and creative approach to marketing. Differentiation also requires speed and flexibility since imitators are many and easily flock to a success. The rapid expansion of Starbuck's Coffee chain in the UK has forced its rivals to follow its pace and focus on building scale, not on making profits. Many companies have felt the competitive pressures of Starbuck's differentiated strategy. According to Mark Hughes, Numis Securities, 'Starbuck's has shaped the UK market and they have done to coffee what McDonald's have done to fast food. It is only after you reach critical mass that you start to make money' (*The Financial Times*, 7 August 2002, p. 19). In such circumstances it is likely that even Starbuck's is not making any money but by rapidly acquiring market share it is in a position to wait for rivals to run into financial difficulties causing the onset of consolidation. There was evidence of that consolidation in 2002 in the acquisition by Caffe Nero of 4.3 per cent share in Coffee Republic. Any further dilution of its shareholding would be an indication that Coffee Republic has not been successful in establishing its brand in what has become a saturated UK coffee market.

A focus on niches and imitation

Small companies sometimes focus on small sheltered market niches in which they are uniquely able to survive. In doing so they attempt to avoid confrontation with major low-cost competitors by occupying niches in a separated market segment which is secluded and profitable.

Imitators are companies that do not have sufficient resources, appropriate market position technical skills or organizational commitment to challenge the market leaders. Market leaders dominate their industries where product and service differentiation and branding are difficult to achieve, where price sensitivity is high and where the market rewards existing suppliers with patronage because the products and services offered are sufficiently established and acceptable to provide satisfaction. In this market structure imitators copy or mimic successful products.

Success does not depend on concentrating exclusively on one competitive position. Many successful companies are cost leaders and differentiators. The buying power and skills and expertise of companies like 3M or Carrefour makes them low-cost companies but they trade on quality, service and brand names. Differentiators can be combined with focus to produce a successful competitive mix: Ferrari and Jaguar in cars; Bang and Olufsen in stereo musical equipment.

Some companies succeed, therefore, by keeping costs down and investing the profits earned in new products and services to stay ahead. Others win by differentiating their products and services to meet the needs of the market in a unique way while smaller companies can sometimes succeed by focusing on special niches with a customized approach. Even imitators can be successful. It is necessary, however, to understand the market, its customers and competitors before choosing a particular approach.

Time-based competition

Time-based competition or speed to market has recently been suggested as a way of increasing flexibility to offer customers more choice and faster delivery of goods and services. By improving on speed to market successful companies can provide the most value for the lowest cost in the least amount of time. To be competitive in such an environment companies strive to provide speedy, low-cost, high added-value goods and services.

Successful organizations choose time consumption as a critical strategic response to stay close to customers which results in increased customer dependence. Time-based competition also allows the organization to rapidly direct value delivery systems to the most attractive customers which may have the effect of further growth with higher profits. In this way the organization can set the competitive standard in the industry. As time compression allows incremental innovation, it does not depend on strategic leaps so slower companies are forced to incorporate a greater number of changes each time a new product version is introduced. Fast companies can innovate incrementally in steps which are less risky and more reliable.

The market benefits to the firm of faster new product development and commercialization are numerous. Faster new product development allows the company:

- to charge higher prices

- to adopt a shorter time horizon for forecasting sales and profits

- to increase its market share

- to provide excitement at retail level and increase consumer satisfaction

- to obtain a greater number of product development experiences.

Customers want products faster than ever; the fashionable buy products only if the latest designs are available before rivals have them and they pay more for the privilege of speed. For the increasing number of faddish, fashionable, innovative customers, many companies have developed fast response manufacturing, marketing and distribution. Benetton, for example, maintains an undyed inventory of clothes waiting to be coloured according to the latest trends. This is not a matter of cutting out unnecessary manufacturing tasks. In developing speed to market it is necessary to examine the entire manufacturing and marketing system and to restructure it systematically. Customers benefit from rapid response time by value providers in a number of ways:

- They need less inventory.

- They can make purchasing decisions closer to the time of need.

- Their customers are less likely to cancel or change orders.

- A rapid market response speeds up customers' cash flows.

- Market share grows because customers like receiving near immediate delivery.

- Quality improves because speed to market encourages being right the first time.

Order of entry and market share

Speed to market allows the innovator greater pricing discretion which is likely to benefit profit margins. Early entry at the pioneering or growth stage of the life cycle results in greater sales than achievable by a late entrant. Further, throughout the remainder of the life cycle, market share tends to be larger for the quicker firm. As competitors introduce new products in response, prices may decline. By then, however, the pioneering company will have moved down the manufacturing learning curve ahead of the competition (Figure 6.4). The pioneering firm benefits from the initial price premium and from a significant cost advantage. This tends to last over the life of the venture. There is, therefore, a continuing price and cost advantage to being first. In sum, pioneering or first mover advantages refer to lower unit costs and greater market control than competitors; the ability to set product standards and thus differentiate the organization from followers; and the decline in unit costs through experience curve effects.

In the beginning the pioneer dominates the market completely but after others enter, it usually continues to hold a large share of the market. There are three major sources of market pioneering advantage; those attributable to relative consumer information advantages, relative marketing mix advantages

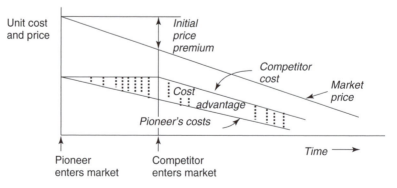

Source: Smith, Preston G. and Donald G. Reinertsen (1991): Developing Products in Half the Time, New York, Van Nostrand Reinhold.

Figure [6.4] Impact of speed to market on costs and prices and, through increased market share, improvements in relative direct costs (Robinson and Fornell 1985). By using the organization's products before competing products become available customers obtain differential information advantages derived by way of product experience or familiarity, which, in turn, may provide market pioneers with higher market shares – customers know and understand how the products function. These represent a product differentiation advantage arising from the demand side of the market.

With relative direct costs held constant, market pioneering may lead to long-lived marketing mix advantages. These represent product differentiation advantages arising from the supply side of the market. Because customers have come to know and understand the pioneer's marketing mix, this provides an additional relative advantage over competitors. A stronger relative marketing mix tends to lead to a higher market share.

A third source of pioneering advantage occurs because of the pioneer's lower relative direct costs. Being first to market may lead to direct cost savings, purchasing, manufacturing and physical distribution expenditure, relative to competition. These direct cost savings can be based on absolute cost or scale advantages. If some portion of the relative cost savings is used to provide a more effective marketing mix, the pioneer can achieve a higher market share. It is now generally accepted that market share is, in general, closely related to order of market entry: 'the first takes the lion's share, the second has to settle for second best, the rest fight over the scraps. We can prove this in our markets. On average, the pioneer achieves twice the share of the second man in' (Fitzgerald 1991).

The protected position built up through early market entry is achieved in the face of inactivity by competitors and allows the pioneering organization to achieve customer loyalty, brand identification and time to build distribution while benefiting from manufacturing-scale economies that may exist. Product leadership, being the first to introduce a new product or innovative product features, can also provide an extended period of market protection.

Challenges in the business system

The organization faces two major challenges in the business system – how to compete with other organizations in the business system and how to co-operate with some of them. In Chapter 1 the business system was characterized as a value-added chain from supplier through the organization to the customer, supported by partners and competitors (Figure 1.5). It was noted that the organization faces other organizations both as partners with whom it co-operates and competitors who are rivals. Consequently, the organization faces co-operative and competitive challenges in the business system. Furthermore, these challenges evolve in stages over time. In the pioneering stage of the evolution of the business system the provision of value is the key consideration; in the growth stage it is developing a critical mass to compete and survive while at the following stage leadership becomes the issue, and at the renewal stage continuous performance improvement is the driving force (Moore 1993). The pioneering organization, the innovating organization that is first to market, is much concerned about providing value that is attractive to a significant group of customers and faces the competitive challenge of protecting from competitors the ideas, patents and processes that produced that value. It is likely that an organization in this stage of development will be a differentiator whose resources and capabilities substantially meet the imitability criterion for valuing its resources and capabilities. The co-operative challenges the pioneering organization faces include the ability to work with customers and suppliers to define and provide new value propositions based on its innovating, pioneering, and speed to market skills.

The natural feed additives firm, Alltech Inc, faced the competitive challenge in the early 1990s of working closely with integrators and large animal feed compounders and its suppliers of scientific knowledge, minerals and trace elements to define new innovative products to reduce the cost of production of beef, pork and poultry while at the same time being friendly to the consumer, the animal and the environment (Figure 6.5). Alltech Inc had to do this while protecting its ideas deriving from its core capabilities based on fermentation technology and other scientific knowledge of biotechnology processes. In contrast, at the start of the new century the competitive challenges were to dominate key market segments and sign agreements with critical lead customers, suppliers and distributors. The co-operative challenges were to continue to work with customers and suppliers to achieve critical mass in its sector. It is possible to speculate that Alltech Inc's ambitions for the maturity

Figure [6.5]   Changes in the business system life cycle

stage might be to become the business system leader and subsequently to establish programmes designed to renew its position by adapting to the evolving competitive and co-operative challenges in its business system.

References

Barney, Jay (2002), *Gaining and Sustaining Competitive Advantage* (2nd edn). Upper Saddle River, NJ: Prentice Hall.

Bradley, Frank and O'Reagáin, Seán (2002), 'Deriving international competitive advantage in SMEs through product-market and business system resource allocation', *Irish Journal of Management*, **22** (2), 19–44.

Brandenburger, Adam and Nalebuff, Barry J. (1996), *Co-opetition*. New York: Currency-Doubleday.

Carson, Stephen J., Devinney, Timothy M., Dowling, Grahame R. and John, George (1999), 'Understanding institutional designs within marketing value systems', *Journal of Marketing*, **63** (Special Issue), 115–30.

Cooper, A. C. and Schendel, D. (1976), 'Strategic responses to technological threats', *Business Horizons*, **19** (1), 61–9.

Fitzgerald, N. W. A. (1991), 'Sustaining competitive advantage', paper presented at National Marketing Conference, Dublin.

Gilbert, Xavier and Strebel, Paul (1988), 'Developing competitive advantage', in *The Strategy Process*, Henry Mintzberg and James Brian Quinn, eds (2nd edn). New Jersey: Prentice Hall.

Hamel, Gary and Prahalad, C. K. (1994), *Competing for the Future*. Boston, MA.: Harvard Business School Press.

Hofer, Charles, W. and Schendel, D. (1978) *Strategy Formulation: Analytical Concepts*. Minneapolis, West Publishing Company.

Hunt, Shelby D. (2000), *A General Theory of Competition*. Thousand Oaks, CA: Sage.

Lanning, Michael J. and Michaels, Edward G. (1988), 'A business is a value delivery system', *McKinsey Staff Paper*, 41 (June).

Moore, James F. (1993), 'Predators and prey', *Harvard Business Review* (May–June), 75–86.

Porter, M. E. (1980), *Competitive Strategy: Techniques for Analyzing Industries and Competition*. New York: Macmillan.

Porter, M. E. (1985), *Competitive Advantage: Creating and Sustaining Superior Performance*. New York: The Free Press.

Prahalad, C. K. and Hamel, G. (1990), 'The core competence of the corporation', *Harvard Business Review*, **68**, 79–91.

Robinson, William T. and Fornell, Claes (1985), 'Sources of marketing pioneering advantage in consumer goods industries', *Journal of Marketing Research*, **22** (August), 305–17.

PART II
Providing the Value

Chapter 7

Building competitive brands

Branding is concerned with identifying and developing the added values associated with products and services. A product is something with a functional purpose. A brand serves a functional purpose but its value derives from a unique balance between functional benefits and differentiated benefits. Uniqueness is the hallmark of a brand. Successful brands balance functional benefits which prompt the customer to use any brand in a product category and discriminatory benefits which prompt the customer to choose one brand rather than another. Because they are more tangible, functional benefits sometimes receive greater attention than the discriminating benefits. Successful firms do not focus exclusively on functional benefits, over which they exercise greater control, at the expense of the added values which may be psychological factors, over which they have only limited control. Building competitive brands requires the organization to seek a balance between the functional and added-value benefits while ensuring that neither are depreciated.

Nature and significance of branding

The creation of successful brands means starting with a tangible product or service which after the organization or owner has incorporated design and quality, and developed appropriate packaging and decided a suitable brand name becomes the basic brand (Figure 7.1). The next stage is to augment the basic brand by providing a range of basic ancillary services not associated with the core brand. These include guarantees, credit and purchase terms, customer service, installation and training and delivery. Associated with the augmented brand is a particular advertising emphasis which contributes to the overall brand image. By manipulating each of these attributes of the brand, adding others yet to be discovered, the company eventually reaches the state of having produced a potential brand which will replace the existing brand sometime in the future. Branding has three objectives:

- To conform to the legal patent protection the inventor may have.

- To guarantee quality and homogeneity in markets where buyers and producers cannot meet face to face.

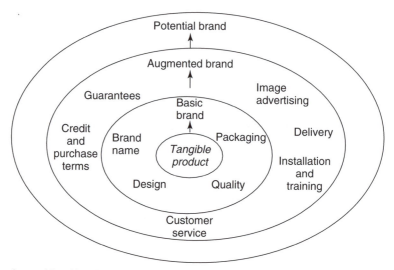

Source: Adapted from Theodore Levitt (1986) *The Marketing Imagination*, New York: Free Press

Figure [7.1]   Creation of successful brands

■ To differentiate products and services in a competitive environment.

Branding has been an important aspect of marketing for centuries but brand names are of more recent origin. They first appeared in the sixteenth century when whiskey distillers burned or branded their name onto the top of each wooden vessel in which the whiskey was shipped, thus identifying the distiller to the customer and preventing tavern owners from substituting cheaper products, two purposes of branding which are still important today. The brand concept evolved in the eighteenth century as the names of places of origin, famous people and even animals replaced producer names in an effort to strengthen the association of the brand name with the product thus making it easier for customers to remember the organization's product and to distinguish it from the competition. More recently organizations have begun to use their brands to enhance the product's perceived value through such associations.

Meaning of branding

A brand is any combination of name, symbol or design which identifies a product or service and differentiates it from competitors. An economist's view, held in regard by marketing managers defines branding as:

> various brands of a certain article which in fact are almost exactly alike may be sold as different qualities under names and labels which will induce rich and snobbish buyers to divide themselves from poorer buyers (Robinson 1933, pp. 180–1).

Alternatively, 'a successful brand is a name, symbol, design or some combination, which identifies the "product" of a particular organization as having a sustainable differential advantage' (Doyle 1991, p. 336). For Lannon and Cooper (1983, p. 205):

> What turns a product into a brand is that the physical product is combined with something else, symbols, images, feelings, to produce an idea which is more than and different from the sum of the parts. The two, product and symbolism, live and grow with and on one another in a partnership and mutual exchange ... as a sort of attachment or "symbiosis" which consumers have for their brands and the advertising surrounding them.

Brand equity is the added value with which a given brand endows a product. The brand also legally protects any unique features the underlying product might have from imitation while at the same time conveying to the customer a set of quality attributes which help to build loyalty and repeat purchases of the brand. A brand is, therefore, a name, symbol, design or mark that enhances the value of the product, thus providing functional benefits and *added* values that some consumers value sufficiently to buy.

The definition of branding provided above emphasizes that only some consumers value the brand sufficiently to buy it. Tastes differ so widely that no brand is likely to satisfy everybody. A manufacturer who maintains a very wide scope runs the danger of producing a brand that is number two or number three over a wide range of attributes, rather than number one over the limited range that matters. It may be more profitable to aim for a limited part of the market with a brand and use a number of brands to cover a greater part of the market; herein lies one of the reasons for segmentation.

A brand is a promise which is distinctive, valued and consistently delivered over time. BMW's brand has been rated as stronger than that of any other luxury car (*Forbes Global*, 22 July 2002, p. 24). Three reasons may be identified for BMW's successful branding – consistency in all that it does, patience and a long-term view of the brand and a simple sophisticated message. For more than a quarter of a century BMW has been offering customers the ultimate driving machine. Furthermore, BMW is very consistent in its product line that reflects the essence of the brand. The distinctive shape of the radiator grille, introduced by BMW in the 1930s, with its dividing line down the middle, while not sufficient to differentiate a car, is nevertheless an indicator of consistency.

Consistency by itself, however, is not enough. Many other manufacturers can provide good quality at a reasonable price. Modern technology allows for competitive product parity. While competitor brands reflect tangible practical attributes, BMW has created an image more emotional in character. It is an emotional reason that encourages customers to pay more for a luxury car than a mass-produced product.

The rewards of branding are, therefore, both tangible and intangible. Successful brands provide eight benefits for the organization:

- Recognition – brands can be instantly recognized and trusted.

- Channel placement – brands may facilitate easier entry into the marketing channel especially at retail level and thus provide an advantage in a battle with competitors.

- Pricing – brands usually command a price premium thus giving the organization a larger margin.

- Sales – brands usually sell more than private-label products.

- Platform – brands provide a platform for brand extensions.

- Licensing – brands may be licensed to other organizations for use on related products.

- Longevity – many brands last a long time, often surviving the company that introduced and built them.

- Value – brands are often the most valuable asset in the company.

Building equity in the brand

Brand value or brand equity is a measure of the intrinsic utility of a brand to customers. It is the outcome of long-term investments designed to build a sustainable, differential advantage for the company relative to competitors. The key components of brand equity are brand awareness and brand image. Awareness derives from the strength of the brand in the customers' memory which is reflected by the customers' ability to identify the brand under different conditions – familiar brands tend to be bought. Brand image refers to the perceptions about the brand held in the customers' memory and is reflected in brand associations. Brand equity has been defined as 'the differential effect of brand knowledge on consumer responses to the marketing of a brand' (Keller 1993). Building brand equity implies a long-term commitment to the brand. Brands must be managed and updated, therefore, to remain relevant to target segments. Marketing communications are an essential ingredient in the brand building process.

In demonstrating a long-term commitment to the brand the organization usually engages in a number of activities such as heavy advertising, brand positioning, brand extensions and product modifications (Figure 7.2). On occasion the organization may have to relaunch the brand and introduce private label branding. In all its activities to manage the brand in the longer term the organization must avoid cannibalizing its existing brands – taking

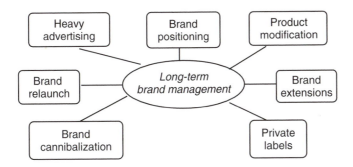

Figure [7.2] Long-term brand management

sales away from existing brands on the introduction of an extension or a private label, for instance. The brand is the organization's truly unique and sustainable competitive advantage.

For the brand provider or manufacturer brand equity may be measured by the incremental cash flow from associating the brand with the underlying product. This arises when the product sells more with the brand than without it. Incremental cash flow also arises from premium pricing and reduced promotional expenditure. Brand equity gives the firm certain competitive advantages. A strong brand can serve as an umbrella under which to launch new products or to license existing products. An important strategic component of brand equity is brand dominance, i.e. the ability of a brand to dominate a product category, thus providing virtual ownership of the category e.g. McDonald's in the fast-food service, Heinz in beans and Electrolux in household dishwashers and washing machines.

One of the tasks facing Hans Strabery, appointed Electrolux's new chief executive in 2002, was to reduce the size of the company's portfolio of brands. The company's best-known brands were Zanussi, AEG and Flymo in Europe and Frigidaire in the US but it had a plethora of smaller brands, in Europe especially. According to Straberg 'we need fewer and stronger brands with Electrolux as the master brand. The starting point is that Electrolux has to be number one, two or three in all its markets. It gains economies of scale in manufacturing and can deal with retailers from a position of strength. The enhanced visibility strengthens the company's brand' (*The Financial Times*, 5 August, 2002, p. 8). The strategy is to stop household appliances from becoming commodity products. It is the difference between a customer going into a shop and saying 'I want a new fridge' and saying 'I want to see the new Electrolux range'.

Brand equity helps the customer in a number of ways: quick recognition – reduces search costs; associations in the customer's mind; inferred attributes – Seiko watch, judged as reliable, inexpensive, durable and fashionable; consistency – BMW; and simplification of the buying decision process.

Brand equity also helps the organization: an ability to charge a premium price or obtain added market share; quicker recognition which reduces the necessity of extensive advertising; quicker new product introductions; increased power in the channel; eases brand extensions; is a competitive barrier and increasingly seen as an important balance-sheet item.

Brands help to create customer loyalty and repeat purchasing behaviour as they help to differentiate the company's brand from competing products. A powerful brand name is said to have a customer franchise. This is apparent when a sufficient number of customers demand the brand and refuse a substitute, even if the price of the substitute is somewhat lower. According to Watkins (1986, p. 36), 'The success of an existing brand may be judged primarily by its price level compared with other brands, as this is the most visible evidence of success of the branding policy.' Companies that develop a brand with a strong customer franchise are somewhat insulated from competitors' promotional strategies. A successful brand also means market power in the distribution channel. A strong brand with a heavy customer franchise receives the respect of an otherwise indifferent or antagonistic retailer.

In retail markets well-known consumer brands pay lower 'entry' or 'slotting' fees and are given more shelf facings for new products than weaker brands. Brand leverage also protects against private labels. Less leverage means that market shares are eroded and less expensive generic brands become dominant.

For customers, brands provide cues in coping with many competing products in the market and the confusion associated with the plethora of advertising messages (Figure 7.3). Habit also has a significant role to play in customer choice, especially with low-involvement products. Sometimes brand preferences are based on perceptions which are highly influenced by branding. Branding positively influences attitudes toward industrial products and services and influences aspirations by concentrating on brand attributes that influence potential buyers who may not be in a position to buy the brand now, but may be in the future.

Branding added values

A brand offers added values that some customers value sufficiently to buy. In branding added values the organization stresses the functional benefits of using the brand associated with the product class. The organization also emphasizes, and often concentrates on, the differentiated benefits of using the brand, which means focusing on the brand itself (Figure 7.4). Added values arise from four sources:

- From experience of using the brand – familiarity, reliability, risk reduction; personality and character.

- From the kind of people who use the brand – rich and snobbish, young or glamorous, and user associations fostered by advertising.

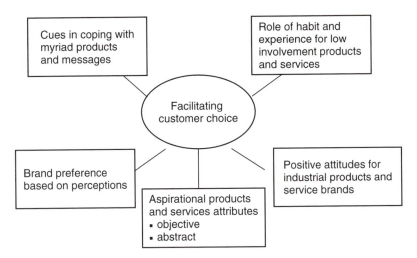

Figure [7.3] Branding functions

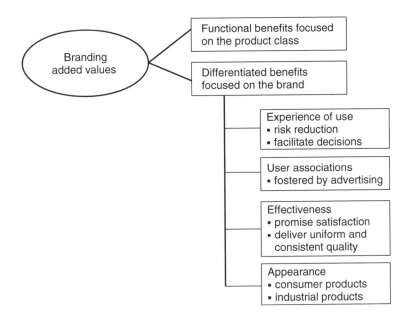

Figure [7.4] Branding adding values

■ From a belief that the brand is effective.

■ From the brand's appearance.

   The choice of brand name can be significant. Added values embodied in a well-known brand name may be transferred to a new product. This is the rationale for umbrella branding in product-line extensions. Umbrella branding saves promotional costs by relying on the added values of other brands carrying the umbrella name.

Branding may also work like an ingredient of its own and is effective. The branding of some proprietary drugs is thought to affect the mind's influence over body processes: 'branding works like an ingredient of its own interacting with the pharmacological active ingredients to produce something more powerful than an unbranded tablet' (Lannon and Cooper 1983). Added values may also come from the appearance of the brand which is the prime function of packaging and applies to consumer markets, e.g. perfumes and industrial products, e.g. industrial compressors.

Brand values are communicated to customers through advertising design and packaging. Advertising communicates and positions the brand. The image or personality of the brand is a strong driving force behind successful brands. These psychological aspects may be just as important as the functional aspects. The image the product has gives rise to conative components of the brand which represent real benefits to the customer. Branding is a claim to uniqueness. The process technology involved in Unilever's Vienetta ice-cream protects this brand from imitators and so gives the brand its uniqueness. Uniqueness, therefore, is the key attribute of branding.

Brands have an image reflecting two dimensions – the rational characteristics associated with the brand and the way brand values are communicated.

- Rational characteristics

  - quality

  - value for money

  - latent influence

  - special position of customer service

- Communication of brand values

  - communicate to consumers through advertising, design and packaging

  - advertising communicates and positions brands

Image is also important in services. In the crowded financial services market asset management companies have resorted to building corporate brands to promote their services. In a cross-country study of 900 people in institutions that use and distribute mutual funds in 2001, Fidelity Investments, Chase/Fleming and Merrill Lynch Investment Managers were identified as Europe's best recognized mutual fund brand names (*The Wall Street Journal Europe*, 8 February 2001, p. 11). Fidelity reached the top ranked position by building its own brand in Europe while the others pursued a strategy of acquisition. Building brand names in the financial services business is about building trust – people seek an acceptable return from an organization that is trustworthy, ethical and possesses longevity attributes. Consistency is also a large element in brand building. Fidelity maintains a consistent message using the slogan 'Trust the World's No. 1 to deliver', in newspaper, magazine and poster advertising.

Building and communicating brand values

In addition to product quality, acceptable prices and value for money, success-ful companies identify other brand values that are important to communicate to customers. Two concepts have been identified as essential for the long-term success of brands – brand popularity and country image (Kim and Chung 1997, p. 361). Brand performance is also a critical factor in brand building. Two additional factors contribute to the brand value mix and, hence, the popularity of the brand – the ability of the company to recruit and retain cus-tomers in different countries and their level and frequency of consumption of the brand (Figure 7.5).

If a brand is to establish itself as a strong contender in the market, it should build or maintain its market position through its presence in the market. Being a brand leader in a market segment could create valuable intangible assets for the same brand in other segments. Brand popularity or leadership in one segment should be considered a key strategic variable for building long-term positions for the brand. Many well-known brands have established their popularity in all international markets of significance: Coca-Cola, McDonald's, Kodak, Heineken, Guinness, Honda, Ford, BMW, to name but a few. Popular brands are those that are widely sought after and are bought by a large cross-section of society.

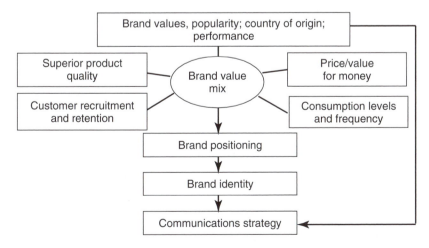

Source: Frank Bradley (2002) *International Marketing Strategy*, 4th edition, London: Financial Times/Prentice Hall, p. 196
Reproduced by permission of Pearson Education

Figure [7.5]   Building and communicating brand values

Brand popularity is considered as the accumulation of market acceptance and brand goodwill over time, promoted by word-of-mouth communication and advertising. Once a brand has become popular, the popularity component brings a positive contribution to the brand's loyalty, image or equity, or sales (Aaker 1991; Kim and Chung 1997). Brand popularity positively influences brand performance not only directly in the short run but also indirectly in the long run by creating a favourable brand image. These factors, taken together, influence the brand value mix.

Once the brand value mix has been established, the company positions the brand in the market, taking account of customer needs and competing brands. The brand is given a clear identity in the market and the organization attempts to develop an effective communications strategy to ensure that having built up the brand its values are properly communicated.

Long-term brand management – an illustration

Markets develop at different rates and in some countries the development starts earlier than others. In such circumstances the consumer brand company faces the predicament that its brand may be at different stages of the development cycle in different markets. Typically in the domestic market or in the first major market entered, it is likely to reach maturity before even taking off in emerging markets. For the purpose of illustration only suppose that if the managers of Baileys Original Irish Cream Liqueur were to apply these principles they would likely discover that the Baileys' brand development, its market share and sales, would differ in different countries. The differences in market development from one country to the next would likely require a different marketing emphasis.

The hypothetical market analysis might show the position of the Baileys' brand is each major country cluster as continuing to evolve (Figure 7.6). In countries such as Hungary, Argentina, the Philippines and South Africa the company's task would be to create an awareness and test the brand proposition. In Sweden, Brazil, the Czech Republic and Korea, Baileys might attempt to penetrate the market perhaps with an emphasis on heavy advertising and promotion. It would continue to be necessary to recruit customers in these markets. In its key maintenance markets such as Australia, Belgium, Switzerland and Denmark, Baileys' marketing endeavours would be focused on increasing consumption frequency and strengthening brand equities to maintain sales volumes. Finally, in its investment markets such as the United States, the United Kingdom, Germany and Spain, Baileys might wish to increase volume by increasing frequency of consumption and encouraging consumers to increase the occasions on which the brand is used. In these markets Baileys would be engaged in changing the positioning of the brand from being a traditional special occasions spirit to being a mainstream spirit drink with an emphasis on pleasure for all sociable occasions.

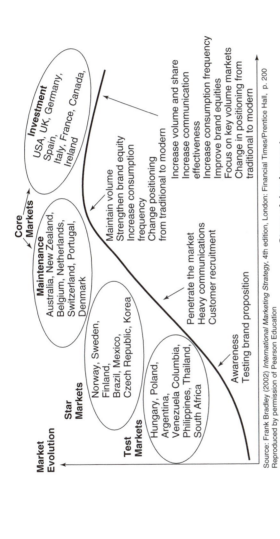

Figure [7.6]   Baileys' brand development

Source: Frank Bradley (2002) *International Marketing Strategy*, 4th edition, London: Financial Times/Prentice Hall. p. 200
Reproduced by permission of Pearson Education

Managing brand extensions

Brand extensions or umbrella branding is a favourite device of companies in the possession of a strong brand which management believes will extend to other areas. Brand extensions are relatively easy to arrange, hence their popularity. In evaluating the wisdom of brand extension it is necessary to examine the company's overall brand strategy and the financial implications as measured by market share changes and advertising efficiency (Smith and Park 1992, p. 298). This evaluation should take account of three sets of characteristics: those associated with the brand itself, those associated with the extension and those concerning the market for the brand extension (Figure 7.7).

Umbrella branding, taking an existing brand and applying it to a different product category, can be very profitable, e.g. 'Les Must de Cartier' for a new line of consumer trinkets such as scarves, wallets, cigarette lighters and writing pens. Firms that are successful in developing umbrella brands exploit the recognition value and reputation of a brand name in a new product area and obtain very high margins in doing so. This strategy is an accepted way of quickly and inexpensively entering a new market.

As a strategy, brand extension offers a number of advantages. A strong brand name gives a new product instant recognition. Brand extensions can be profitable as they save money. The company saves the advertising costs involved in familiarizing customers with a new name.

An established brand name makes a new product attractive by promoting a range of desirable associations and images. Not only do umbrella branded products need less advertising but consumers are also more willing to give brand names they already know an initial trial.

Figure [7.7]   Effect of brand extensions on market share and advertising efficiency

In this regard the Smirnoff Vodka brand extension, Smirnoff Ice, in 2002 was considered such a successful launch by its owners, Diageo, that they planned several similar extensions based on its Captain Morgan rum brand. The rum industry was dominated by Bacardi (>50 per cent market share) while Captain Morgan (>20 per cent) and Allied Domecq's Malibu (5 per cent). Diageo, it appears, was attempting to take some market share from Bacardi.

There are dangers, however, in umbrella branding. It can undermine the credibility of the original product. Customers either may not believe that the new product shares any of the desirable characteristics of the established brand, or they may simply forget what was attractive about the original brand. The brand name may be inappropriate to the new product, even if it is well made and satisfying. Furthermore, the brand name may lose its special positioning in the customer's mind through overuse.

The extension of the Starbucks brand to coffee beans, tea, croissants and scones, coffee, ice-cream, fruit juices, sandwiches, greeting cards and CDs may contribute back to the original brand in addition to taking support from it. The same may be said for Virgin's branding of air travel, train travel, travel packages but it is questionable whether extending the Virgin brand to cinema, soft drinks, financial services and telephones will have a long-term success. The danger is that these categories are too far apart and may result in diluting the original Virgin brand. In the luxury market the Mont Blanc brand extension from fountain pens to pencils, jewellery, and possibly to perfume and felt-tip pens may succeed. The extension to felt-tip pens, however, may dilute the brand somewhat as felt-tip pens would not be considered as belonging to the luxury category.

Badly thought-out brand extensions can be hideously inappropriate. Imagine a Pepsi single-malt whiskey or Chanel galoshes or Texaco olive oil or Harpic dairy products! Brands risk hurting themselves if they indulge in too many acrobatics. On the other hand, strong brands can take a tremendous amount of mismanagement to destroy.

Threats to branding

The major threats to branding arise from three sources: perceived product parity, lack of innovation and proliferation of undifferentiated products and the rise of own or private label brands. In regard to perceived product parity the argument is made that there now is no discernible difference between rival brands across a broad range of products. Manufacturing technology has raised the quality of many products while innovations are minor and easy to imitate. Lack of brand uniqueness and the better technology available result in an abundance of new undifferentiated products. At the same time advertising reinforces the belief that brands are similar.

The second major threat, lack of innovation and increased product proliferation of undifferentiated products, leads to dominance of promotion in the marketing mix. Overdependence on undifferentiated products that are not innovative means that retailers are able to auction access to customers by demanding discounts and marketing support for new products seeking shelf space. In this situation advertising budget tends to be diverted into sales promotions and less money is available for advertising. This shift gives greater power to retailers and it also gives them greater price discretion which often results in brands being sold below cost.

The third threat arises from private or own-label brands. Private-label brands tend to increase their share in times of recession, when customers are more price conscious. The shift to private-label products is the result of a fundamental shift of attitude among high cost-conscious and low brand-conscious customers. There is also a strong private-label tradition in some countries in selected product categories. Private-label brands pose a significant threat to established manufacturer brands. They may also be used to access an untapped market, so that the organization's brand continues to serve a designated market niche. Private-label branding may often be used to determine whether a new market segment exists for which the company might develop an exclusive own brand at some future date. The challenge for branded products under these circumstances is to ensure that the premium they charge reflects customers' perceptions of the competitive superiority of their products. It is important to emphasize that customer perceptions depend not only on price but also on advertising.

Scourge of brand debasement

For these and other reasons it is relatively easy, however, for a company to neglect the valuable equity created over years and to precipitate the decline that leads to brand erosion and eventual demise of the brand. Six interrelated factors, often under the organization's control, are thought to contribute to brand erosion, here referred to as the vicious circle of brand debasement (Figure 7.8). Financial pressures and the need to serve short-run targets often force organizations to adopt a harsh short-run perspective. Long-term brand building in such circumstances is virtually impossible. As a result brand managers must increase short-run sales instead of investing in image advertising to develop and nurture brands. In such circumstances many companies shift budgets away from advertising into sales promotions such as coupons, contests and lotteries.

Where companies experience great pressure to produce quarterly sales results, the impact of image-building advertising is frequently difficult to see and its value is not so obvious compared to price discounts or coupons which result in a quick, easily measured sales response. Such developments often lead to a brand being turned into a commodity, sold on the basis of price only.

These short-term corporate objectives play into the hands of the powerful retailers. By denying their brands the support required, manufacturers

Figure [7.8] Vicious circle of brand debasement

abrogate their right to brand control to the retailers who demand even higher percentages of promotion budgets for in-store promotions and other locally focused activities. Brands are further weakened thereby placing greater pressure for corporate imposed short-term financial returns.

Brand management has traditionally been the responsibility of middle and junior managers who must also show short-term results. These managers, because they are relatively junior, may not have the experience or corporate clout to protect company brands. Sometimes companies reduce advertising believing that the brand can sustain itself without such support.

Spending less on advertising is the third factor which directly contributes to the erosion of brands. The risk in cutting advertising budgets is that the brand will go into decline. With less money to spend and a greater pressure to show short-term returns, product line and category extensions under family brands multiply but with no accompanying image building effort. As a result, brand values dissipate and decline.

In an effort to defend customer franchise and forestall the evil day of complete decline, organizations have little choice but to turn to in-store price and sales promotions to encourage trial of well-known brands. While this has immediate benefits in terms of short-term financial objectives of the firm, it has decidedly sinister long-term effects.

Retailer power has arisen in large part due to checkout scanning devices which enable supermarkets to see which products sell and to allocate shelf space accordingly. To hold on to valued shelf space suppliers often agree to trade discounts, contributions to retailer advertising budgets or fees for in-store displays and other sales promotions. These fees have grown enormously because the increase in the number of new products has made shelf space that much more scarce. Having to pay for it leaves manufacturers with much less for brand advertising. Many companies now spend a very high proportion of their marketing budgets on promotions leaving very little for advertising.

With brand proliferation and a seemingly endless stream of brand extensions, more and more categories have moved towards commodity status. Brand image convergence occurs when organizations fall into the trap of diluting brand values. Many organizations rely too much on promotional programmes, often demanded by sales departments in the organization and large retailers. Price-orientated promotions such as coupons and discounts please distributors but the more the organization focuses on discount deals, the more it debases the brand. At the same time the organization is not helped by advertising agencies hell-bent on producing clever advertising, based on state-of-the-art graphics to prevent the curse of the 'zapper', instead of concentrating on designing advertising campaigns emphasizing how a product differs from its rivals.

Branding decisions

Brands depend on the strength of the company behind them – no amount of positioning will change that! The return on brand investment depends on the ability of the brand to keep the promises it makes and the expectations it creates among customers. Choosing the brand name and spending enough to imprint it on the minds of customers are the easy parts; living up to expectation is the more difficult part because, as we have seen, a brand is more than just a name.

Three principal approaches to branding may be identified: manufacturer brands, e.g. Heinz, Cadbury, Komatsu; private-label brands, e.g. Safeway, Carrefour, St Michael; and generic brands, e.g. Yellow Pack.

Manufacturer brand decisions

Manufacturer brands usually contain the name of the manufacturer, e.g. Miele electrical products. These brands appeal to a wide range of consumers who desire low risk of poor product performance, good quality, status and convenience shopping. Manufacturer brands are quite well known and trusted because quality control is strictly maintained. The brand name is identifiable and presents a distinctive image to customers. Manufacturers normally provide a number of product alternatives under their brand names.

There are advantages and disadvantages in using individual or family brands or a combination of the two. Sometimes organizations use individual brand names. The Mars company, for example, produces and sells, Mars, Twix, Milky Way, Bounty, Snickers and Marathon each with a distinctive image. Individual brands, e.g. Procter & Gamble (Tide, Bold, Daz, Oxydol) and Guinness (Guinness Stout, Smithwicks Ale, Harp Lager) require large promotional costs and there may be loss of continuity as individual brands are replaced from time to time. The brands do not benefit from an established identity and there are few scale economies involved.

A major advantage of an individual brand-name strategy is that the company does not tie its reputation to an individual product's acceptance. If the product fails, it does not compromise the manufacturer's names. A manufacturer of good-quality watches, such as Seiko, can introduce a lower quality line of watches (e.g. Pulsar) without diluting the Seiko name. The individual brand-name strategy permits the firm to search for the best name for each new product. A new name permits the building of new excitement and conviction.

Equally popular is the practice of using family brand names. With family brands one name is used for several products, e.g. Heinz Beans and Heinz Tomato Ketchup. Other companies which follow the family brand-name policy are General Electric and Philips. The cost of introducing a new product is less. There is no need for name research or for expensive advertising to create brand-name recognition. Furthermore, a well-known and reputable family brand will tend to guarantee an acceptable level of sales for the new product. The major disadvantages are that a company's overall image may be adversely affected when individual products fail the acceptance test.

Thus Campbells introduces new soups under its brand name with extreme simplicity and instant recognition. On the other hand, Philips in Europe uses its name on all of its products, but since its products vary in quality, most people expect only average quality in a Philips product which damages the sales of its superior products. This is a situation where individual branding might be better, or the company might avoid putting its own name on its weaker products.

A combination of an organization tradename combined with individual product names is a policy followed in the breakfast cereals market by Kellogg's e.g. Kellogg's Rice Krispies, Kellogg's Raisin Bran and Kellogg's Crunchy Nut Corn Flakes, and by Weetabix, e.g. Weetabix Ready Brek, Weetabix Fruit and Fibre, Weetabix Wholebran. In these cases the organization's name legitimizes, and the individual name individualizes the new product. Thus Quaker Oats in 'Quaker Oats' 'Cap'n Crunch' and Guinness in 'Guinness-Kaliber' use the company's reputation in the breakfast cereal field and beer markets respectively, while Cap'n Crunch and Kaliber individualize and dramatize the new products.

Finally, organizations frequently follow a multibrand strategy. In a multi-brand strategy, the seller develops two or more brands in the same product category. This marketing practice was pioneered by Procter & Gamble when it introduced Cheer detergent as a competitor for its already successful Tide. Although the sales of Tide dropped slightly, the combined sales of Cheer and Tide were higher. The emphasis in a multibrand strategy is to focus on the product category not on the brand. Manufacturers adopt multibrand strategies for several reasons:

- They can gain more shelf space, thus increasing the retailer's dependence on their brands.

- Few customers are so loyal to a brand that they will not try another – capture 'brand switchers' by offering several brands.

- Creating new brands develops excitement and efficiency within the manufacturer's organization. Brand managers in P&G, Opel and Beechams, for example, compete to outperform each other.

- Each brand is focused on a different market segment. Hence, Mars' four brands of ice creams are aimed at different segments of the market.

In deciding whether to introduce another brand as part of a multibrand strategy the manufacturer considers:

- The uniqueness of the background to the development of the brand.

- Its credibility among consumers.

- The degree to which the new brand is expected to cannibalize competitors' brands rather than the manufacturer's other brands.

The company must also want to determine whether the new brand's sales will cover the cost of product development and promotions. A major pitfall in introducing new entries is that each might obtain only a small market share, and few might be profitable. Ideally a company's brands should cannibalize competitor brands and not each other.

Private-label brands

Private-label brands means that retailers have greater control over pricing. They also have greater control over the supplier since in their dealings with manufacturers they have become more powerful.

The increased power of retailers, especially in the food sector, is part of the reason for the growth of private brands. As more and more grocery sales have become concentrated in the hands of fewer retail chains such as Aldi in Germany, Carrefour in France, Tesco and Safeway in the UK, they began to market products under their own private brand names and thereby transfer customer loyalty to the supermarket from the manufacturer.

Private-label branding generally does not adversely affect the brand leader in any category. Private labels are usually sold side by side with brand leaders. Indeed most supermarkets could ill-afford to be without the product category brand leader. If a private label competes with the No. 3 and No. 4 brand, the brand leader may welcome the arrival of strong private-label brands.

Generic brands

A further development of private brands has been the growth of generic brands especially for grocery products. For most products, generic brands are of lower quality than manufacturer or private brands. In packaged food products, for example, contents may vary in size, have less strength and use more filler. Pharmaceutical generics are an exception to this, being a close approximation of manufacturers' brands. Labels and packages are simplified, assortments are limited and brands are not well known. Distribution costs are much lower. Generic brands are not well advertised and receive secondary shelf space. The major marketing goal is to offer low-priced, lower quality items to consumers interested in economy.

Brand and category management

The brand management system evolved out of the notion that brands within a company should compete with each other. Such competition creates strong incentives to excel among brand managers but it also introduces conflict and even inefficiencies as brand managers compete for corporate resources such as advertising budgets, plant capacity and delivery services. Brand proliferations and fragmented markets combined with increased power among retailers have forced many consumer packaged goods companies to consider competing on the basis of product categories.

Rise and fall of the brand manager

Traditionally brand managers were responsible for all aspects of brand development, growth and maintenance. They were responsible for integrating all management functions to ensure the success of the brand. This ranged from research and development, production, sales, advertising, pricing and sales promotion activities. The brand manager had to be able to communicate effectively with the other functional areas of the business. In this world the manufacturer was dominant, the retailer weak and the middlemen subservient to both. In such an environment the brand manager was king.

As margins dwindled and costs became a major issue, particularly the rising cost of advertising, and as retailers became more powerful, the power of the brand manager has been dramatically reduced.

Prevalence of category management

Principally because of their growing power, retailers are no longer passive observers of inter-brand competition at the manufacturer level. Retailers are not brand oriented but category oriented as they are concerned about entire categories – the confectionery category, the detergent category, the dairy foods category. They are not really concerned about whether consumers reach for Mars or Cadburys, Tide or Cheer, Yoplait or Danone. The retailer is also in a position to demand shelf promotion allowances and 'slotting' fees. Very few manufacturers can afford the advertising and promotional inefficiency of two or more of its own brands competing for the customer's attention. To the retailer, therefore, it makes sense to have a Cadburys coupon this week, a Danone money-off promotion next week and an end-of-aisle display of Mars products the week after. Category management has become the important criteria not brand management, for both manufacturers and retailers.

Under a system of product category management, advertising, sales, manufacturing and research and development report to the product category manager. Marketing strategies are developed by integrating brand management into category management rather than developing competing brand strategies which must also compete for resources. As an example of how brands sometimes compete, note that claims on appeals are often fought over by brand managers. In detergents 'clean' or 'whiter' are words which competing brands would like to use. In cereals 'crunchy' or 'wholesome' are competitive claims among brands. Arbitrating such disputes between brand managers can be a waste of resources whereas promoting the category might be more profitable.

By focusing on categories instead of on brands, consumer products companies direct their attention to what competitor companies are doing. Devoting time to what rivals are doing is central to successful competition. Category management allows the company to rationalize its product line so that instead of overlapping, each brand can have a unique and distinct market position. Under category management the marketing manager has some control over other functions such as research and development, finance and manufacturing. Such a system also allows for better planned, faster, new product launches.

Positioning the brand

As discussed in Chapter 3, positioning is the process by which the company defines what it wishes a product or service to stand for in the market relative to competing products. The ability of an organization to compete effectively in any given market is determined in large measure by its ability to position its products, appropriately, relative to the needs of specific market segments and relative to competitive brands. Product positioning, therefore, requires a synthesis of customer analysis and competitor analysis. The organization also attempts to identify a range of benefits customers use to make decisions which helps to identify relevant market segments. The organization evaluates the relative importance of each benefit in each segment.

Analysis of competitive offerings involves not merely a review of product features and other marketing mix strategies, but also an evaluation of competitive advertising content. The image generated by advertisements and the nature of the slogans employed may constitute a major positioning tool, especially for personal products such as cosmetics, liquor and apparel.

Effective brand positioning

Following this analysis of customers, management must consider the degree to which existing products in the category are perceived to deliver a strong performance on each of the benefits of interest to customers. In choosing a position for a product, the company must match an appropriate package of benefits, clearly differentiated from competitive products on important dimensions, with a specific target market segment whose needs are not fully satisfied by existing products. Positioning permits a firm to develop a more effective and parsimonious approach to competition rather than competing head-on.

Product positions often reflect not only intrinsic product characteristics but also the image created by promotional strategies, pricing decisions and choice of distribution channels.

Effective positioning is essential to a product's success. If the company does not consciously position its products, customers will be confused and will do the positioning unaided which may not suit the organization. In such circumstances, competitive products which are accurately positioned may enjoy an advantage. At the same time, a product's positioning must not be too rigid. Positions are held relative to other competitive products and relative to customer needs. Both may change, necessitating a change in positioning. Different tastes make truly standardized products and brands a rarity; for example, the global brand Nescafé is sold in 50 combinations of strength, taste and flavour in different European markets. The brand and its values, of course, are constant throughout these markets.

Repositioning of the brand

As an alternative to physical modification of an existing product, firms sometimes elect to reposition their products simply by changing some or all of the elements of the marketing mix: advertising and promotion, distribution strategy, pricing or packaging. A revision of the entire marketing mix, including a change in product features may also accompany a repositioning strategy. Sometimes repositioning may represent a deliberate attempt to attack another firm's products and erode its market share; in other instances the objective may be to avoid head-to-head competition by moving into alternative market segments which are attractive but which are not well served by existing products.

Repositioning along price and quality dimensions or function served is generally referred to as 'trading up' or 'trading down'. However, repositioning may also involve sideways moves in which price and quality remain little changed but modifications are made to the product's tangible benefits or image to enhance its appeal to different types of consumers or for alternative end uses. Repositioning a traditional brand which has been neglected for many years and overstretched can be very expensive but may be necessary if the brand is to survive. An example of such repositioning of an existing product occurs when a deodorant formally promoted only to women is advertised as 'the deodorant for all the family'.

Relaunching the brand

For numerous reasons brand sales expectations sometimes do not materialize. In attempting to redress the situation organizations often relaunch failing brands. A brand relaunch does not, however, always succeed. Sometimes companies leave it too late to relaunch a previously poorly supported brand. The reason for the fall in share or decline in sales of the brand must be clearly understood. A decline due to a temporary withdrawal of marketing support or due to concentrated competitive attention is one thing but longer-term neglect is another. The brand must not be obsolete in all applications or market segments for the relaunch to work. It must have a franchise that still commands loyalty. The relaunch should not be the first of a long series of repairs but should pave the way for durable market performance.

When the brand is relaunched, product improvements added may be evaluated alongside the established and accepted battery of functional benefits the brand provides. Relaunching a brand gives the company an occasional opportunity to sharpen the attention of existing and potential users. Relaunching the brand also allows the introduction of new variants, e.g. types, flavours, colours, which can add market share without cannibalizing existing sales. In most relaunches of a brand, organizations make adept use of the word 'new', a concept that apparently holds its value for a long time afterwards!

There are a number of ways a company might relaunch a brand. A face lift for existing products under the brand and a quick introduction of line extensions may bring a positive response. Aggressive, new-look advertising and promotion are sometimes used in successful relaunches. A careful revision of the pricing structure which may involve a total repositioning is another way of relaunching a product.

References

Aaker, D. (1991), *Managing Brand Equity: Capitalizing on the Value of the Brand Name*. New York: Free Press.

Doyle, Peter (1991), 'Branding', in *The Marketing Book*, M. J. Baker, ed., Oxford: Butterworth-Heinemann.

Keller, Kevin Lane (1993), 'Conceptualising, measuring and managing customer-based brand equity', *Journal of Marketing*, **57** (January), 1–22.

Kim, Chung Koo and Chung, Jay Young (1997), 'Brand popularity, country image and market share: an empirical study', *Journal of International Business Studies*, Second Quarter, 361–86.

Lannon, J. and Cooper, P. (1983), 'Humanistic advertising: a holistic cultural perspective', *International Journal of Advertising*, **2**, 195–213.

Levitt, Theodore (1986) *The Marketing Imagination*. New York: The Free Press.

Robinson, Joan (1933), *The Economics of Imperfect Competition* (reprinted 1950). London: Macmillan.

Smith, Daniel and Park, C. Whan (1992), 'The effects of brand extensions on market share and advertising efficiency', *Journal of Marketing Research*, **29** (August), 296–313.

Watkins, Trevor (1986), *The Economics of the Brand: A Marketing Analysis*. London: McGraw-Hill.

Chapter 8

Developing new products and services

The task of managing the development of a new product is one of balancing efforts devoted to three objectives: product performance, speed to market and product cost. Concern rests with determining whether the organization is a technology leader or follower in regard to new product development and innovation. Product performance refers to the extent to which a product meets its customer-based performance specifications or how well a product is rated in the eyes of the customer. The second objective, speed to market, is measured as the time which elapses between an unsatisfied need appearing in the market and a product being made available to a customer to satisfy this need. The impact of speed as a competitive tool has already been discussed in Chapter 6. The third objective, product cost, refers to the total cost of delivering the product to the customer. A product with a low manufactured cost but a high marketing cost may still be a failure. In designing and developing new products all three criteria must be fulfilled.

Dimensions of the product

A product is anything that can be offered to someone to satisfy a need or want – a set of tangible and intangible attributes, including packaging, colour, price, quality, brand, and the services and reputation of the seller. A product is, therefore, anything tangible or intangible that satisfies the customer's needs.

The concepts of products and services are often confused which leads to considerable misunderstandings. Much of the difficulty arises from the mistaken view that products are tangible physical goods only. Using tangibility as the dominant distinguishing feature between products and services led Shostack (1977) to place products on a tangible–intangible spectrum ranging from goods and services on one end to intangible services on the other. Tangibility is the principal critical factor in the marketing of products and services.

The products that people buy are mostly tangible goods like furniture, beer, cars, newspapers and books. Intangible items like medical care, education, shoe repair, entertainment and hotel accommodation are services which are also bought – here these are also treated as products.

Core products and benefits

Fundamental to every product is a core benefit that is the basic service or benefit the customer seeks. The core benefit is the first and central dimension of the product and involves the physical appearance of the product, its quality, and its ability to satisfy user needs including functional utility (Figure 8.1). The core product allows customers to solve problems and satisfy basic needs, e.g. in the case of a car it may be transport to work, shopping trips or socializing.

Generic and expected products

Having identified the core benefit, the task facing the company is to convert the core benefit into a generic or basic version of the product which will eventually be sold. Thus, a car consists of a box-like body made of steel, plastic and glass and other materials which has an engine and four wheels. Associated with the concept of generic product are benefits to be obtained from its use. Product features are not stressed. Generic product concepts evolve with time. The generic product concept 'computer', for example, has evolved from being a large machine with complicated software which dominated a specially equipped room to a hand-held unit which doubles as a mobile telephone and personal organizer. Generic products are easy to recognize. The names by which they are known immediately convey a sense of recognition

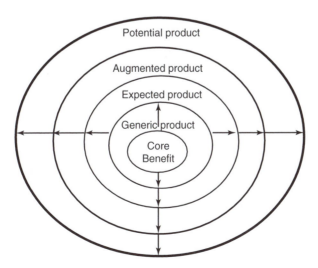

Figure [8.1]   Dimensions of the product

for most people: a race horse, a bicycle, a cup, a hair cut, a rock concert, a parliamentary speech.

The third dimension refers to the expected product or the set of attributes that customers normally expect when they purchase this product. Car buyers, for example, expect that the vehicle they purchase will travel at certain speeds, carry a certain number of passengers and their baggage safely, cost so much to run and maintain and will not corrode or rust. Image is also an important feature of cars and country of origin image may be a key determinant in making a purchase. The expected product generally reflects the minimum acceptable standards in a particular product market.

Differentiated products and the future

By adding additional services and benefits the company turns the expected product into an augmented product which is the fourth product dimension to be considered. It is these additional benefits and services that help to distinguish the company's product from those of competitors and form the basis for product differentiation. As was seen in Chapter 3, product differentiation allows the organization to segment the market – one segment that competes on the basis of augmented products and another which competes on the basis of the expected product. As an example, witness the growth of low-price low-service economy supermarkets paralleling the growth of premium price and service food outlets. Similarly, car manufacturers produce differentiated products for the premium or luxury end of the market while also producing economy models for the expected product market. These product markets may exist side by side within the same country or region.

Product differentiation is related to the image in the market of the organization's products and its ability to charge a price premium. The organization that provides differentiated products raises its image among customers and may be able to charge a premium for its products. There is a strong interrelation among differentiation, price premiums and image effect (Figure 8.2).

Basic staple products in consumer markets such as salt, sugar or a bus ride are homogeneous products and services which are difficult to differentiate and hence are unlikely to attract a price premium. Similarly, in industrial product markets commodities and raw materials, agricultural products, basic chemicals, metals and electricity or gas are difficult to differentiate and obtain a price premium. Low differentiation is possible for consumer products such as shampoos, oil, petrol, tyres or a taxi ride and for industrial products such as components, corrugated packaging material or rail freight.

In contrast, medium differentiation and a slightly higher price premium may be obtained for consumer products such as branded packaged food products, vacuum cleaners, televisions and video players and hair styles while the same applies for industrial products such as personal computers, food processing equipment and refrigerated container services. High product

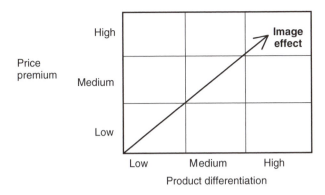

Figure [8.2]   Product differentiation, price premium and image effects

differentiation and high price premiums are possible for consumer products such as clothing, perfume, watches, cars and premium hotels and similarly for industrial products such as special fine chemicals, customized machinery and integrated distribution systems with computerized information and control systems.

The fifth dimension of the product refers to all possible future innovations in the product. The potential product refers to the evolutionary process through which the product may pass. As companies search for new ways of satisfying customer needs, potential new products are identified which help to distinguish the company's products.

Role of product design

Product design means searching for a set of key features or appeals that are special or even unique to the product or customer group. By agreeing on the basic benefits, the organization is in a better position to serve customer needs. Product design is considered as 'the designation of the key benefits the product is to provide, the psychological positioning of these benefits versus competitive products, and the fulfilment of the product promises by physical features' (Urban and Hauser 1980, p. 155). These key benefits form the foundation on which all elements of the marketing strategy are built.

Product design and quality

Quality is what the customer thinks it is, and design contributes to it. It is necessary, however, to be precise in the meaning of quality and how it should be implemented. In this regard it is necessary to translate technical proficiency into product and service attributes desired by the customer. Quality relates and contributes to customer satisfaction. At the same time the organization must also benefit from providing quality products and services. This means decomposing customer demand into its elements and relating those elements to the functions performed by the product objectively and compared to competitors. This evaluation allows the organization to judge how well the customer is being satisfied.

Many organizations realize that, while they can manufacture reliable products, they fail to get products right the first time. Increasingly these organizations understand that they do not adequately take customer needs and preferences into account, and hence rely very little on market research, one of the unwelcome consequences of short-term financial pressures. New products that fall short of customer requirements, however, have to be redesigned which is costly both in terms of resources and the market opportunity costs. Quality function management demonstrates how design considerations can be used to eliminate the need to redesign faulty products and produce competitive products the first time.

An example of a hypothetical pencil company Writesharp illustrates the procedure (*Business Week*, 2 December 1991, pp. 28–9). Assume that Writesharp has two major competitors: X and Y. The company recognizes that the attributes desired in a pencil by customers are 'easy to hold'; 'does not smear'; 'the point lasts'; and 'the pencil does not roll in the user's hand' (Figure 8.3). Company research has shown that customers attach different weights to each of these attributes. Writesharp's research has also shown certain correlations between these customer demands and physical characteristics that a pencil might possess: pencil length; time between sharpenings; lead dust and hexagonality. For example, there is a strong correlation between lead dust measured as particles for each line of text written and smearing. Furthermore, there is a possible correlation between pencil length and rolling.

In terms of satisfaction levels Writesharp is perceived to be better than competitors on 'easy to hold' so the company's target is to maintain that standard. Competitor Y and Writesharp deliver the same high level of satisfaction in regard to smearing so there is no scope for improvement here. Competitor X provides greater satisfaction levels in regard to 'point lasts', so Writesharp expects to improve on this attribute. Writesharp has no competitive advantage on 'rolling' so it will attempt to improve satisfaction levels relative to competitors.

At present Writesharp's price is 45 cents, its market share is 16 per cent and profit on each pencil is four cents. With the improvements it expects price to be 46 cents, share to be 20 per cent and profit to double.

The company expects to achieve this level of performance by improving the quality of its product and has prepared a set of benchmarks to use in its evaluation. Writesharp's aim is to significantly improve on its own performance on each functional characteristic and to exceed its two competitors on three of them and to match Competitor X on hexagonality. If Writesharp's

FUNCTIONAL CHARACTERISTICS

CUSTOMER SATISFACTION

*** strong correlation ** some correlation

* possible correlation

scale 1 - 5 (5 = best)

CUSTOMER DEMANDS	Pencil Length (inches)	Time Between Sharpenings (written lines)	Lead Dust (particles per line)	Hexagon-ality	Importance Rating (5 = highest)	Writesharp (now)	Competitor X (now)	Competitor Y (now)	Writesharp (target)
Easy to hold	**			**	3	4	3	3	4
Does not smear		**	***		4	5	4	5	5
Point lasts	*	***	**		5	4	5	3	5
Does not roll	*			***	2	3	3	3	4
BENCHMARKS									
Writesharp (now)	5	56	10	70%					
Competitor X (now)	5	84	12	80%					
Competitor Y (now)	4	41	10	60%					
Writesharp (target)	5.5	100	6	80%					

	Writesharp (now)	Competitor X (now)	Competitor Y (now)	Writesharp (target)
Market Price	45c	48c	44c	46c
Market Share	16%	12%	32%	20%
Profit	4c	6c	4c	8c

c = cents

Source: Adapted and up-dated from *Business Week*, 2 December 1991, pp. 28-29

Figure [8.3] Integrating design and quality in product development analysis is correct and if it meets the benchmarks set and if customer satisfaction materializes as expected, company performance in terms of price, share and profit should improve as a result of the improved quality.

Quality can be built into all kinds of products and services. The above example illustrates the need to be precise in the meaning of quality and to translate elements of quality as perceived important by customers into physical reality.

Special position of packaging in product design

Prepackaging brings with it considerable advantages to marketing organizations; they can make direct contact with customers through the medium of the package, creating images and appeals to stimulate purchase. Initially, prepackaging provided assurance to customers that the contents were unlikely to have been adulterated or interfered with in any way; protection was the objective.

Having chosen a design image for the product the organization attempts to preserve that image for as long as possible so that customers can feel sure that a consistent level of quality is being delivered. Packaging is seen, therefore, not just in its protective role but as a vehicle to carry information and as a way to promote the product through the creation of a unique image. Three factors contribute to image formation:

- the outline design of the package

- the use of strong colour

- the overall shape.

Designs in glass have fostered a strong brand image, e.g. Coca-Cola, Bovril, Orangina. Packaging colour plays a crucial role in immediate recognition – the yellow of Colmans Mustard, the red and white of Campbell's soups.

In the early years of mass merchandising the overall design of many packaged products relied on a typographic statement of the company's name and general information about the product. Complex package designs were used, however, on many of the packaged versions of well-known brands. These designs remained substantially unchanged as the brands established themselves in the market. In some cases the packaging is still the same, e.g. Lyle's Golden Syrup.

There are distinct promotional advantages which stem from effective design, shape and colour. Packaging helps to identify products especially at point of purchase. The advertising copy on the package lasts as long as the product remains in the package. For some products the package is the only way to differentiate the product contained. In photocopying paper, for example, one brand is considered as good as another, so the package may be used to differentiate one supplier from another.

Innovation and evolution of markets

Competition in markets based on innovation has led to products which perform old functions better and products that make new functions possible (Roman and Puett Jr. 1983, p. 256). There are numerous product examples: Teflon, velcro fasteners, synthetic wash and wear fabrics, accelerated freeze drying. Procedural innovations can also be very significant in services marketing – the way customers are served can result in a more effective use of resources and increase customer benefits.

Seldom is there a single dominant product technology underpinning a product market. In most instances companies have the choice of pursuing quite different product technologies, sometimes incremental and sometimes radical. While many organizations excel in developing and implementing sustaining technologies, many more avoid radical or disruptive innovation. The fear is based on the costs involved and the larger the market share already held, the more there is at stake if the disruptive innovation does not work or is not accepted in mainstream markets. This occurs even when the radical technology embodies a new and improved value proposition for customers in rapidly growing non-mainstream market segments. For these reasons large established organizations are rarely at the forefront of radical new product innovation whereas small entrepreneurial organizations are.

Large organizations, however, can successfully adopt radical or disruptive product innovation according to Stringer (2000) if they employ a combination of the following strategies:

- Make breakthrough innovation a strategic and cultural priority in the organization:
  - set stretch goals that can only be achieved by doing things differently
  - challenge divisions to increase the proportion of revenues derived from new products
  - develop benchmark measures that show how important radical innovation is likely to be in the business system
- Create informal project laboratories within the organization:
  - provide innovators with time, flexibility and discretionary R & D funds
  - modify the performance management system so that promoters of radical ideas that do not have immediate pay-offs are not penalized
- Establish knowledge markets within the organization:
  - small teams of internal entrepreneurs with responsibility for driving radical innovation

– collect the best ideas from throughout the organization and independently develop and commercialize likely winners.

The concept of informal project laboratories was at the heart of 3M's success at innovating. The project laboratory strategy, however, is contrary to management practice which seeks justification for all expenditures based on short-run financial returns only.

Product innovation and diffusion, discussed in this chapter, and product life cycles, discussed in Chapter 9, are closely related concepts. Many products evolve from simple to more sophisticated forms with time. This development takes place due to changes in production techniques, new developments in packaging, the availability of new ingredients or components or more simply as a result of changes in fashion, customer preferences or attitudes. The extent of innovation in products such as computers, telecommunications and aircraft is highly visible and the impact on our daily lives is considerable. The innovation that has occurred in machine tools and robotics is less obvious but has an equally positive impact on our lives. Innovation also occurs in ordinary consumer products which is sometimes taken for granted.

The only insurance against obsolescence for any organization is a consistent policy of product innovation. According to the Chairman of Unilever plc and Unilever NV:

> Detergents is a technology driven business: we can prove it. All the development since the 40s that have permanently and profitably shifted market standing, have had at their core a better product. The competitor who delivers superior technology, and delivers it first will win. This means sinking large capital sums into the ground in anticipation of demand, often on scant evidence. When we get it wrong it leaves us with an expensive white elephant – or an expensive car park in one of our factories! It means entering the new markets which recent geopolitical changes have opened up while there are still economic and political risks. It means extending our brands around the world without necessarily collecting the finest points of market research evidence in Uruguay or Vietnam (Fitzgerald 1991).

Special position of high technology products

In new product development, especially in rapidly changing technologies, the focus should be on the customer benefits and problem solving, not on the product itself. In rapidly changing technologies this may mean that success in new product development can depend on how well the organization anticipates future requirements that customers may not be able to articulate in the present. The case of the mobile telephone may be cited to support this point. Before the introduction of mobile telephony it is unlikely that conventional consumer research studies would have indicated a need or want for such products. In such circumstances some organizations draw on the advice of technology 'opinion leader-users' who have an economic incentive to explore advancement on current products and services. For such innovations it is necessary to study that segment of the market that is likely to give the information required, not just the average customer.

It is often argued that the successful high technology organization abides by the principle of creative destruction. Such an organization takes a long-term view of the market and competition by continually seeking, through planned obsolescence, to surpass its own profitable existing technologies and thereby replace them with something superior in technology and market appeal. In this respect it is argued that the 'high tech firm really has no choice. If it does not create superior products, someone else will' (Shanklin and Ryans 1984, p. 100).

Conditions resembling supply-side marketing dominate the early stages of the marketing of high technology products. 'In high tech, Say's Law (the supply of a product can create its own demand) appears right on target' (Shanklin and Ryans 1984). High technology products and services appear to create a demand where none previously existed. According to these authors, 'the infancy of every high technology market has been characterized by supply-side conditions in which the marketer's job is to stimulate primary or basic demand for the product, process or service at hand' (p. 102).

Manufacturing and engineering people, however, frequently miss the broader context of markets by concentrating on individual users. Marketing people must decide if there are others who are similar and if the segment to which they belong is sufficiently large and profitable. Marketing managers must also determine relative priorities for product and service attributes in the context of the entire market to complement the technical perspective of manufacturing and engineering.

Diffusion of innovation

An innovation is the adoption of a new idea, product or process which is prospectively useful. The presence of a number of factors increases the likelihood that an innovation will be adopted. The innovating company must seek to satisfy an existing or latent demand or need and the solution provided must be compatible with the norms and rules of society. The greater the perceived complexity of the innovation, the slower the rate of adoption. Providing the innovation in small quantities, if that is possible, may reduce risk and encourage product trial and adoption. If the customer can observe the benefits of the innovation, it is more likely to be adopted; and product innovations that can be easily and frequently communicated through the media are likely to be adopted much more rapidly than innovations which require strong sales and extensive merchandising support.

Macro level diffusion

It is generally accepted that the diffusion of most products into a market follows an S-shaped pattern. At the initial stages few people are aware of the innovation, many who are aware delay adoption because of risk or lack of information, others are much too loyal or are otherwise committed to existing products. With time, industry sales begin to increase slowly, accelerate and finally converge on a market potential which is difficult to define. It is possible to relate the diffusion of an innovation to classify adopters into categories according to when they first try the product. The diffusion process is generally envisaged as consisting of five stages (Figure 8.4).

Innovators are the first customers to adopt a new product. Besides being venturesome, innovators are willing to take risks; they may be outward-looking, communicative, and sometimes thought of as socially aggressive, and involved in many networks of people. Customers in this category form only a small proportion of the total population in the market.

Customers who are early adopters enjoy the prestige and respect that early purchasing of an innovation brings. They tend to be opinion leaders, who influence others through word of mouth to purchase. This group represents the larger proportion of society.

The mass market for a product is divided into two customer groups. Early majority customers are generally thought of as having status within their social class and are gregarious, communicative and attentive to sources of information. They represent a large proportion of the total population. Late majority customers, also a large part of the total population, tend to be less cosmopolitan and responsive to change. Customers in this group tend to be less well off, older and usually belong to one of the lower socioeconomic groupings.

The last customer group to purchase a new product, not surprisingly, are called laggards. This group, which may be a relatively substantial proportion of the population, tend to be price conscious, suspicious of novelty and

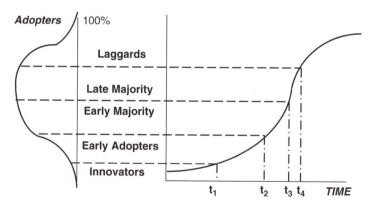

Source: Richard P. Bagozzi (1991) *Principles of Marketing Management*, New York: Macmillan Publishing Co, p. 102

Figure [8.4]   Contribution of adopters to product sales over time change, have low incomes and are conservative in most of their behaviour. Most products have reached the maturity stage of the life cycle, i.e. a saturated market, before being purchased by laggards.

Micro level diffusion

At the micro level in the market, potential buyers are viewed as passing through an adoption process for the product or service that results in a trial and eventually may culminate in a purchase. One of the most popular forms of the adoption process, popularized by Rogers (1962, pp. 81–6) involves six stages (Figure 8.5). Potential buyers become aware of a product or brand when they learn of its existence but do not have any further information about it. In some cases the customer takes an interest in the product and is motivated to seek information about it. It then becomes necessary to evaluate the product and the customer decides whether to try it. At the trial stage the customer purchases the product to test it. Adoption is said to have occurred when the customer uses the product on a regular basis. During the confirmation stage the buyer seeks reinforcement of the adoption decision but may reverse it if for any reason a dissonance arises.

The probability of adoption of an innovation is influenced by a number of characteristics of the innovation itself (Rogers 1983; Tornatzky and Klein 1982). Products are considered to be relatively easy to adopt if they:

- are compatible with existing lifestyles

- are relatively unimportant in total purchases

- are suitable for mass advertising and distribution

- are consumed quickly

- are easy to use

Figure [8.5] Product adoption in consumer markets

- can be tried in small quantities

- have desirable attributes which are obvious.

Barriers to adoption can be substantial when there is loyalty to existing products or the innovation is sufficiently incompatible with prevailing values among customers that acceptance is retarded even though other factors are supportive.

The success among users of the innovative Linux computer operating system, which is free, has been a challenge to Sun Microsystems, the dominant Unix supplier, and Microsoft which supplies Windows. Linux is continually improved by volunteer programmers around the world who believe software should benefit society. Addressing the challenge, Sun Microsystems claims that Linux is a 'bathtub of code' whereby the myriad designers will ultimately cause Linux to splinter into incompatible versions. Similarly, Microsoft agues that 'all the noise and optimism of the early adopters doesn't in any way guarantee Linux will cross into the mainstream' (*USA Today*, 5 August 2002, p. 2B).

With customer awareness of Linux growing, hardware and software developers have been forced to develop Linux strategies or risk losing out on a new growth market. In mid-2002, Oracle, the dominant supplier of database software for Unix systems, announced an alliance with Dell Computers and Red Hat, the leading Linux distributor with the objective of promoting inexpensive Linux servers equipped with a large Oracle database to do the same back-office functions normally done by Unix servers, such as store data, perform accounting functions and interact with employees, suppliers and customers. This alliance may give the Linux system the credibility it needs to become a mainstream product and move firmly through the innovation cycle.

New products as marketing innovation

New products serve to increase sales overall, contribute to company growth and reduce risk through diversification. They also make more efficient use of distribution channels and may enhance the company's image as an innovator. An innovation is anything perceived as new by potential adopters. The newness may be incorporated in products, services or ideas. The perceived innovative characteristics of a new product determine the rate and extent of adoption. A number of characteristics of the new product itself influence the likelihood of adoption – relative advantage, compatibility, complexity, trialability, observability, uncertainty and diffusion barriers (Figure 8.6).

For an innovation to be adopted there must be an advantage associated with its use that is higher or better than that of competitors. The perceived superiority of the new product over that which it replaces is a

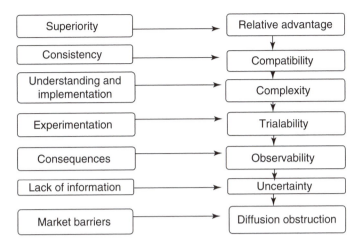

Figure [8.6] Adoption of a marketing innovation

measure of its relative advantage in the market. Consistency with existing lifestyles and ways of working and procedures indicates how compatible the new product is likely to be with customers. Successful innovation must be compatible with the lifestyles of the target market, its culture, religion, mores of the society and behaviour and industrial practices. Lack of information about the innovation and its application can result in marketing and artificial market entry barriers and thus obstruct the diffusion of the innovation.

New products that are difficult to understand and implement may be perceived as too complex for adoption. Complexity should be avoided – the innovation must be understood by potential users and easy to implement. In industrial markets many products are highly complex, sometimes much too complex for the intended task. Before adopting something new, customers or users often want to try the innovation without committing to it, particularly if it involves a large cost or a significant change in work practices and behaviour among buyers.

To what extent is it possible to experiment with the new product before adoption? If the investment is high, adopters may wish to place the new product on trial for some time before deciding to purchase. Experimentation with the innovation before final commitment allows potential customers to test the innovation for usefulness which is a desirable feature of any innovation. To accomplish trialability companies often make the product available as samples. In consumer markets food products are frequently available in prepared form in supermarkets by way of a sales promotion to allow potential customers to try them. In industrial markets potential customers may be allowed to use a piece of equipment or observe it in use for some time before deciding whether to purchase it.

If the consequences of adopting the innovation are clearly observable, e.g. greater efficiency of new equipment or complimentary glances from passers-by for a new outfit, the innovation will have met the observability criterion.

Successful new products meet customer needs competitively whereas failures tend to be based on an illusory innovation. The six most important variables that contribute to new product development success are:

- new product synergy with existing marketing skills

- new product synergy with existing technical and manufacturing skills

- high product quality

- significant customer/user benefits

- appropriate targeting and pricing strategies

- distribution channel support.

New product-market decisions

By improving technology only without changing market decisions the organization is merely reforming the product. A new technology would mean a product innovation. By deciding not to change the product and at the same time changing the marketing in some way, the company is re-merchandising. Entering a new market the organization is attempting to reposition an existing product or brand.

A combination of improved technology and a new marketing mix allows the company to introduce an improved product. An improved technology in a new market means deciding to extend the market while a new marketing mix and a new technology mean an extension to the company's product lines. A combination of a new technology for a new market involves a decision to diversify. The further the company moves from serving existing product markets, the greater the risk involved. The decision to diversify involves the greatest risk.

New products and market share

A larger market share at any stage in the life cycle enables the firm to achieve greater production and marketing economies. A company whose share falls radically in a particular segment soon joins the marginal suppliers in the industry and experiences the disadvantages such a role implies, including the loss of pricing initiative.

Firms usually seek to establish themselves in the market early in the product life cycle. Market share is easier to obtain for innovators. In more mature markets, as the sales curve flattens, gains in market share only come at very high cost. Each extra percentage share point of a mature market costs much more that a similar gain at the introduction or growth stages. Buying market share at the mature stage of the life cycle may not be justifiable in profit terms. Innovative organizations seek ways to circumvent this predicament.

Generally car companies rely on a single model for their sales in the sub-compact category but in Japan Toyota has six models, Honda plans as many as five and Nissan has two with a third on the way. This mania for multiple models arises because Japan's car sales are shrinking due to a declining population. The market remains crowded with nine domestic manufacturers, all seeking a share of a medium-sized market. In the mid-1990s a shake-out appeared likely as Nissan and some smaller companies were close to collapse. This shake-out never occurred, however, but competition intensified and the introduction of new models emerged as the car makers' key marketing weapon. The manufacturers have conditioned Japanese customers to expect a steady stream of new models but yet they remain profitable and have the world's most efficient factories and cars in demand that are on the top of customer satisfaction lists.

With few high-volume models, Japanese manufacturers have learned to make a profit on a range of sub-compact niche cars such as Toyota's Vitz, built in small quantities. Doing so requires them to reduce the time they spend on developing new vehicles and launching them. The shorter lead-times, in turn, allow them to respond quickly to new design trends and to respond to even short-lived fashion demand.

The new competitive model that puts pressure on Japanese manufacturers poses a dilemma for foreign manufacturers. Should they plan the same strategy and risk the losses, or drop out and forfeit the competitiveness dividend to the Japanese? In late 2001 General Motors joined the fray with the Cruze, a mini SUV, especially designed for Japan but Rolf Eckrodt the CEO of Daimler-Chrysler's Mitsubishi Motors affiliate believes it is dangerous to be drawn into the new competition – 'You have to shorten development times, and so you make it quick and dirty. Then you have quality problems and a vicious cycle is on. I don't want to have that race' (*The Wall Street Journal*, 5 August 2002, p. A8).

Process of new product development

The process of bringing new products to the market can be very risky and often involves large investments of money and time. In calculating the cost it is necessary to include the cost of the time spent in research and development, capital investment in plant and equipment, warehousing and distribution costs, packaging and advertising development costs and launch and promotional support costs. The new product development process may be divided into six stages:

- new idea/concept generation and screening
- development and testing of new idea/concept
- business and marketing analysis
- product development and testing
- test marketing
- commercialization.

Idea generation and screening

In the process of new product development the organization first analyses the current market situation and the capabilities in the organization and simultaneously carries out a market opportunity analysis and search (Figure 8.7). The first step in the process is to generate new ideas and concepts which involve a continuous, systematic search for new product opportunities. In this regard it is generally believed that customers are the best source of new ideas, followed by competitors and the sales force.

The organization then refines the new concepts or ideas and screens them using criteria such as product features, market opportunities, the competitive situation, organization capability and the availability of finance. Ideas which have been screened through research and corporate-fit criteria and have survived must pass through several further stages of refinement:

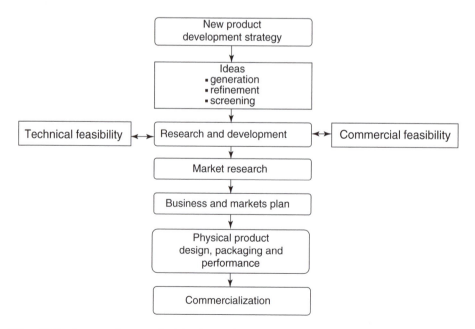

Figure [8.7]   Process of new product development

- identity of market segment

- product description

- technical features

- customer benefits

- competitive advantage

- manufacturing process to be used.

Concept development and testing

During the second stage the company carries out two types of feasibility study: a commercial feasibility study to judge if the new idea proposed is commercially viable and a technical feasibility study to determine if the appropriate technical requirements and standards can be met. It is also necessary to produce designs and samples for quantitative research during this stage. This development and testing of the new idea move the process from the stage of considering a product idea to dealing with a product concept to deciding an appropriate product image.

The commercial feasibility assessment is a form of business analysis which attempts to identify product success requirements and organizational competencies. Financial projections, market analyses, sales projections, estimates of profit margins and likely costs are made at this point. During this stage the company attempts to identify the product features and market opportunities while assessing competitive factors, company capability and the financial requirements associated with proceeding further.

The company faces the possibility of making two types of mistake. It may decide not to proceed with a new product development idea that is taken up successfully by a competitor. Alternatively it may decide to proceed with an idea which turns out to be a failure. Either way the organization faces a dilemma that it must resolve.

Business and marketing analysis

The third stage of the process involves a business and marketing analysis to produce a marketing plan. Financial and sales projections are part of the process and estimates of profit margins and development costs are provided. At this stage also the company describes the target market in considerable detail. It determines the appropriate positioning for the new product, its likely sales, market shares to be achieved and profit objectives. The marketing mix is also specified during this stage.

Product market testing

During the fourth stage the product is developed and tested. Numerous functional tests are carried out and selected consumer tests are administered. Two sets of activities take place simultaneously. One set of activities involves deciding the appropriate packaging requirements for the product, its design and tests of performance while the other set of activities involves product design, and technical and production factors involved in production planning and the development of a sample product. At this stage too the proposition may again be tested leading to some revision particularly if retailers or other channel members have an opportunity to express their opinions.

During the fifth stage the company market tests the new product having briefed the sales force. The product and the proposed mix of marketing activities are introduced into authentic buyer settings to test product acceptance and market size. Revisions may still be necessary, hence, the need for a flexible approach.

It will also be necessary to carry out quantitative research through consumer surveys or interviews with buyers in industrial markets depending on the nature of the new product. At this stage the company attempts to measure the extent to which potential customers are interested in the product, how they assess it compared to competing products, the features they like and dislike, the extent to which they are likely to purchase and the price they would expect to pay. Other aspects of the marketing mix will also be researched as the product moves through the development process, e.g. packaging, advertising copy and merchandising.

Commercialization of a new product

Market testing presumably gives management enough information to decide whether to launch the new product. If the company goes ahead with commercialization, it will face its largest costs to date. The company will have to contract for manufacture or it will build or rent a full-scale manufacturing facility. The size of the plant will be a critical decision variable. The organization can build a plant smaller than called for by the sales forecast, to be on the safe side, but it will then run the risk of missed market opportunities if the product takes off. In such circumstances the company is in danger of handing over the potential of a well-cultivated market to flexible competitors that are capable of moving fast to imitate the company's new product. Another very large cost is the marketing cost associated with commercialization which can be very high depending on the size of the market and the marketing tasks to be performed.

The final stage is to commercialize the product by launching it in the market. At the launch stage the entire sales promotion activity working with the trade and sales force and, particularly, retailers, converges with the advertising support process. The timing of market entry, the geographic market segments to be served, the target customer groups in each segment and the introductory marketing strategy are determined at this stage. Successful firms are known to evaluate new product development ideas using four important criteria:

- prospects for sales and profits

- capital or investment cost associated with the new venture

- competitive feasibility

- strategic desirability.

The new product development process described above is quite typical of the situation facing most companies. The details vary by company and circumstance. In addition to the above requirements it is usually necessary to consider the technology capabilities of suppliers and their ability to respond within the business system to integrate the new product development process. Based on a study of different industry sectors around the world Handfield *et al.* (1999) report that while many organizations realize the importance of supplier integration in the new product development process, they have not discovered the means to successfully implement it. In attempting to integrate the supplier, the organization not only must understand the supplier's ability to meet cost, quality and product launch and timing goals but it must also assess the supplier's technology plans, their level of design capability and the volatility within the particular technology being integrated.

Developing a new cereal food ingredient for the confectionery industry brand leader, Quaker Oats, on a co-packing basis, was a problem faced by Tipperary Cereals Limited in the early 1990s. The product development sequence resembles that discussed above in considerable detail. In industrial markets new product development is usually carried out in close co-operation with existing and potential customers. The development sequence for the introduction and launch of a co-packing agreement whereby this small cereal manufacturer prepared ingredients to be used in branded confectionery items for a large consumer products company demonstrates the resource and time commitment and level of interaction involved (Figure 8.8).

New product development myopia

Understanding customers' needs is often a costly and an inexact process, as was seen in Chapter 5. Even when customers know precisely what they want, they often cannot transfer that information to the organization clearly and completely. Furthermore, the pressure for short-term returns and considerations of speed to market to compete innovatively with others have led some

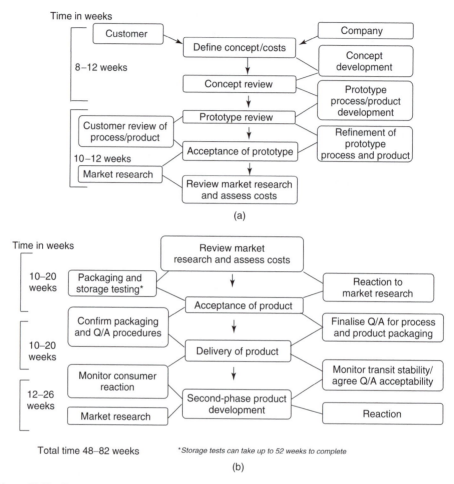

Figure [8.8] Time and action sequence for co-pack cereal product: (a) from concept to market research; (b) from market research to second-phase product development

organizations to abandon their efforts to understand exactly what products their customers want. They have instead equipped customers with tools based on computer simulation and rapid prototyping to design and develop their own products (Thomke and von Hippel 2002). Such an involvement of customers generates value but capturing that value is not straightforward since the organization has relinquished a fundamental operation – designing a new product – to customers, thereby running foul of the appropriability criterion regarding resource value discussed in Chapter 1. This creates a new business model in which the organization may be forced to focus more closely on providing competitive customized manufacturing. The location in the marketing system where value is both created and captured changes, and the organization may need to reconfigure its business model accordingly.

Traps in new product development

It is a relatively simple matter to fall into one of the five traps associated with developing new products: competitive delusion, market scope, competence, illusory innovation and marketing analysis and strategy (Figure 8.9). Competitive delusion refers to the situation where companies believe that their approach is right and that they can capture a large share of the market without much opposition. Under such assumptions development launch plans are likely to be much too ambitious. For this reason, to avoid competitive delusion companies may be advised to adopt a roll-out sequence through a series of smaller test markets first before going national or tackling large international markets.

Competitive delusion also arises from corporate pride. On occasion a new product about to be launched is tipped in the trade press to be a loser and market research may have already indicated as much to the company but for reasons of corporate pride the product is launched when it should have been dropped.

The second trap arises when the organization adopts an overly restricted market scope for its new product development. Without being overly ambitious and falling into the competitive delusion trap it may be advisable to design the new product in such a way that, without heavy modification costs, it can be subsequently introduced into wider markets. Organizations attempting to maintain control over market scope tend to carry out product and market tests in a number of markets early in the process to obtain a wider vision of the overall potential for their new product.

The third new product development trap refers to the company's competence in the area and its cost structure. In many markets there are strong competitors who are difficult to dislodge. It may be foolhardy to attack market leaders particularly if the company does not have a distinct competence in a

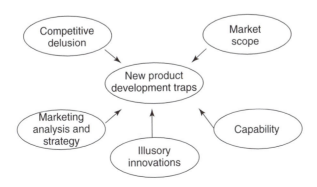

Figure [8.9] Traps in new product development

number of areas. Success may depend on a competence which includes cost leadership, quality or access to distribution outlets.

The most likely trap, however, in new product development is that the innovation is a market illusion. Unfortunately many companies develop products based on technology push which have no real points of superiority. The danger is that technically excellent products may be produced which are perceived as not having any exceptional customer value. An allied danger of this approach is that the product may be matched or rendered obsolete by competitors sooner than expected. There are many examples of products which have fallen into this trap. For example, very soon after the launch of Kodak's failed Photo CD product, doubts were cast on its market viability. For some it was thought that the product was 'over-engineered', too sophisticated and expensive for the task to which it would be devoted, particularly when many more accessible and competitively priced alternatives existed.

The most fundamental trap in new product development arises due to weak marketing analysis and incorrect marketing strategy. Weak marketing in the organization is often the reason why they fall into the traps listed above. In some cases market research is inadequate and sales projections are overly optimistic. In other cases a marketing strategy of aggressive entry level pricing may achieve initially high sales but at the cost of low profits. In general, such organizations do not have adequate marketing know-how or distribution capabilities for the product or fail to implement them properly. Sometimes organizations and even entire industries misjudge trends among customers or misinterpret them so badly as to produce highly sophisticated and technical solutions when customers seek simple solutions to their problems, e.g. mobile telephony.

In summary, many reasons have been cited for product failure. The seven most frequently encountered are:

- inadequate market research
- high development costs
- short life innovation
- lack of marketing skills
- high production costs
- lack of competitive advantage
- corporate pride.

References

Fitzgerald, N. W. A. (1991), 'Sustaining competitive advantage', paper presented at National Marketing Conference, Dublin.

Handfield, Robert B., Ragatz, Gary L., Petersen, Kenneth J. and Monczka, Robert M. (1999), 'Involving suppliers in new product development', *California Management Review*, **42** (1), 59–82.

Rogers, Everett M. (1962), *Diffusion of Innovation*. New York: The Free Press.

Rogers, Everett M. (1983), *Diffusion of Innovation* (3rd edn). New York: The Free Press.

Roman, Daniel, D. and Puett Jr., Joseph F. (1983), *International Business and Technological Innovation*. New York: North Holland.

Shanklin, William L. and Ryans Jr, John K. (1984), 'Organizing for high-tech marketing', *Harvard Business Review*, **62** (6), 64–71.

Shostack, G. Lynn (1977), 'Breaking free from product marketing', *Journal of Marketing*, **41** (2), 73–80.

Stringer, Robert (2000), 'How to manage radical innovation', *California Management Review*, **42** (4), 70–88.

Thomke, Stefan and von Hippel, Eric (2002), 'Customers as innovators', *Harvard Business Review*, **80** (4), 74–81.

Tornatzky, Louis G. and Klein, Katherine J. (1982), 'Innovation characteristics and innovation adoption – implementation: a meta analysis of findings', *IEEE, Transactions on Engineering Management*, **EM-29** (1, February), 28–45.

Urban, Glen L. and Hauser, John R. (1980), *Design and Marketing of New Products*. Englewood Cliffs, NJ: Prentice Hall.

Chapter 9

Managing the product through the life cycle

Before a product is launched the company incurs considerable costs, many of which continue after the product is available in the market. Three sets of cost arise prior to product launch: marketing research, market testing and promotion costs; product research, engineering and development work; and the manufacturing costs of prototypes and samples, based on primitive designs which are subsequently modified and finalized. After launch, sales in a normal life cycle increase slowly at first and if expectations are realized they soon begin to take off and increase rapidly, quickly reaching a revenue-rich period of maturity from which they decline under management control. During the initial stages, advertising costs tend to be very high relative to sales. Other marketing costs also are significant during these stages. The result is that direct marketing and other organization costs continue to rise for a considerable period.

According to this framework investment recovery begins after the product is launched but the product is in the maturity stage or near it before break-even is reached. There is considerable debate regarding the precise point at which the investment recovery line reaches the point of break-even. The broad thrust of the framework has been accepted: products reach profitability later in the life cycle and the greatest level of profits occur in the mature and decline stages depending on how the product is managed throughout the life cycle.

The profile or shape of the life cycle is determined by the organization's marketing actions. For some organizations the product life cycle can be a dangerous self-fulfilling concept, though it need not be. Some organizations with a product in the maturity stage of the life cycle, believing in the inevitability of its prediction, tend to withdraw marketing support too soon in favour of newer products with the result that the mature product unnecessarily goes into a terminal decline. Management then believes that their actions were anyway justified whereas the product might have stayed in the mature stage for much longer. The renewal stage results from the organization's marketing strategy rather than from some inevitability. Weak marketing support for products late in the maturity stage and in the renewal stage is frequently the major determinant of premature demise.

Innovation and product life cycle

When innovations occur and many new products enter the market, organizations offer many different versions of the product, the rate of product innovation is high, and market shares change rapidly. Despite continued market growth, subsequent entry of firms slows, exit of firms overtakes entry and there is a shake-out in the number of producers, the rate of product innovation and the diversity of competing versions of the product decline, increasing effort is devoted to improving the production process, and market shares stabilize. This evolutionary pattern has come to be known as the product life cycle.

The product life cycle is driven by the way new technologies evolve (Abernathy and Utterback 1978; Utterback and Abernathy 1975). When a new product is introduced there is considerable uncertainty about the preferences of users, even among the customers themselves, leading to demand uncertainty, and the technological means of satisfying them are also uncertain. As a result many organizations producing different variants of the product enter the market and competition focuses on product innovation.

In the business system, organizations co-operate in developing capabilities around a new innovation to develop and support new products, satisfy customer needs and at some point begin the next round of innovation.

Managing products through the life cycle

The product life cycle concept implies that in managing its products the organization recognizes that products follow a cycle of some kind and that they are finite in some way. The product life cycle provides the firm with an understanding of the behaviour of products in the market. Fundamental to understanding the product life cycle concept is the belief that market and competitive characteristics change from one stage to the next and that these changes have significant implications for marketing strategy. Each stage, therefore, presents a different challenge to the organization. By identifying the location of a product in the cycle, an appropriate marketing plan can be developed. The different stages also recognize that profits and cash flow increase and decrease at different rates throughout the life cycle.

In this regard high perceived value strategies may be more appropriate in the emerging stages of the product cycle when the manufacturing process is not a significant competitive factor. Technology is still evolving, the business system may not have stabilized and competition tends to be confined to product innovation and development at this stage. Low delivered cost strategies, however, are more appropriate to the mature or standardization phase of the product life cycle which is characterized by rapid market development. In a low delivered cost strategy, the organization's attention is focused on the manufacturing processes and resources are directed to the entire business system with process technology, market positioning and distribution efficiency becoming critical.

By following a planned sequence of moves emphasizing high perceived value now and low delivered cost at a later stage where one set of circumstances creates the conditions for implementation of the other, the organization successfully develops a strategy which identifies elements of perceived value that are not worth the delivered cost. These can then be unbundled and produced outside the organization at a lower cost. Additional elements of perceived value desired by the served segment can be included in the competitive formula at an acceptable cost (Gilbert and Strebel 1988).

Usually the different stages of the life cycle are indicated where changes in the rates of sales growth or decline become pronounced (Figure 9.1). Time is the variable on the horizontal axis but time is not the determinant of product sales. Time is a proxy variable for changes in product characteristics, competition, marketing strategies, environmental variables and market-related variables which occur over time (Meenaghan and O'Sullivan 1986).

Stages in the product life cycle

Analysts of the product life cycle generally divide it into four distinct stages: the pioneering stage, the growth stage, the maturity stage, and the renewal stage – each with different characteristics.

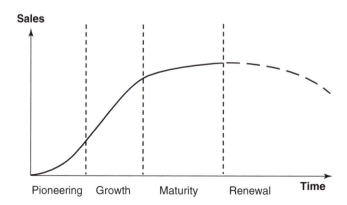

Figure [9.1]   Generic product life cycle

Pioneering stage

New products or product versions in the pioneering or introductory stage of the life cycle are unique and face a competitive situation which is quite different from that faced by them later in the life cycle. New and innovative products are a feature of the pioneering stage of the life cycle. During this stage new product forms or new product classes are introduced and developed. As such, these products are new to the world and usually do not have any direct competition when they first appear.

During the pioneering stage the organization expects sales to grow slowly, profits to be very low or non-existent and cash flow to be negative. Furthermore, there is normally a great deal of risk and uncertainty associated with its future acceptance by customers. This is a high cost period in the development of the product market since investment is needed to develop the market. At this stage it is unlikely that the organization would have many competitors and customers tend to be innovative. At this stage the organization concentrates on relatively high priced undifferentiated products sold through few outlets with a marketing communications mix concentrated on creating awareness. Customers and intermediaries must be informed of the product's existence and of any unique features it possesses; awareness is emphasized in promotional messages. It may, however, take a relatively long time to make the product available in all relevant markets and to fill the distribution channels. Sales growth may be very slow as inventories build up and the first sales materialize.

Several reasons for slow growth during the pioneering stage have been identified: delays in achieving adequate distribution, the novelty associated with the new product, and customer reluctance to change existing buying patterns.

During the pioneering stage firms focus on identifying what customers want, i.e. the value of a proposed new product or service and the best way of delivering it. Success in this embryonic phase often goes to those firms that best define and implement customer value requirements; identifying and selecting customer value are central to success.

Growth stage

It is difficult to state exactly when a product moves from the pioneering to the growth stage. Generally speaking, the organization knows when it has entered the growth stage; the most telling phenomenon is the rapid growth in sales. Purchase patterns and distribution channels tend to change rapidly and market share can be increased relatively quickly and at low cost by focusing on incremental sales, especially among new users instead of existing users. For consumer products repeat orders begin and the less innovative consuming majority begin to show an interest in the product. Strong market growth attracts new competitors into the market. These competitors are product imitators who are attracted by the opportunities for large-scale production and profit.

The marketing activity of imitators and the new product features they include give credibility to the innovator's product and further expand the market. The competitive pressure may not be an issue at this stage because growth is so strong and customers seek the relatively new products. As the market expands there may be temporary room for many competitors, each producing a product version customized to particular market segments. The increased number of competitors leads to an increase in the number of distribution outlets and industry sales increase rapidly to fill distribution channels.

Real prices tend to fall in the growth stage. In some product markets the lower real price is combined with an improved product in intensive distribution to create brand preference. Brand preference established by an innovator in the growth stage is difficult to dislodge. Promotional expenditures tend to remain the same or increase as organizations continue to educate the market and meet new competition. Sales, however, increase much faster causing a rapid decline in the promotion-to-sales ratio. Profits tend to increase in the growth stage as promotion costs are spread over a much greater volume and unit manufacturing costs fall faster than prices. The accelerating growth rate eventually slows down and declines, however. As growth decelerates, a new approach to the market is warranted.

During the growth stage companies usually continue to innovate the product in order to remain ahead of imitators because without continued investment imitators may reach the stage of product parity, leaving the pioneer with no competitive advantage. Inadequate attention to continued product and market development in the growth stage may shorten the life cycle and dissipate any leadership position obtained.

With a slowdown in growth, the battle for market share and survival tends to precipitate a shake-out among competitors leaving only the stronger to share a relatively large and stable market. A shake-out in the late stage of the growth stage of the life cycle refers to the failure or disappearance of a significant number of marginal competitors as a result of intense competition which seems to occur as sales growth slows down as the market approaches maturity.

Maturity stage

There comes a point when the rate of sales growth slows down to the equivalent of the general rate of growth in economic activity in the market; the product has entered the stage of maturity. During the maturity stage purchasing patterns and distribution channels stabilize, as a result of which a substantial increase in share by one company at the expense of another is strongly resisted. Share gains during the mature stage of the life cycle are time-consuming and expensive. In maturity, sales growth declines and profits begin to wane, but cash flow is at its strongest. Unit marketing costs are at their lowest. The marketing objective is to manage low-priced, differentiated products in intensive distribution for long-term brand loyalty.

Companies prolong the maturity stage by improving the product in various ways or by adapting it to new segments or uses, by developing line extensions to cater for new segments and by attempting to change customer needs and sometimes by price decreases to attract the more price-sensitive segments of the market. In effect, the firm may reposition its product to defend its market. The maturity stage of the life cycle is normally associated with strong cash flows which provide funds for further new products and profits.

The mature stage of a market normally lasts longer than the previous stages but it still poses formidable challenges to the company. It is generally believed that products with high shares in low growth markets generate more cash than is needed to maintain their position in the market. These products are referred to as cash cows and are most valuable to the company. The usual marketing strategy for cash cows is to provide support so that market share is maintained.

Cash cows are businesses or products with a relatively high market share in a low growth market which yield cash in excess of reinvestment needs to develop the product or business. Successful cash cows are managed for their positive cash flow. These products or businesses generate the cash required for profits or contribution to overheads or dividends. Cash cows support acquisitions and the necessary cash flow to invest in more recent product introductions, still classified as questionable. The dilemma facing the organization is to know how much cash to take from the cash cow to support other products and how much to reinvest in the cash cows themselves to ensure their continued health. Many companies fail in this regard by bleeding cash cows to support questionable ventures.

Renewal stage

New formats or new innovations which threaten the existing business system provide evidence that the renewal stage of the product life cycle has arrived. Sudden environmental changes, e.g. government regulations, rapid changes in customer buying patterns or in general macroeconomic conditions may also speed up the onset of the need for renewal. The ultimate challenge for a dominant company is presented in the renewal stage. Leading successive generations of innovation is crucial to a business system's long-term success and its ability to renew itself.

But despite the difficulties of such a complex and changing business environment, managers can design longevity into a business system. During the growth and maturity stages, for instance, all the companies in the business system devote much effort to microsegmenting their markets, creating close, supportive ties with customers, building relationships. These customers tend to remain committed to a particular business system long enough for its members to incorporate the benefits of innovation and new approaches.

Superficially, competition among business systems is a contest for market share. But below the surface, these competitive struggles are contests over who will direct the future. People make decisions – there is conscious direction; the larger patterns are maintained by a complex network of choices among organizations. This is the principal reason why this stage is referred to as 'renewal' instead of the more traditional 'decline' stage as 'decline' conveys a sense of necessary demise whereas most organizations seek to renew or refresh their products during this stage. The symptoms of 'decline', however, are very much worth noting.

The renewal stage should be predictable and under company control. Ideally the organization wishes to have its product in a leadership or strong competitive position in the chosen market segments by this stage as marketing strategies in the maturity stage revolve around deepening the company's position in the market and extending the maturity stage as long as possible.

Products eventually reach the stage where they can no longer be maintained in the market in their current form. The market loses interest in them, the organization fails to upgrade and support them or they are actually phased out deliberately in favour of new products at the pioneering stage. Whatever the reason, most product versions reach the renewal or decline stage and disappear from the market in the form they entered it.

Sales decline for many reasons, most of which may be outside the manufacturer's control. Technological advances, shifts in consumer tastes and competitive activities account for most of the reasons why organizations discover they have too much capacity, suffer from increased price cutting and see their profits erode.

Mismanagement of the renewal stage, especially if it involves too much investment in the product to retain it artificially beyond its profitable life, can result in a serious financial trap for the organization and damage its reputation among customers.

The sales decline may be slow, rapid, or lingering. Careful management of the process in the decline stage usually involves the reduction of product models, the reduction of product variations and options and the maintenance of reasonable margins. Organizations may also withdraw from smaller market segments and weaker channels. In the renewal stage firms stress low costs and production and marketing efficiency. Prices may even be raised for restricted product versions in selective distribution. Reinforcement advertising is stressed. Such a combination usually produces adequate cash flows for the company to invest in new products or renew existing ones.

Ideal product life cycle

The ideal product life cycle shows a short initial period of development involving losses followed by a short period of rapid introduction and growth leading to a relatively long tranquil period of positive cash flow, sales and

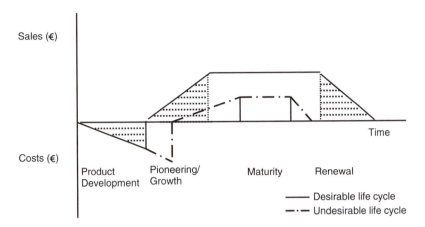

Figure [9.2] Desirable and undesirable life cycles

profits (Figure 9.2). Because the product development period (Dp) in the ideal product life cycle is short, product development costs tend to be low. Development time is shorter and less costly, however, for routine products than for high technology products. New perfumes, new snacks, and so on, do not involve much development time, whereas high technology industrial products may require much research and development, engineering time and cost.

The pioneering and growth stages of the ideal product life cycle are also short. Sales therefore, reach a peak relatively quickly, which results in the maximization of revenues. The maturity period lasts much longer, giving the company an opportunity to earn profits over an extended period. The renewal stage tends to be prolonged indicating that if profits fall, they do so gradually rather than suddenly.

The shape of the life cycle may depend on whether products are classified as low or high learning products. For low learning products sales lift off quickly as little learning is required by the customer and the benefits of purchase are readily understood. The result is a rapidly rising life cycle during the pioneering stage. Because considerable education of the customer is required, high learning products tend to have an extended pioneering stage and sales are slower to materialize. The result is a rather flat life cycle during the pioneering and growth stages. The length of the pioneering and growth stages tends to be short when:

- The product does not require setting up a new distribution channel.

- The channel readily accepts and promotes the new product.

- Customers have an interest in the product, adopt it early and give it favourable word-of-mouth promotion.

These conditions apply to many familiar consumer products. They are less valid for many high technology products, which therefore require longer pioneering and growth stages.

The length of the maturity stage depends on the extent that customer tastes and product technology are fairly stable and the company maintains leadership in the market. Organizations make the most money from products that experience a long maturity period. In circumstances where the maturity stage is short, the organization might not even recover its full investment. The renewal stage tends to be long if consumer tastes and product technology change only slowly. The more loyal the customers, the slower the potential rate of decline. The lower the exit barriers, the faster some firms will exit, which slows down the rate of decline for the firms remaining in the market.

Many organizations face market entry barriers when they attempt to launch their new products. An entry barrier arises when product development time is longer than anticipated, when development costs are steeper than expected, when a longer time than expected is spent in the pioneering and growth stages and an uncertain and possibly a rapid decline due to demand technology changes or competitive market entries occurs (Figure 9.2).

Life cycle for frequently purchased products

For frequently purchased low learning products like a packaged ice-cream bar, the product life cycle sales that can be expected resemble Figure 9.3. The number of first-time buyers initially increases and then decreases as fewer are left, assuming a fixed population. Repeat purchases occur soon, provided that the new product satisfies some fraction of people who become steady customers. The sales curve eventually falls to a plateau representing a level of steady repeat purchases.

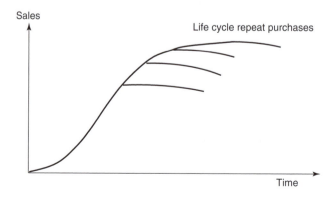

Figure [9.3] Product life cycle for frequently purchased products

For a frequently purchased new product, the seller has to estimate repeat sales as well as first-time sales. This is because the unit value of frequently purchased products is low, and repeat purchases take place soon after the introduction. A high rate of repeat purchasing means that customers are satisfied; sales are likely to stay high even after all first-time purchases take place. The organization notes the percentage of repeat purchases that take place in each repeat purchase class – those who buy once, twice, three times, and so on. Some products are bought a few times and dropped. It is important to estimate whether the repeat purchase ratio is likely to rise or fall, and at what rate, with each repeat purchase class.

Product category life cycle

Markets develop at different rates and in some countries the development starts earlier than others. In such circumstances the organization faces the predicament that its brand may be at different stages of the development cycle in different markets. Typically in the domestic market or in the first major market entered, it is likely to reach maturity before even taking off in emerging markets. In this context it may be relevant to examine the evolution of the product category as well as the brand as it would be expected that a product category would have a life cycle. If the managers of Baileys Original Irish Cream Liqueur were to follow this advice, they would examine how the development of the product category for cream liqueurs differs in different countries. An application of these principles is shown in Figure 9.4.

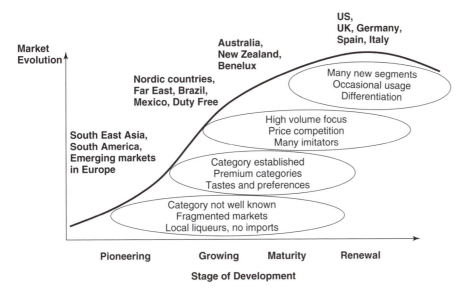

Figure [9.4]   Development of the cream liqueur product category

In regard to the development of the cream liqueur category by country or area in South East Asia, most of South America and in emerging markets in Eastern Europe, the category is not well developed and the markets are very fragmented. In contrast Nordic countries, the Far East and Mexico are growing rapidly while markets in Australia, New Zealand and the Benelux countries are reaching maturity. Along with the US, the EU, Germany and other countries are core cream liqueur markets.

Management implications of the life cycle

The product life cycle provides the company with an insightful framework for considering the growth and development of a new product; it is used primarily in planning the company's marketing strategy but it also affects other areas in the business including manufacturing, finance and human resources because of the differential demands it places on them. For example, different patterns of life cycle have a different effect on manufacturing requirements in terms of volume, variety and the dominant form of competition. Decisions regarding product customization, sales of each version and time to replacement are affected.

The stage of the life cycle affects product design, the combination of product attributes used, and the commonality of components. At the early stages greater emphasis is placed on uniqueness and differentiation. The maturation of a market tends to lead to fewer competitors and greater price competition among survivors. In this context it is important to ensure that marketing effort is of the correct form for each stage of the cycle. During the pioneering stage advertising themes are likely to emphasize educational aspects which would be wasteful in the mature stage. The life cycle concept assists the company in making financial forecasts for different stages. In the mature stage, for example, sales revenue is unlikely to increase unless price is increased.

Expansion of business system

During the growth stage of the product life cycle, business systems expand to capture new markets. Some business expansions meet little resistance but in other situations rival business systems may be closely matched and choose to target the same territory. At this point direct battles for market share start and turbulent times are typical as each business system attempts to exert pressure on suppliers and customers to commit to the particular business system. In the end, one business system may triumph, or a business system may reach an uneasy accommodation with its rival. The existence of two conditions is necessary for expansion:

- A business concept that a large number of customers value.

- The potential to scale up the concept to reach this broad market.

During the growth stage, established companies tend to dominate the business system in regard to marketing, sales and the management of large-scale production and distribution. One of the most important managerial challenges in the growth stage is to stimulate market demand without greatly exceeding the firm's capacity to meet it. This was the very great fear R. & A. Bailey and Company had in launching Baileys Original Irish Cream Liqueur brand in the US market. At the start Baileys did not attack new competitors arising within its business system through special promotions, or by lowering prices. Indirectly the company encouraged competition because the extra investment in the market would help educate and expand the total market and also compel the business system to recognize its brand as the product standard in the market.

In general, the growth stage rewards the organizations that are quick to expand which squeezes other firms to the margin. Time and speed become important competitive factors. It is necessary, however, for managers to prepare for future leadership and leverage during the next stage. To do so, organizations need to maintain careful control of customer relationships and core centres of value and innovation. Moreover, they must develop relationships with their suppliers that constrain these followers from becoming dominant during the maturity stage.

Managing the maturity stage

Product mix decisions

The product mix is the composite of products and services offered for sale by the organization. In a well-managed organization each product in the mix serves a specific purpose. Sometimes an individual product item in the mix may not itself be profitable but it may contribute to goodwill and the overall well-being of the company by enhancing the product mix. In the process, the firm is careful to take account of cost and demand interactions which may exist within its portfolio of products.

The company can expand its business by deepening the product mix by adding new versions of selected products, by broadening the product mix by adding new product lines, making each product line longer, and by changing the product line consistency. The depth of the product mix refers to the average number of product items offered by the organization within each product line. By increasing the depth of the product mix the company may attract customers with very different needs and wants. The breadth of the product mix refers to the number of different product lines found in the firm. By increasing the breadth of the product mix the company may capitalize on its good reputation and skill in existing markets. Johnson and Johnson has a very wide product mix ranging from anaesthetics and birth control drugs to Band-Aids, baby powder and oils to contact lenses. The consistency of the product mix refers to how closely related the product lines are in customer use, distribution channels, technology and production techniques. By increasing consistency the company may acquire an unparalleled reputation in a particular area of endeavour, whereas reducing consistency allows the firm to compete in several areas.

Product line extensions

Product line extensions are favoured by some firms since a new introduction to the product line may be made with relative ease. Product line extensions are a low risk way of gaining share in a crowded market provided the new product item does not cannibalize the organization's existing products. The objective is to take share from a competitor. The approach works in some situations but not always. Product line extensions capitalize on the organization's existing capabilities and resources in design, manufacturing, distribution and marketing. A product extension launch in ideal circumstances can be relatively quick, inexpensive and without much risk. The great advantage of speed may be increased by companies that can buy in under their own brand, an increasingly popular way to stay ahead in new product development as market changes become more rapid and the cost of new product development rises. Line extensions are sometimes an overused approach to new product development, however, especially when there is an attempt to exploit product line gaps which may not exist.

The principal way of extending the length of the organization's product line is by stretching it upwards or downwards. Trading up means adding a higher priced, prestige product to a line to attract a higher income market. One of the major difficulties encountered in attempting to stretch the product line upwards is that of credibility among customers. They may not believe that the firm is capable of producing products for the high end of the market. In addition the company's sales people may not be adequately trained and competitors are unlikely to remain passive; they may counter-attack in the lower end of the market.

Other organizations, initially located in the premium end of the market, stretch the line downward by introducing promotional versions of their products to attract customers on price. Trading down like this means adding a lower priced item to the firm's line of prestige products. Behind downward product line stretching is the view that buyers will trade up once they see the better versions of the product. In such cases the promotional version of the product should support the organization's high market image. One of the dangers of downward line stretching is that of product line cannibalization.

The company could ultimately be worse off if customers switch away from high market items toward the promotional versions of the product.

Successful product line extensions are ideal for companies with a strong brand but limited product range. By way of illustration, L'Oréal's successful scent for men, 'DRAKKAR', was quickly extended to include 'DRAKKAR Noir' for men preferring a heavier scent. Such product line extension is unlikely to work in the dairy cabinet in supermarkets or in certain sectors of the car market. The danger of too much dependence on product line extensions as a way of developing and launching new products is that very quickly customers could face a proliferation of indistinguishable products which serve only to dilute the organization's image and damage its costs position.

There are, however, a number of traps associated with an undisciplined approach to product line extensions. With the onset of maturity, sales begin to stagnate. At this point some organizations introduce product line extensions and enter new niche markets. This in turn causes product management complexity to increase. Complexity and the consequent need for additional management resources increase the cost of the product range. The final stage in this process is that competitiveness declines. This completes the vicious circle which emphasizes the short term with the result that further sales stagnation occurs and decline becomes inevitable (Figure 9.5). In contrast, the virtuous circle which emphasizes the longer term depends on capturing cash flows arising from successful products reaching the mature stage of the life cycle and investing them in product innovation. Innovation leads to new investment in products and markets and a new round of evolution of the life cycle.

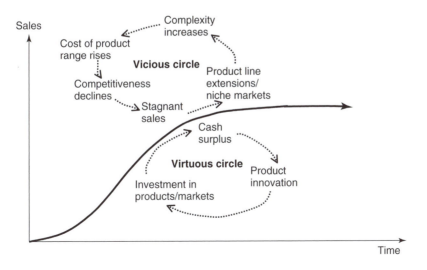

Figure [9.5]   Product life cycle – vicious and virtuous

Managing the renewal stage

The organization that wishes to actively manage the renewal stage should consider the possibility of relaunching the product or if the product is likely to fail it may be necessary to consider a product deletion.

Product deletion

Too many weak products in the firm's portfolio eventually weaken the company's ability to introduce new products which adversely affects future prospects. Before removing a weak product from the product portfolio a number of factors should be considered. First, the product under threat may help to fill out and complete the organization's product line. Second, sometimes because of cost interactions a product may help to cover fixed costs even though its own sales performance is not up to standard. Third, a weak product may sell as a complement to other products in the product mix and may be indirectly contributing to profits. Finally, a significant group of customers may want the product which for goodwill or other long-term reasons the firm may wish to delay a decision to eliminate, e.g. General Motors' decision to drop the 'Oldsmobile' brand in the United States.

Managing cash flow

Products which are growing rapidly require relatively large amounts of cash while those which are growing slowly in mature markets tend to generate cash. The investment required to maintain market share in any market, therefore, is a function of the growth rate in that market. If the growth rate is high, a high level of investment in plant, equipment and inventory is required, if sales of the product are to grow as fast or faster than the market, i.e. to retain or improve share position. Furthermore, in a given market or product category the profitability of competing products is a function of their market share. Products with large market shares, which dominate the segment, tend to have high margins and thus generate a substantial amount of cash.

Two cash flow management principles emerge. First, products which have a high market share but experience slow growth should be managed to generate cash. The low growth rate means that the reinvestment needed in the products themselves is less than the earnings being generated. Deliberate control is required to ensure that the earnings from such mature products are not totally reinvested in themselves but are liberally applied to new products in the pioneering and growth stages of the life cycle.

Second, products with high growth rates are unlikely to be able to produce their own investment funds. In high growth markets there is a high demand for funds to maintain or extend market share. In such circumstances companies transfer cash from the sales of mature products to be used to support products with rapidly growing sales to ensure that they grow faster than the market and thereby achieve a dominant position. Current profits are sacrificed for market position and longer-term profits. In this way the product portfolio is managed as a whole to provide a balance between cash generation now and future cash generation by aiming for dominant share positions in growth markets.

References

Abernathy, William J. and Utterback, James M. (1978), 'Patterns of industrial innovation', *Technology Review*, **80** (June/July), 41–7.

Gilbert, Xavier and Strebel, Paul (1988), 'Developing competitive advantage', in *The Strategy Process*, Henry Mintzberg and James Brian Quinn, eds (2nd edn). New Jersey: Prentice Hall.

Meenaghan, John A. and O'Sullivan, P. J. P. (1986), 'The shape and length of the product life cycle', *Irish Marketing Review*, **1** (Spring), 83–102.

Utterback, James M. and Abernathy, William J. (1975), 'A dynamic model of process and product innovation', *Omega*, **3** (6), 639–56.

PART III
Communicating the Value

Chapter 10

Marketing communications

The marketing communications environment changes constantly and aspects such as the changing behaviour of customers, demographic changes, income levels and their distribution are usually monitored by most organizations. At the same time markets fragment and the concentration of selling power among the large retailers in consumer markets and among key manufacturers and users in industrial markets has given rise to different emphasis in communications. Organizations acknowledge the increase in media proliferation, sales promotion, direct customer contact and the use of the Internet. The underlying force in this changing communications environment that the organization attempts to understand is its audience – what is it communicating and to whom?

The importance of marketing communication has increased in recent years primarily because many organizations have acknowledged that their products have reached the maturity stage in the life cycle and are, therefore, at parity with each other. As a result, points of difference to distinguish brands related to inherent product attributes have become more difficult to discover.

Marketing communications process

To communicate effectively with buyers it is necessary to develop a promotion strategy which implies an understanding of the communications process itself. The organization communicates with its customers to ensure that they know about the value provided by the company. It is necessary to establish communications objectives, determine the nature of the message to be communicated, select the audience to be addressed and specify the expected response. There are five major elements in the communications process: the source of the message; the message; the media or channel used; the sender and the receiver (Figure 10.1). There are also four principal functions: encoding and decoding of messages; response by the receiver and feedback to sender. Every marketing decision and every communication initiated by the organization has a positive or negative impact on the overall image of the organization's brand in the eyes of at least some of the target audience.

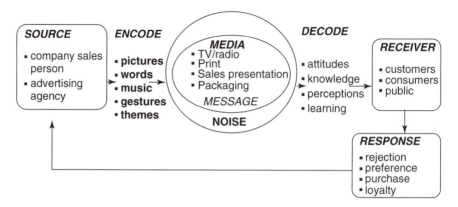

Figure [10.1]   The communication process

Marketing communications is unconcerned with the methods or tools by which companies attempt to derive an intended response from a customer. The tools of marketing communication include advertising, sales promotion, public relations, direct marketing, personal selling and most importantly word of mouth. Each element of communications should be evaluated on the basis of how it helps, cost effectively, to establish or consolidate the desired position. No one element is superior to the other – it is the communications mix that counts. There is no optimum mix but there is one certainty in marketing communications – word of mouth has the potential to undermine even the best communications plans but it may also consolidate and confirm positive results.

In the marketing arena the sender is the organization wishing to advertise its products and services. The receiver is the party who receives the message, usually a household, an individual or another firm. The message consists of a set of symbols which the sender wishes to transmit, e.g. 'Diamonds are forever' (De Beers); 'the pause that refreshes' (Coca-Cola). The media consist of the channels of communications used to convey the message from sender to receiver, e.g. newspapers, sales conferences, television, outdoor posters. Senders of messages must know what audience they want to reach, why and what responses they anticipate.

Common tasks in communications

Organizations pay a great deal of attention to these five elements of the communications process. The encoding process, converting thought into symbolic form, i.e. deciding the appropriate set of words and illustrations to be used, requires great care, attention and planning. Encoding the message must take account of the way the target audience is likely to decode it. Similarly, decoding the message or the process by which the receiver assigns meaning to the symbols transmitted by the sender, raises the possibility of misunderstanding or misinterpretation. The receiver uses language, symbols and illustrations to internalize the meaning of the message being transferred. The possibility of error is greater when the communication is between different language or cultural groups.

The sender of messages in marketing is very concerned about the possible responses by receivers of the message. Here a range of reactions may be anticipated depending on the communications objectives. The sender may seek awareness, interest, desire or action on the part of the receiver.

First, the customer must be made aware of the communication itself, and hence its content. For example, deliberately irritating advertisements, provocative headings and catchy jingles are noticed. In developing interest, the company faces the possibility of considerable waste unless the communication is very focused. Advertising on television for new car models faces this dilemma since only a small number in the audience are potential buyers at any one time.

Feedback refers to that part of the receiver's response which is communicated back to the sender, e.g. a request for further product information or product purchase. Throughout the communications process there is a danger of interference or noise in the system which distorts the message received and so gives rise to unexpected or undesired responses. Many distractions produce 'noise' or barriers to effective communications – other competing communications, inappropriate use of symbols in the message sent, or a preoccupied receiver of the message.

In marketing communications, senders of messages must know which audience they want to reach and what responses they desire. They must understand how to encode messages in such a way as to skilfully avoid misunderstanding, especially if strong cultural factors are present. The message must be transmitted through efficient and effective media directed at the target audience. It is necessary also to develop a mechanism by which the responses are understood.

Marketing communication objectives

When setting promotion objectives it is necessary to specify the target audience, the desired response, the message and the media. It is necessary to decide who the target audience is before sending a message. By knowing the audience it is possible to know what to say and how to say it. Frequently the audience for marketing communications are influencers, deciders, users or buyers. These may be individuals, households, other organizations or the general public. The nature of the product and the target audience influences the organization's decisions on marketing communications. For example, in crowded mature markets marketing communications has a special position. By transcending the common inherent attributes of the myriad products on the market, marketing communications can provide information to create points of difference that otherwise would not be possible. In a cluttered, complex marketplace, marketing communication may allow brands to stand out and help customers appreciate their comparative advantages (Keller 2001, p. 823). In the crowded instant coffee market, Maxwell House has been very successful with its 'Good to the last drop' claim. The basic issues in marketing communication may be identified by answering a number of questions based on who, what, how and when:

- Who does the organization wish to inform?

- What outcomes does it wish to influence?

- What message best achieves these objectives?

- What media are most appropriate?

- When should the organization communicate?

- How much should the budget be?

- How effective is the marketing communication?

Marketing communications objectives may be divided into three categories:

- Those dealing with the pre-purchase situation such as the level of aware-ness, product or service knowledge and established preferences – conveying information to potential buyers.

- Those dealing with the purchase situation itself and the level of satisfaction involved – creating brand preferences and sales.

- Those dealing with the post-purchase situation which relate to issues of loyalty.

The firm must also seek an effective means of communications which means deciding among the various media involved such as advertising, pub-licity, sales promotion and personal selling. The company may concentrate on one of these but is more likely to consider a mix of them. These are complicated objectives and difficult to separate from one another. In reality different effects may result from a particular promotional expenditure. Setting objectives for promotion requires an understanding of the influence process.

Effect of marketing communications

The organization expects three types of response to communications. First there is a cognitive response ensuring that the message is considered by the target audience and understood. The second refers to an affective response whereby the customer's attitude is changed in some favourable way. Third,

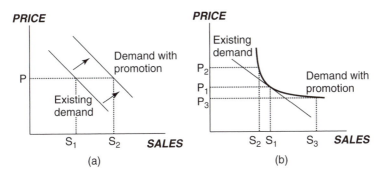

Figure [10.2] Effect of promotion on product or service demand

there is a behavioural response whereby a desired action takes place. This behavioural effect of marketing communications changes the demand curve for the company's products and services. Using marketing communications two effects on the demand curve may be observed (Figure 10.2). First, the demand curve shifts up and to the right so that greater quantities are purchased at the same price. In Figure 10.2(a) sales increase from S_1 to S_2 at price P with the introduction of marketing communications. Second the shape of the demand curve changes (Figure 10.2(b)). For price increases, from P_1 to P_2 the demand curve becomes more inelastic with than without marketing communications. A decline in price from P_1 to P_3 shows demand becoming more elastic than before. A price increase with marketing communications results in a smaller decline in sales from S_1 to S_2 than would have been expected had the old demand curve remained in place. A price decrease with marketing communications results in a greater increase in sales from S_1 to S_3 than would have been expected had the old demand curve remained.

Influence of marketing communications on the customer

Buyers are thought to go through a number of stages in being influenced by promotion. A three-stage model is frequently assumed in which there are different objectives at each stage. In the first stage, objectives refer to cognitive issues such as awareness, attention, knowledge and exposure to the product or brand (Figure 10.3). During the next stage, objectives switch to issues of affection. In the affective stage, issues such as interest, desire, liking, preference, conviction, evaluation, attitude and intention associated with the product or brand are central to advertising objectives. The third stage, the behaviour stage, deals with action, purchase and other behavioural objectives.

Based on concepts discussed there have been numerous models developed purporting to show how customers reach decisions about products. One of the most popular of these is AIDA that suggests, drawing on the material above (Figure 10.3), that when considering a purchase the human thought process

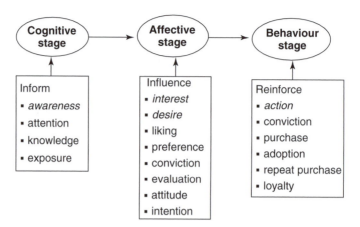

Figure [10.3]   Stages in customer decision process and marketing communications emphasis

goes through four stages: awareness, interest, desire and action. The AIDA model is fairly simple, which partly explains its longevity and widespread use. Before customers make a purchase they need to be aware that the product exists, what it is, what it does, and perhaps also where and when it is available.

At the next stage potential customers must be stimulated to take some interest in the product. Here it is important to know the special features of the product, the benefits it offers and how it might serve a variety of needs and wants. During this stage the potential buyer develops a reaction favourable or unfavourable to the product.

If the response is favourable and the marketing communication is successful in awakening interest, it then attempts to create in the potential customer's mind a desire to purchase. It does this by successfully connecting the benefits of the product with the customer's needs and wants. This is frequently the most difficult aspect of designing a marketing communications programme. It is one thing to portray a product in an attractive manner that stimulates interest in potential customers; it is quite another to persuade them that they actually need it. While most of us would find the BMW 7 Series 'interesting' in that it is an attractive well-engineered car, few of us actually own one or are likely to, if only because we cannot afford it. This phase of the marketing communications must, therefore, both show potential customers that there is a product available which will satisfy their needs and show them that they can satisfy that need by purchasing the product in question. This leads to the final stage – action – where customers actually make the effort to seek the product and buy it.

The most common problem experienced in the AIDA model is the failure to make the transition from interest to desire, both of which are influences in the affective stage of the customer decision process (Figure 10.3). There are many marketing communications that offer interesting and attractive products we

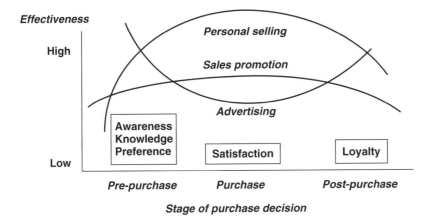

Figure [10.4] Impact of communication mix on buyer

particularly do not want to buy. The model does, however, recognize that not all of our thinking occurs on a conscious, rational level.

The different forms of marketing communications affect buyers in different ways depending on the purchase decision stage. At the pre-purchase stage the organization wishes to increase awareness, knowledge and even preference for its products and services. At the buying stage the aim is to create satisfaction and at the post-purchase stage the company seeks to promote loyalty among its customers. The different forms of marketing communications vary in their effectiveness in achieving these aims at each stage of the buying process (Figure 10.4). Advertising is more effective in creating awareness, raising the knowledge level and establishing preferences than is sales promotion or personal selling.

Personal selling and sales promotion, because they are interactive and provide incentives to buy, are more effective in increasing satisfaction at the purchase stage. Advertising again dominates the influence in the post-purchase stage. By reinforcing the desired attributes, advertising reassures and is very effective in raising loyalty and hence repeat purchases.

It is difficult to judge how much emphasis the advertiser should give to each objective at each stage. It is possible to over- or under-promote in any of the stages. At the pre-purchase stage it is possible to create too much awareness and too high a preference for a new product. Advertising money may be wasted if the product is not available. Also it may build up resentment among retailers and consumers.

Methods of marketing communication

Promotion is any form of marketing communication used by an organization to inform, influence or remind people and other organizations about its products, services, ideas, image and identity and impact on society. Marketing communication may be by means of the organization's brands, its sales force or the mass media and emphasizes information, persuasion or reinforcement of various themes such as product performance, sociability, fear, humour or comparisons with competitors. There are several categories of audience: consumers, owners, government, consumer associations, suppliers, company staff and the general public. Because each of these audiences is different in terms of objectives, knowledge and needs, the promotional method and emphasis in communications are likely to be different.

The most popular of these methods, advertising, is a high profile promotions medium used to reach a mass market. Other aspects of communications may complement the role of advertising. Public relations are sometimes used to capitalize on good news concerning the company and are also effective in dampening the effects of bad news. Increasingly companies are turning to sponsorship of events which promote a self-image developed by the company. Organizations tend to associate themselves and their products and services with the characteristics and lifestyles of people who feature in such events.

In many circumstances, word-of-mouth promotion, which arises as people transform from being passive to active participants in the communications system, can be successfully used by the organization. Effective word-of-mouth promotion works best in conjunction with some other communication media. Pharmaceutical firms often use scientific conferences to launch and promote a new drug to medical practitioners while at the same time advertising the product in magazines read by the target audience. The combination of the educational element of the scientific communication and the discussion among target customers and between them and their doctors generates significant 'buzz' or word-of-mouth promotion for ailments previously unnoticed or neglected (Dye 2000).

Marketing communications as investment

Most marketing communications expenditure is an investment, an outlay made today to produce future benefits, so the important consideration from the advertiser's point of view is future cash flows accruing from the communications. Advertising is normally a matter of strategy aimed at the long-term objective of increasing the number of customers and their loyalty to the brand. In contrast, sales promotion works by stimulating sales in the short run, essential for cash flow but they are important for other reasons too. Short-run sales stimulate brand purchases by consumers, brand use and the long-run accumulation of added values which arise from brand use.

Advertising may, therefore, be viewed as an investment in which the returns are increased sales spread over time. Sales decline slowly when advertising is reduced or withdrawn because they also respond to the history of the company's advertising (Vidale and Wolfe 1957). A substantial carryover effect implies that the company should devote relatively more resources to advertising as a strategic variable and not just a tactical response to short-term considerations.

Marketing communications mix

Four factors are taken into account in deciding on the appropriate communications mix: the available funds, the market, the product and the stage of life cycle. As indicated already, irrespective of the desirability of a particular communication mix, the funds available are often the determining factor (Rossiter *et al.* 1991). An organization with adequate resources is usually better placed to produce more effective communications than a company with limited resources. Smaller companies with scarce resources are likely to depend on personal selling, joint manufacturer–retailer promotions and general-purpose displays at point of sale. Such companies often rely on personal selling even though television advertising would be preferable but because of resource considerations the company can afford a sales person but not an advertising budget.

The nature of the market also influences the communications decision. Personal selling may be adequate for a small local market. For an extensive market television advertising may be necessary. The geographic scope of the market is, therefore, an important factor. Related to the scope of the market is the degree of concentration in the market. The smaller the number of potential buyers, the more effective is personal selling compared to advertising.

The type of customer also influences the decision. The communications decision depends on whether the company is attempting to reach final consumers, intermediaries or industrial users. Related to this consideration is audience heterogeneity. A target audience consisting of a homogeneous customer group requires a different communication mix than a market consisting of many different customer groups.

In allocating the promotion budget consumer products manufacturers are likely to spend most of it on advertising with a considerable amount on sales promotions, less on personal selling and a relatively small amount on public relations (Figure 10.5). For industrial products, personal selling dominates with advertising and sales promotion absorbing a smaller proportion. The proportion spent on pubic relations tends to remain the same. These proportions tend to fluctuate with changes in the environment and the circumstances facing individual companies. As national or international advertising becomes expensive and ineffective in reaching target audiences, some firms prefer to target customers more closely by using sales promotions and even personal selling.

The objectives of marketing communications also change with the different stages of the life cycle. For new products or services, customers must be informed and product attributes recognized before customers can develop

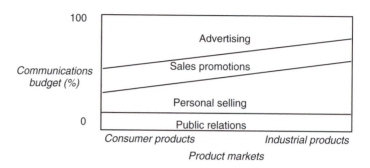

Figure [10.5]   Communications mix in consumer and industrial product markets

a favourable attitude toward them. For products at a later stage in the life cycle, consumer awareness is less important but persuasion or the conversion of product knowledge into product liking becomes important. For mature products, the emphasis is on reminding customers and reinforcing existing positive beliefs.

Marketing communication budget

Two alternative ways of developing a promotional budget may be identified. The top-down approach is used when the company applies an upper limit on the amount to be spent for promotion. This approach and the percentage of sales approach are similar and very popular in situations where company planning is dominated by a financial view of the world whereby financial managers allocate a certain fixed proportion of forecast sales to promotion without a detailed statement of how the money should be spent.

The bottom-up approach is a more logical approach involving decisions on the combination of message content, context and media required to achieve specified communications objectives; the objectives and task method. The total cost of the plan becomes a recommended communications budget to be reviewed by senior company management for approval. Like other investment decisions the use of funds for promotion is balanced against other ways of spending money.

The objectives and tasks method of setting marketing communications budgets is very popular among consumer packaged product firms. The organization starts by determining the desired market share from return on investment and break-even calculations. For packaged goods the percentage market share is equal to the percentage of the audience who are aware, multiplied by the percentage who tried the brand multiplied by the percentage who repeat purchase. Using this formula it is possible to determine how much awareness is needed. An example will illustrate the method. Assume that the break-even share required is 9 per cent. Assume further that market research indicates that only 30 per cent of those who are aware of the organization's product try it. Furthermore, the organization knows from past experience that as many as 60 per cent of those who try become repeat purchasers. Using the formula described above it is possible to determine how much awareness the organization needs:

$$[\text{Aware (\%)}] \times [\text{Try (\%)} = 0.30] \times [\text{Repeat (\%)} = 0.60] = 0.09$$

$$\text{Aware (\%)} \times 0.18 = 0.09$$

which implies that Aware (%) should be 0.5 or 50 per cent!

Communicating through advertising

Advertising is mass media paid communications used to convey information, develop positive attitudes and encourage customers in the target audience to respond in a desired way. It is a cost-effective way of communicating a simple message to large audiences and may create images and symbolic appeals to help in differentiating the organization's brands. Furthermore, because the organization is able to control the advertising message, its timing and frequency, it contributes to the creation of brand equity.

The advertising process consists of a number of stages. The company must decide the appropriate advertising strategy to employ, establish a set of objectives to be attained, decide the message to be communicated, select the mix of media to use and decide the budget and advertising support necessary. It is important to distinguish between the advertising idea and its implementation or execution. Many organizations acknowledge that they do not devote sufficient thought to selecting the advertising idea – the enduring creative thought – 'We try harder' (Avis), 'Have a break' (Kit Kat). The executional idea follows and deals with the way the thought is expressed. Too many advertising campaigns depend on the latter and pay little attention to the former.

Considerable thought has been devoted by US pharmaceutical companies to the advertising idea since the Food and Drug Administration in 1997 allowed them to name both the drug and the disease it treated in the same commercial without having in addition to list every single side-effect. By concentrating their advertising budgets on a small number of very successful drugs these companies have created branded drug franchises, supported by line extensions that help to prolong patent life. AstraZeneca now advertises both its ulcer drug, Prilosec, and its successor, Nexium, as 'the purple pill' – an easy slogan for customers to recall. The effect is to force off-patent medicines to leave the market. Doctors and health services agencies worry about safety and the threat to their position as experts and are opposed to direct-to-consumer advertising of drugs, complaining that patients demand potentially unsuitable drugs they have seen advertised. Research in 1999 published in the magazine *Prevention*, however, showed that 87 per cent of patients who asked doctors for an advertised drug were prescribed it (*The Economist*, 21 April 2001, p. 66).

Deciding an advertising strategy

In deciding an advertising strategy successful companies concentrate on systematically reaching the right audience with a clear convincing message. Many companies fail this test by being preoccupied with popular or fashionable advertising whereby the audience is attracted to the theme but not the product or service advertised. It is necessary, therefore, to set specific communication objectives for each advertising campaign and these should not be confused with the company's marketing objectives. Good advertising usually means using specialist agencies. Successful companies tend to be meticulous in their choice of agency and very critical in evaluating creative work and media plans submitted. They insist on pretesting where feasible to measure the probable impact of a campaign. In such circumstances it is necessary to have an advance plan for measuring the final results of a campaign which is implemented by a disinterested party.

Effective advertising

For advertising to be effective it should establish brand preference in the customer's mind for one particular brand to persuade them to try it and to continue using it. The Unilever Company has developed 10 principles for good advertising.

1 Consumer/user orientated

2 Concentrate on one selling idea

3 Emphasizes most persuasive idea

4 Presents unique/competitive feature

5 Involves the consumer/user

6 Is credible and sincere

7 Is simple, clear and complete

8 Associates the selling idea with the brand name

9 Exploits the medium

10 Makes the sale.

Advertising should be presented in a way that addresses the needs of customers: the case for purchasing a product or service should be presented as the customer sees it, not as the organization sees it. Good advertising concentrates on memorable reasons for trying a product, the emphasis is placed on selected customer benefits to avoid a scatter-gun approach which would diffuse the impact of the advertising. The company should also emphasize the product attribute with the greatest appeal to customers which implies pretesting of advertising and research to ensure that this property exists in the advertisement.

Successful advertising contains a promise of some unique benefit, quantity or quality not available elsewhere and it appeals to the customer's interests by attempting to solve some problem experienced. Advertising must also be credible and sincere and must be perceived to be honest and should not mislead.

Most advertisers also attempt to avoid misunderstanding by saying what is intended so advertisements should be simple, clear and complete. It is also necessary to link the brand name with the central selling idea. Some advertising fits better with one medium rather than another so it is important to take full advantage of the physical characteristics and the mood to which the particular medium predisposes customers. Finally, for advertising to be good, it should establish among customers a wish to buy so strong that simple merchandising techniques will be sufficient to serve as a gentle reminder.

In measuring advertising effectiveness there are a number of factors to take into account. Many organizations assess the effectiveness of creative strategies by measuring day-after recall using telephone surveys among a sample of the target audience. Successful creative strategies demonstrate the product, mention the brand name, outline the positive attributes, show how to use the product, avoid unpleasant connections with the product and clearly inform potential customers where and how they can buy it. Awareness is measured on the basis of aided and unaided recall and also during surveys. Overall effectiveness, impact on sales, is usually measured on a cross-market basis whereby advertising is increased in some geographic markets and the sales results compared against a control market where advertising expenditure levels are maintained.

Communicating through publicity and public relations

Publicity refers to free promotion of the organization's products and services in the media. It is usually the result of a newsworthy aspect of the organization's activities being captured by the media. Publicity covers all those situations where somebody outside the company gives it credit for some good thing or event. Media coverage of newsworthy items such as the development or introduction of a new product by a company falls into the realm of publicity. It takes the form of press releases, press conferences and press exclusives. Organizations frequently orchestrate their own publicity in situations where the event or circumstance has broad appeal. Publicity may help to promote a positive image of the company among relatively detached third parties. Like public relations, publicity may be managed in the company itself or by a specialist company.

Public relations which are closely related to publicity are also part of the organization's communications mix and used to inform selected groups about the company and its products with a view to building a basis of understanding and trust for product-specific communications activities. Public relations is not 'free advertising' or 'propaganda' but rather a communications vehicle which must be planned and implemented as part of a marketing communications strategy. Public relations helps to develop personality for the organization.

Public relations, described as being good at getting credit for something, refers to activities aimed at creating, maintaining or enhancing the organization's reputation among groups in its environment, e.g. the government, the financial institutions, employees, whose goodwill and understanding promote its future prosperity. Large well-established organizations whose prosperity is tied to the development of the economy at large pay special attention to public relations. Public relations are generally more restrictive in the types of objectives which can be achieved. Because it uses news stories in the media there is little opportunity to present persuasive reasons for buying a product or service. It is impossible to make a direct appeal to customers to buy the product. Public relations in these circumstances plays an educational role rather than a persuasive role in the marketing communications process. Public relations may be managed within the company or on an agency basis by a specialist company.

Communicating through sponsorship

A casual observer of the marketing communications scene would be forgiven for believing that sponsored cultural, social, sporting and educational events are now the way companies advertise themselves, their products and their services. In recent years there has been much growth in marketing expenditures by sponsors of such events. A sponsor is a organization who pays for a broadcast programme into which its advertisements are introduced. Commercial sponsorship has been defined as 'an investment, in cash or in kind, in an activity, in return for access to the exploitable commercial potential associated with that activity' (Meenaghan 1991, p. 36). The sponsor obtains the audience exposure potential which the activity sponsored has and the image associated with the activity in terms of how it is perceived. Like advertising, the company invests money in sponsorship for an expected return on the investment and by combining it with advertising, the organization may

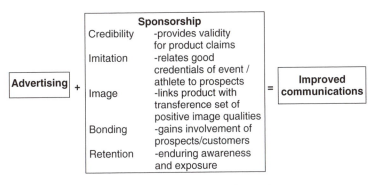

Source: Marshall, D.W. and Cook, G. (1992) 'The corporate (sports) sponsor',
International Advertising, **11**(4), 307–24.

Figure [10.6]   Adding value through sponsorship

achieve improved communications with its customers and other stakeholders
(Figure 10.6).

Sponsorship and self-image

Successful sponsorship means that the activity sponsored must reflect the
company's vision of itself and its products and services. Some activities are
acceptable and some are not. In recent years sports sponsorship has become
very significant in total communications expenditures. An organization may
decide to sponsor sports but not the arts, individuals but not teams, rock
music but not classical. These are general policy criteria which are company
specific. In recent years there has been a rush to sponsor sporting activities,
which possibly indicates a shift in lifestyles which attract certain kinds of
commercial sponsorship.

Sports sponsorship combined with athletic endorsements provide organizations with opportunities to promote themselves and their products. For
organizations seeking a broad, low-risk approach that also provides opportunities to interact with customers on a large scale, event sponsorship may
be the most effective. If rapid brand awareness and loyalty are the objectives, for example, during a product launch, athletic endorsements may be
preferred. Business-to-business organizations with only a small number of
clients soon discover that having celebrity athletes on a retainer to meet with
key clients is a successful approach in bonding and customer relationship
building. It is necessary, however, to ensure that the celebrity's personality
reflects the personality desired in the brand. Whichever approach is used,
sponsorship or endorsement, the organization should recognize that the cost
involved is merely the cost of admission. A multiple of the cost of the original sponsorship or endorsement is required for public relations, advertising
support, entertainment and travel expenses.

While both approaches are often used, it should be recognized that they are very different. The greatest advantage of sponsorship over athlete endorsements is that sporting events provide the organization with face-to-face contact with large numbers of customers through on-site activities such as consumer promotions and sampling. Organizations can also showcase an industrial product or service on a grand scale through sport sponsorship. Avaya Inc built the data and voice infrastructure for the final stages of the World Cup soccer championship held in Japan and South Korea in 2002. Sport sponsorship is the less risky of the two as there are many more marketing opportunities associated with events that do not depend on winning. On the other hand, an endorsement by a well-known athlete can raise brand awareness and credibility quickly and often works well when an organization introduces a new product or repositions its brand. According to Matt Yonan, a sports marketing specialist, 'Nike built its golf product line through its endorsement with Tiger Woods. He's young, exciting and has the right demographic following him. Sponsorship of the PGA Tour could not have done that for Nike' (*Marketing News*, 22 July 2002, p. 4).

Communicating through sales promotion

Sales promotion is eminently suited for supporting short-term marketing objectives. Other factors encouraging the use of sales promotion include the ability to tailor promotions to almost any marketing situation at different stages of the product life cycle and for different product-market situations.

Sales promotion refers to marketing activities other than personal selling, advertising and publicity that stimulate consumer purchasing and dealer effectiveness, e.g. display, shows, exhibitions and demonstrations. In practical terms sales promotion consists of couponing, refunds and rebates, sweepstakes and contests, allowances, educational programmes, promotional public relations, meetings, premiums and incentives promotional packaging (Bowman 1985). Sales promotion has been defined as 'the direct inducement or incentive to the sales force, the distributor, or the consumer, with the primary objective of creating an immediate sale' (Schultz and Robinson 1988, p. 8).

Sales promotions activities serve to complement advertising, as a substitute for competitive advantage, to assist new product launches and often as a somewhat reluctant response to the power of retailers (Figure 10.7). As image-building advertising is a slow process and sales promotion is designed to produce immediate effect, sales promotion complements advertising. Advertising effects are weak if there is no competitive advantage. As a substitute for competitive advantage, sales promotion offers a form of differentiation, at least in the short term. It may also be quite effective in supporting the launch of new products, however, particularly if it attracts the attention of customers

Figure [10.7]   Role of sales promotion

at the point of sale. Finally, the concentration of retail power in a small number of organizations and the introduction of modern communications technologies have given retailers access to market information that allows them to develop a sophisticated understanding of customers not readily available to manufacturers. In this regime retailers use their power to force their suppliers to use sale promotion on the understanding that customers benefit.

Sales promotion is most effective, therefore, in the short term. Demand from retailers and competition from private label and other manufacturers combine to encourage manufacturers to use sales promotions much more frequently than heretofore. The decline in brand loyalty among more fickle consumers and the fragmentation of media also contribute to the growth of sales promotion. Furthermore, there has been increased pressure from shareholders for short-term financial returns which motivates managers to favour the short term and hence, sales promotions.

In a general way sales promotion endeavours are designed around attempts by organizations to complement their marketing communications at the point of sale. The need for this form of promotion is to encourage consumers or users to select the company's product, service or brand from among the myriad others available in cluttered retail situations calling out for attention. Sales promotion in effect becomes a silent sales force encouraging people to select one offer over others. Sales promotions are most effective when:

■ A new brand is being introduced.

■ A major product improvement in an established brand is being communicated to the market.

■ The brand being promoted is already enjoying competitive success.

■ The company is trying to increase store distribution, and sales promotion is used to help sell to intermediaries.

■ A branded product is being advertised, and sales promotion is used to amplify the results of the advertising.

Complementary role of sales promotion

Sales promotion complements other marketing mix elements at various points in the marketing channel. Trade promotion is used by the manufacturer to encourage distributors to behave in a certain way with respect to the manufacturer's products and services (Figure 10.8). The manufacturer also designs sales promotions which are implemented directly at consumer level. Sales promotion to the retail trade and directly to consumers are the most common versions in use; sales promotion is predominantly a consumer market phenomenon. Trade promotion attempts to move product through the channel, provide price incentives, merchandise, assist in co-operative advertising and implement dealer contests. The objectives of trade promotion are to do the following:

- provide in-store sales support

- increase the level of trade inventories

- improve product distribution

- motivate channel trade.

Consumer promotion uses various forms of direct incentives to encourage the final customer to buy the manufacturer's product rather than some other. The objectives of consumer promotions are:

- to obtain product trial

- to encourage loyalty

- to introduce new or improved products, new packaging or new product sizes

- to encourage customers to trade up

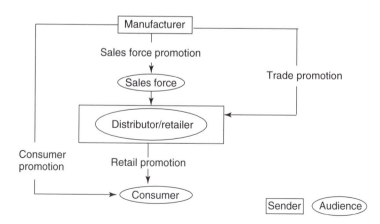

Figure [10.8]   Sales promotion in the marketing channel

- to promote more frequent purchase

- to capitalize on special circumstances, e.g. a local festival or sports event.

Very often the mass media are used to advertise the sales promotion itself.

The task for the manufacturer is to ensure that all types of promotion are co-ordinated and that no element conflicts with any other. This is very difficult to achieve since retailers typically have very different objectives than manufacturers. In circumstances where profit goals are unlikely to be achieved, it is a relatively easy matter for an organization to cut advertising expenditure, which has a longer-term effect, than sales promotion budgets which have a more immediate and visible effect on sales volumes. A second contributory factor for the popularity of sales promotion is that sales volumes, not values, are still used by many companies as the basis on which to evaluate and reward retailers and compensate sales people. Evaluation methods based on volume usually do not reflect a profitability criterion especially when heavy sales promotions are involved. At the same time brand managers operate under performance criteria which are essentially in conflict. They are often held accountable for a combination of profit and volume or share gains. This inconsistency in performance criteria and associated compensation systems for brand managers and sales managers leads to inevitable conflict and damage to the organization.

Another reason for the relative growth of sales promotions may be due to the relative ease with which effectiveness may be judged compared to advertising. By depending solely on intuitive and qualitative measures to judge effectiveness rather than quantitative techniques, advertising agencies and brand managers have weakened the case for brands.

There are life-cycle effects in the use of sales promotion. Sales promotion can be effective in the pioneering and late maturity or renewal stages of the life cycle. In general the ratio of advertising to promotion tends to change over the life cycle. Frequently, when product categories reach maturity, brand differentiation declines and many indistinguishable brands proliferate the market.

Market maturity leads to less differentiation and, therefore, an increase in price and promotion responsiveness. Furthermore, customers learn, as a result of manufacturers' initiatives, to respond to promotions. The lower the differentiation among brands, the higher tends to be the ratio of sales promotion expenditure to sales (Quelch *et al*. 1984). It may also be true that the effect of advertising may decline as markets mature. With increases in advertising, its marginal productivity declines compared to trade and consumer sales promotion. Higher levels of promotion relative to advertising are associated with brands that:

- have a profit contribution rate below the company average

- have little brand loyalty

- have little competitive differentiation

- are directed toward children

- are purchased with little planning

- are in the introductory or renewal stages of the life cycle

- have a pronounced seasonal sales pattern

- have a small share of the market

- compete in markets where private labels are important (Strang *et al.* 1975).

Extra costs and brand debasement

Engaging in sales promotion gives rise to additional costs at manufacturer level as it is necessary to produce in peaks and troughs to meet the increased demand and subsequent decline. Trade promotions have often been referred to as costly affairs for manufacturers. Powerful organizations strike back by reducing discounts offered to retailers for some but not all products in the portfolio, thereby leaving the total purchase cost to retailers about the same as before.

By following this pricing and sales promotion approach these companies expect that the lower prices will eliminate the manufacturing and distribution inefficiencies caused by sales promotions, allow a decrease in regular retail prices to customers and eventually restore brand loyalty among buyers. Such a strategy can work only if the organization has a portfolio of well-known brands in demand which the retailer is reluctant to boycott. The fear from the organization's viewpoint is that competitors will continue to offer retailers attractive concessions in order to control greater shelf space. If more powerful manufacturers withstand this pressure, weaker competitors could then face increased competition from discounts if they continue to offer deals to powerful retailers.

While the direct costs implications of sales promotions may be considerable, a more fundamental cost is the possible debasing of brands created by continuous sales promotions which encourages many shoppers to purchase products only when 'on sale'. There has been considerable debate concerning the effects of sales promotion on brand equity. The generally accepted view is that sales promotion has a negative effect. While advertising is believed to increase market share, heavily sales-promoted brands tend to lose market share (Strang *et al.* 1975). Product sampling tends to be an exception since it can help to build awareness especially for a new product. In the case of packaged goods, retail promotions benefit brand leaders over weaker brands (Blattberg and Neslin 1990). The buyer perceives a strong brand to be a quality product and thus can claim a higher price. A sales-promoted brand, however, is often perceived as being of lower quality, otherwise it would not need to be promoted (Dobson *et al.* 1978).

In recent years some retailers have adopted an everyday low-price policy to avoid the haggling over sales promotion deals. Replacing sales promotions, which often produce wide swings in sales and prices, with relatively stable, low prices, eases the time and cost pressures of implementing price promotions and reduces any mistrust that exists between manufacturers and retailers and between retailers and customers. Retailers with strong private label brands are not so accommodating, however, in situations where the real competition is between private label and brands ranked third or fourth. Accommodation is easier to find for dominant brands where mutual interest exists. For example, Elida Gibbs tried the everyday lower price strategy but was forced to return to promotions as it lost share to brands on promotion.

Permanent or temporary gain

Sales promotions are not always successful; they may succeed only in attracting one-time new users or provide the product at a lower price to some regular customers who are subsequently lost when they refuse to pay the normal price for the product at the end of the promotion period. As a general rule, brand loyal buyers use sales promotions to 'stock up' and to adjust the frequency of purchase to the size of the inventory built up from promotional purchases. It is feared that sales promotions do not provide much long-term incremental volume to the company, and the incremental volume from promotions comes from infrequent users of the brand rather than from loyal users or non-users. These are hardly very good reasons to encourage the use of sales promotion except in limited circumstances. Organizations engaging in sales promotion, however, expect there to be a permanent gain as a result of a sales promotion.

Supermarkets can jeopardize manufacturers' sales promotion plans by forward buying special wholesale deals which allows them to stock up far more product than they expect to sell during the promotion. After the promotion period these supermarkets can obtain a wider margin by selling the surplus product at the regular price. Of course, most organizations attempt to avoid such consequences by agreeing mutually acceptable terms in advance during the negotiations phase.

Integrated marketing communications

Managers have expressed the need for integrated marketing communication. The increased emphasis on the integration of marketing communications stems from a realization that there has been a shift from transactions marketing to relationship marketing accompanied by the requirement to build greater loyalty among customers. Furthermore, many customers have been critical of mass media advertising as being irrelevant. Organizations seek an impact greater than efficiency and cost effectiveness in fragmented markets.

Integrated marketing communications means considering all aspects simultaneously where once the organization examined public relations, sales promotion, direct marketing separately. Integrated marketing communication has been defined as 'The process of unifying all of the marketing communications tools to send to target audiences a consistent persuasive message that promotes company goals' (Burnett and Moriarty 1998). This means treating the integration task at two levels – the level of the marketing mix and the communications mix. Integrated marketing communications is based on the recognition that customers do not distinguish among different kinds of communication. It is important, therefore, that consistency is maintained in all messages sent to all audiences through the various channels used. Integrated marketing communications is an essential ingredient in building a strong brand.

For example, a failure to treat sales promotion as an integral part of marketing strategy may give rise to unrelated selling and advertising plans in the company and the dilution of decision-making authority over the sales promotion budget. This lack of integration may prevent the establishment of cohesive marketing communications strategies and an inappropriate balance in the allocation of marketing efforts.

The barriers to effective integrated communications arise from too much specialization within the organization and the communications agencies. Managers perceive that integration is too complex and difficult or impossible to plan and co-ordinate. Strategic direction and strong internal communication within the organization are required to drive an integrated consistent and effective communications policy.

References

Blattberg, Robert C. and Neslin, Scott A. (1990), *Sales Promotion: Concepts, Methods and Strategies*. Englewood Cliffs, NJ: Prentice Hall.

Bowman, Russell D. (1985), *Profit on the Dotted Line: Coupons and Rebates*. Chicago: Commerce Communications Inc.

Burnett, John and Moriarty, Sandra (1998), *Introduction to Marketing Communications: An Integrated Approach*. Upper Saddle River, NJ: Prentice Hall.

Dobson, Joe A., Tybout, Alice and Steinthal, Brian (1978), 'Impact of deals and deal retraction on brand switching', *Journal of Marketing Research*, **15** (February), 77–81.

Dye, Renee (2000), 'The buzz on buzz', *Harvard Business Review*, **78** (6), 139–46.

Keller, Kevin Lane (2001), 'Mastering the marketing communications mix: micro and macro perspectives on integrated marketing communications programs', *Journal of Marketing Management*, **17**, 819–47.

Marshall, D. W. and Cook, G. (1992), 'The corporate (sports) sponsor', *International Journal of Advertising*, **11** (4), 307–24.

Meenaghan, Tony (1991), 'The role of sponsorship in the marketing communication mix', *International Journal of Advertising*, **10**, 35–47.

Quelch, John A., Marshall, Cheri T. and Chang, Dae R. (1984), 'Structural determinants of ratios of promotion and advertising to sales', in *Research on Sales Promotion: Collected Papers*, Katherine E. Jocz, ed., Cambridge, MA: Marketing Science Institute Report No. 84–104.

Rossiter, John R., Percy, Larry and Donovan, Robert J. (1991), 'A better advertising planning grid', *Journal of Advertising Research*, October–November, 11–21.

Schultz, Don E. and Robinson, William A. (1988), *Sales Promotion Management*. Lincolnwood: NTC Business Books.

Strang, Roger A., Prentice, Robert M. and Clayton, Alden G. (1975), *The Relationship Between Advertising and Promotion in Brand Strategy*. Cambridge, MA: Marketing Science Institute.

Vidale, M. and Wolfe, H. (1957), 'An operational research study of sales response to advertising', *Operations Research*, **5** (3), 370–81.

Chapter 11

Direct marketing and personal selling

Direct marketing is an approach to marketing that involves the company knowing precisely who its customers are, understanding that not everybody is a customer, communicating in relevant ways with customers and prospects, enhancing and refining the relevance of the communications and doing all of the above through a database. Successful direct marketing can be accomplished with any and all combinations of media and distribution channels. Direct marketing is not, therefore, a medium, nor is it a channel, nor is it a methodology; it is a comprehensive approach to marketing and to identifying and serving the needs of customers.

Direct marketing is like advertising in a number of respects. Properly used, it can reinforce the brand values created and maintained by advertising. Like advertising it is also an above-the-line expenditure since it represents actual outlays as opposed to sacrificing profit. In both of these respects direct marketing is different from sales promotion which is a 'below-the-line' expenditure which may erode brand values if used excessively.

In a similar vein selling is a dynamic two-way communication which provides information in a flexible way which can be adapted to the specific needs of customers. The difference is that the personal involvement of a salesperson is present in selling. Selling is part of the communications mix but is much more focused than mass communications like advertising. It is customized as occurs in direct marketing but performed by an individual or a team in personal contact with customers. Managing the selling process means understanding and agreeing the roles and tasks of the sales force such as prospecting, communicating, negotiating, collecting information and servicing accounts.

Communicating through direct marketing

The principal benefits of any direct marketing technique are the accuracy with which customers can be reached due to the targeting involved based on computer databases; the measurable effect of direct marketing allowing the

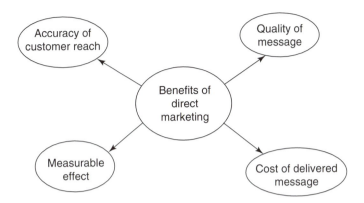

Figure [11.1]   Benefits of direct marketing

company to determine its impact in the short term; the quality of the message due to the ability to provide sophisticated copy appropriately printed; and the low cost of the delivered message, especially compared with advertising (Figure 11.1).

The attractions of direct marketing for many companies are that short-term sales effects are easy to quantify whereas the short-term effects of mass communications such as advertising are less easy to measure. Advertising, as was seen in the previous chapter, addresses longer-term brand values and is essentially a social phenomenon because it is public. Direct marketing by its nature, however, is essentially a private form of communication which ignores the social aspect of consumption. In 1999 Highland Distillers reviewed the promotion of its Macallen whisky brand and decided to switch its entire advertising budget into direct marketing. It built a database of 100,000 of its more frequent drinkers, at least five bottles a year, mailing them every few months with interesting facts about the brand, whisky memorabilia and offers.

The key element of direct marketing is the development and maintenance of a detailed customer database outlining historical buying behaviour that can be statistically manipulated to produce market segments which can be directly served by a customized marketing package.

The growth of direct marketing may be attributed to the rising cost and possible ineffectiveness of mass communications in some situations. With direct marketing there is also the possibility of an accurate focus on individual customers. Direct marketing requires a sophisticated up-to-date database capable of being exploited by advanced computer, mail, telecommunications and web-based technologies. As the use of direct response advertising becomes more widespread, it can be used to support direct marketing activities. Direct marketing has, therefore, become an important element of marketing communications.

There are a number of important distinctions between general marketing and direct marketing (Roberts and Berger 1989). Many of these differences are a matter of emphasis and refer to the organization's communication objectives at a particular time:

General marketing	Direct marketing
▪ Reaches a mass media audience through mass media	▪ Communicates directly with the customer
▪ Communications are impersonal	▪ Can personalize communication
▪ Promotional programmes are highly visible	▪ Promotional programmes (especially tests) relatively 'invisible'
▪ Amount of promotion controlled by size of budget	▪ Size of budget can be determined by success of promotion
▪ Multiple desired actions often delayed	▪ Specific action always required: inquiry, purchase
▪ Incomplete/sample data for decision-making purposes, e.g. sales call reports, marketing research	▪ Comprehensive database drives marketing programme
▪ Analyses conducted at the segment level use surrogate variables to measure effectiveness: advertising awareness, intention to buy	▪ Analysis conducted at organization or individual level. Measurable and highly controllable

Building direct customer relationships

The aim of most direct marketing activities is to create and encourage a personal relationship between the company and its customers which will last a long time. Such relationships encourage people to become increasingly receptive to information about new products and services. Skilfully prepared and well-designed communications are an ideal way to build organization–customer relationships.

Direct marketing is a form of marketing in which the organization bypasses all intermediary channels of distribution in reaching the buyer. It is aimed at building long-term bonding relationships with customers. In doing so it exploits high technology communications to build enduring relationships with customers.

Catalogue companies were the first to recognize the power of building direct relationships with customers. In more recent times a number of financial houses have followed their example. Many service organizations make extensive use of direct marketing to communicate, e.g. airlines, car hire companies, hotel and holiday resorts. In addition, many retailers and manufacturers have experimented with direct marketing, some with greater success than others.

Direct marketing is not just concerned with the first order or sale. The aim of most direct marketing activities is to create and encourage a personal relationship between the company and its customers which will last a long time. Such relationships encourage people to become increasingly receptive to information about new products and services. Skilfully prepared and well-designed mail shots are an ideal way to build company–customer relationships. The banks and other financial institutions have discovered the value of direct marketing and increasingly the manufacturers of expensive consumer products such as cars are also using it. Dell Computer Corporation provides an excellent example of the value of direct marketing based on price competition as a way of entering a new market for a relatively expensive durable product. Organizations like Dell can very quickly achieve a share of the market through price competition where incumbents are vulnerable. Other consumer packaged goods companies are beginning to apply more extensive use of direct marketing.

According to Bauer and Miglautsch (1992, p. 10) 'Direct marketing is a relational marketing process of prospecting, conversion and maintenance that involves information feedback and control at the individual level by using direct response advertising with tracking codes.' This operational definition emphasizes four activities. First, there is a regular repeat contact with customers by direct response advertising, mailings or telephone calls to customers and repeat orders from customers. Prospecting, or name acquisition, is an activity of finding new customers to build the customer file.

Prospecting, seeking new customers to add to the existing database of customers, is fundamental to direct marketing since it helps to provide a source of future sales and revenues. Prospecting means acquiring new first-time customers or locating new sales leads, converting leads and enquiries into first-time customers and minimizing the cost of developing a customer database while maximizing the number of new names. Prospecting costs money; the objective is to find the most likely customers at the lowest possible cost.

Prospecting or customer and lead acquisition has been referred to as 'front-end' marketing since the people in the company involved are different from those at the 'back-end'. The responsibility of the front-end marketing team is to acquire new, first-time customers, acquire new leads or inquiries, convert leads into first-time customers to maximize the number of new names on the customer list while minimizing the cost of building the list (Schmid 1992, p. 39). Few direct marketing companies expect to make money in the prospecting side of the business. The central objective is to locate the highest quality names at the lowest possible cost.

The second major activity is conversion that focuses on changing the status of a respondent to a higher disposition towards purchase and loyalty while the third activity refers to the need to maintain customer interest and purchase. This means building an information feedback loop at the individual level providing detailed customer information and transaction data that constitute the company file on customers. When these transaction data are analysed and used in marketing decisions, it becomes information feedback. Based on this information organizations can develop customer segmentation models to select particular customers for various types of special contact. With such information it is also possible to use true experimental research designs in field research with clearly defined measurement properties.

Fourth, direct marketing involves direct response advertising with tracking codes. Connecting direct response advertising to tracking codes is the basis for developing a customer file of transaction information for future marketing decisions. The tracking code is unique for each direct response advertisement in order to identify the source of the response. Some kind of tracking code is necessary to monitor, measure and analyse responses to a particular direct response advertisement and a set of direct response advertisements for customer lifetime value analyses.

Components of direct marketing

Direct marketing consists of three components: the development of an effective customer database; direct response advertising which leads to the sale; and the direct building of customer relationships to increase sales and profits. Direct marketing is an approach to marketing which is driven by a database which implies that the company knows who its customers are, and communicates with them in appropriate ways through enhanced and refined means of communications; the driver is the database. It is a highly targeted approach to marketing which also implies that the company knows who are not among its customers. Customer information management is critical and two-way communication with customers may lead to high loyalty.

In addition to an effective database, it is also essential to have an efficient medium and an efficient delivery system (Figure 11.2). The delivery medium requires access to sophisticated printing services which can personalize mailings and target customers at competitive prices.

While direct marketing makes extensive use of e-mail and other Internet services, telemarketing and direct mail are the two most popular forms of direct marketing. Telemarketing is most often used in conjunction with other direct marketing techniques where customers call a company in response to a publication in a magazine insert or advertising. A very high proportion, as high as 75 per cent of direct marketing organizations in the UK, use

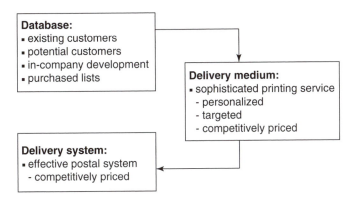

Figure [11.2]   Requirements for effective direct marketing

e-mail marketing. New techniques such as the ability to send video-clips have enhanced the attraction of e-mail marketing and wider adaption of broadband is likely to extend its use. Promotion by mobile phone text messages (SMS), especially among teenagers, is popular among food and drinks brands companies.

It is likely that these technologies will bring about the convergence of direct marketing and advertising. Developments in Internet and cable technologies are likely to make it easier to target different advertisements to different customer groups – advertising will in effect become direct marketing.

Direct marketing process

The general process of direct marketing involves a manufacturer, a direct marketing company, a channel and a consumer (Figure 11.3). Many direct marketing companies do not manufacture the products they sell, but of course they may. The direct marketing firm sends an advertising message, usually in the form of a direct response advertisement, to the consumer. This message is usually transmitted through the mass media, press, radio and television. It is possible, however, for the message to be sent person-to-person directly or by telephone. Direct marketing may, therefore, use any channel of communication to transmit the direct response advertising message.

The consumers who decide to respond usually transmit their responses by mail or by telephone to the advertiser. If an order is placed a tracking code becomes part of the transaction to identify the specific sales message and source of the consumer's name and other details. When the direct marketing company has received the order the merchandise is sent directly to the customer through the fulfilment channel, usually the mail system.

Source: Adapted from Connie L. Bauer and John Miglautsch (1992) 'A conceptual definition of direct marketing', *Journal of Direct Marketing*, 6, 2, Spring, p. 15 Reproduced by permission of John Wiley & Sons. Ltd

Figure [11.3] Direct marketing process: message response and fulfilment channels

Increasing customer loyalty

The degree to which customers are loyal or not depends on a number of factors but loyalty itself is most important for the direct marketing company as repeat purchases and lifetime sales are the life blood of direct marketing companies. Direct marketing may be used to increase customer loyalty in a number of ways (Figure 11.4).

At the first stage, awareness is the important feature. At this point, as already discussed in Chapter 10, customer loyalty does not exist since the customer is unaware of the company or its products. Awareness results from obtaining a greater 'share of mind' than competitors. Appropriate images may be created through advertising. At the awareness stage advertising is perhaps the most powerful communications medium. Advertising also helps to identify the values in the product or service being offered. By appealing to higher level needs, advertising can produce interest in the product or service, desire and action. By identifying the value and communicating it in

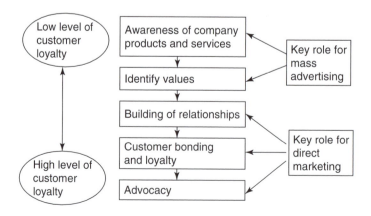

Figure [11.4] Direct marketing increases customer loyalty

this way, advertising obtains strong product identification. The key role for mass advertising is evident in these two early stages in the development of customer loyalty.

During the next stage a relationship between the company and the customer is established. There is a direct exchange of benefits. The company provides customized products, services and information. In return customers provide more information about themselves and their needs. Greater loyalty is established and sales increase. At this stage the first important role for direct marketing arises. The opportunity now exists for two-way mail or telephone communication based on a database.

In the next stage the company attempts to establish a strong link between the customer and the company by integrating the company's products and services with the customer's lifestyle. During this period the relationship between company and customer are highly interactive. The relationship becomes a private one leading to a customized, exclusive treatment. Regular two-way communication becomes essential to this exclusivity. There are numerous ways of building customer loyalty through direct marketing, e.g. frequent buyer benefits, gifts and preferred service are perhaps the more popular.

Direct marketing activities allow these benefits to be packaged in a customized way that can be tailored to the needs of the individual customer with the objective of building and strengthening loyalty. Mass advertising is less important at this stage and may detract from the relationship.

The expected results of customizing the marketing programme in this way is the establishment of trust and close relationships between the company and its customers. These valued relationships receive commercially significant expression in word-of-mouth promotion and advocacy for the company's products and services. When customers reach the stage of being advocates for the company's products and services, the ideal partnership has been established.

Applications of databases

The application of a database in direct marketing implies a statistical modelling of customer behaviour through in-depth quantitative analysis. It is necessary to manipulate the database statistically first. It is also necessary to note that the data are collected and maintained at the individual level, i.e. individual customer, household, or business organization. The analysis is performed and the marketing activity is designed at the level of the individual unit.

The database also allows the organization to monitor and evaluate the effectiveness of each contact with customers or prospects which thereby enables better management decisions regarding product design, pricing, segmentation and media choice. Database marketing should also be viewed as an investment in relationships (Roberts 1992, p. 53). A carefully planned programme of marketing communications can be used to acquire new customers, to obtain repeat purchases from existing customers, to cross-sell, upgrade and otherwise promote the sale of substitute and complementary products and services.

Databases in direct marketing

Maintaining a database of marketing information is essential for the company that wishes to know who its customers are as well as who are most likely to become customers. A database is a collection of information about customers and prospects. That collection of data takes on value when the company uses it to determine audience segments, their unique needs and consequent financial performance. Some customers respond better than others, some are consistently more profitable than others. A database allows the company to determine which is the true situation.

The database is the engine which drives direct marketing. It enables the company to differentiate between customers and non-customers and to communicate with them in different ways. Mass communications can be a very blunt instrument. Direct marketing hones mass communication into a refined and precise tool.

In addition to an effective database, it is also essential to have an efficient medium and an efficient delivery system. The delivery medium requires access to sophisticated printing services which can personalize mailings and target customers at competitive prices. An efficient delivery system usually means having an effective postal system which is competitively priced. The value of direct marketing is, moreover, due in no small way to the revolution in contemporary technologies, most notably data processing and telecommunications.

Monitoring existing and new customers

There is a direct link between direct marketing and an effective database. Database marketing was recognized as a separate marketing entity when companies realized that they could statistically analyse their customer data to produce sophisticated segmentation models which allowed them to offer a given product or service only to those people who demonstrated a high probability of purchase. As a result, database marketing was recognized as an effective way of soliciting sales and of qualifying sales prospects.

Modern information technology, especially database marketing, are dynamic tools which require constant updating and maintenance. A database list which is not maintained ceases to be a useful marketing tool. It is essential to keep the list current and to add new names to it on a regular basis. To have currency, a database must be updated with information on new prospects who are emerging as possible buying influences for future purchase decisions. At the same time the names of people no longer interested in the product should be dropped from the database. Many organizations use a 'bounce back' card or its electronic equivalent, giving prospects an opportunity to request additional information or a sales call or have their names removed from the list.

The most successful database marketing companies use their lists for tele-marketing surveys to monitor market trends and identify emerging customer needs. The time gained and the speed to market allow such companies to outpace rivals who may be only beginning to recognize the gap in the market. Telemarketing also allows the company keep the customer list up to date.

Many companies also frequently advertise in the media, use public rela-tions efforts, attend trade shows and exhibitions to maintain contact with existing customers and to reach new ones. Usually it is necessary to develop a communications strategy balanced between the need to reach short-term and longer-term prospects (Figure 11.5). A typical approach might be to adopt a narrow angle vertical focus through various media to reach short-term prospects. This vertical or narrow focused effort concentrates scarce resources where short-term results are likely to be greatest. A wide angle horizon-tal approach using the same media is necessary to identify new emerging segments with sales potential. By following this procedure the company ensures that its database is maintained with a balanced mix of short-term and long-term prospects for each segment served.

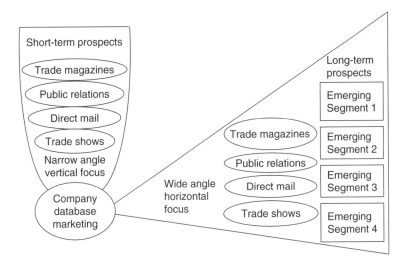

Figure [11.5]   Balanced communications mix to identify prospects

Communicating through personal selling

Selling is a consultative activity between the organization and its customers emphasizing relationships and loyalty and is not just about short-term sales gains. Hence, it is important that the company pays meticulous attention to the recruitment, remuneration and renewal of its sales force. Because selling is an expensive function, it is also necessary to seek high productivity levels which derive from sales support by way of back-office staff, personal computers and access to relevant databases. In organizational terms strategic marketing attempts to integrate the sales force with the other marketing activities by according them a degree of marketing autonomy in recognition of their flexibility and understanding of local customer bases. An effective sales force is one that serves two masters well – the organization and the customer – where both of these meet, in the marketplace.

Nature of personal selling

Personal selling means informing and pursuing customers through interpersonal communications directly associated with a particular transaction especially where advice and demonstration are required, e.g. consumer durables, pharmaceutical products, industrial components and equipment. Because the sales person is trained to be flexible, knowledgeable and adaptable concerning the organization's products, personal selling can be very effective and provide a powerful means of communication. By understanding the sales and communication objectives of the organization the sales person can adapt the communication message as the need arises. Selling is a dynamic two-way communication which provides information in a flexible way which can be adapted to the needs of specific customers. The sales person is in a position to customize the communications message to suit the needs of individual customers. Personal selling is most effective where close relationships between supplier and customer are necessary. The more complex and technical the buying–selling relationship, the more likely personal selling is to be more effective than other means of communication. Because it is focused and feedback is possible, selling can be less wasteful than advertising but is complemented by it.

Sales objectives and tasks

The objectives of the sales force are prospecting, information gathering, selling, servicing and communicating. Arising out of these objectives a number of selling tasks may be identified (Figure 11.6). Tasks which are treated with a certain degree of glamour are the 'front-end' tasks of prospecting, similar to direct marketing, negotiating and selling. The other more 'back-end'

Figure [11.6]   Key tasks in selling

tasks such as collecting and disseminating information, communications, time and resource allocation and servicing accounts are no less important if they are less glamorous. They are essential to the success of selling. Companies sometimes provide a sales support staff to carry out some of these tasks.

Personal selling has been described as the most effective tool of the promotions mix (Reeder *et al.* 1987) while others describe it as the 'art of persuasion', in which the role of the sales person ranges from 'seducing' the would-be customer, to actually delivering the product and providing a back-up service. The art of selling has not really changed over the years. Hutt and Speh (1985) outline emerging industrial selling styles as: consultative, negotiation, systems selling and team selling. In regard to industrial products Shapiro and Posner (1976) have developed a systematic procedure for 'making the major sale':

- Develop a profile of a company's needs and key personnel.

- Justify the purchase to the buyer.

- Co-ordinate the company's resources to present a more attractive sales package.

- Make the sales 'pitch'.

- Close the sale and maintain the account.

Furthermore, in regard to time and resource allocation the organization must decide how much attention should be given to customers, products and activity. Consideration is given to the following factors in allocating resources to customers:

- Which industry to target.

- Which volume segments to consider – high and/or low volume; national and/or smaller accounts.

- Which profitability segments to consider – high profitability and/or less profitable.

- New and/or existing accounts.

- High and/or low penetration accounts.

- Which geographic area to target.

A similar checklist must be considered in regard to product allocation decisions:

- New and/or existing products.

- High and/or low-volume products.

- Easy-to-sell and/or difficult-to-sell products
  - familiar/unfamiliar products
  - products with high short-term impact and low carry-over effects and/or products with low short-term impact and high carry-over effects.

The organization must also decide how to allocate its sales force resources among the various selling activities:

- Hunting for new accounts and/or farming existing accounts.

- Selling to customers and/or servicing customers.

- Developing relationships, product knowledge, industry capacity and/or financial skills.

Evolution of consultative selling

Increasingly the ability of the company to match performance with customer expectations depends on the ability of the sales force to orchestrate the company's response to customer needs. In such circumstances sales people must demonstrate trustworthiness and an ability to solve problems even if the solution does not include the company's products or services.

The most important characteristics that customers seek in sales people are business and product knowledge, communications skills, a customer

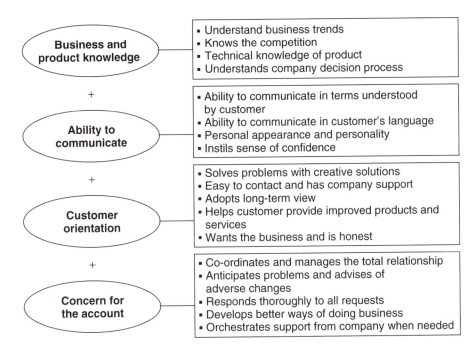

Business and product knowledge
- Understand business trends
- Knows the competition
- Technical knowledge of product
- Understands company decision process

+

Ability to communicate
- Ability to communicate in terms understood by customer
- Ability to communicate in customer's language
- Personal appearance and personality
- Instils sense of confidence

+

Customer orientation
- Solves problems with creative solutions
- Easy to contact and has company support
- Adopts long-term view
- Helps customer provide improved products and services
- Wants the business and is honest

+

Concern for the account
- Co-ordinates and manages the total relationship
- Anticipates problems and advises of adverse changes
- Responds thoroughly to all requests
- Develops better ways of doing business
- Orchestrates support from company when needed

Figure [11.7] Characteristics of a sales person sought by customers

orientation and concern for the longevity of the account (Figure 11.7). All four characteristics rely on the sales person's consultative ability to understand the customer's business, to be a problem solver and an efficient provider of services aimed at satisfying customer needs.

The consultative ability requires sales people to be willing to share their knowledge and understanding of the business and product environment so that organizations can better serve their customers. Usually it is necessary to share state-of-the-art information without pressing for a sale. The purpose is to keep the customer informed of business developments. The service thus provided becomes the key to future sales. Consultative sales people must be able to combine selling skills with consultative skills but they must, however, continue to prospect, enquire, support and close deals. Successful sales people are able to strike an acceptable balance between achieving short-run sales targets and cultivating and maintaining long-term relationships with customers. The ultimate goal of sales people is to master the basic skills of selling to be used within a consultative framework.

Companies attempting to shift from product-driven to customer-driven selling based on customer consultation are faced with a dilemma: how to manage the trade-off between short-run sales revenues and long-term customer relationships. By allowing the sales force to negotiate price, credit terms and other conditions to improve customer satisfaction, there is a danger of jeopardizing the predictability of revenues and production schedules.

Developing a sales team

Successful consultative selling means being part of a team with the resources to satisfy customer enquiries and needs. Customers expect consistent, dependable performance from products and services and the sales person is the one cast in the role as provider. The sales person orchestrates the company's resources, people and information, to address the customer's needs. Rather than a simple dyad of sales person–customer relationship, it becomes an integrated marketing programme where concern centres on the longevity of the account and the underlying relationship.

Selling technical products

In industrial markets companies use personal selling as the traditional means of communication between themselves and buyers. Personal selling is dominant in industrial markets because the number of potential customers is relatively small compared with consumer markets. Purchases in value terms are usually considerably larger. The task of the industrial sales force differs from that of the consumer sales force in two important ways:

- They make fewer sales calls than the consumer sales force.

- They spend much more time with each customer in liaising and problem solving.

For consumer products, a 'pull strategy' based on advertising and other non-personal techniques is normally used. In consumer mass marketing, where the selling process relies heavily on demand stimulation by brand and heavy merchandising, the pure selling function has dwindled to a pale shadow of what it was before the advent of self-service. Personal selling is also most effective in any market where the product or service is technical in nature and requires a considerable amount of knowledge on the part of the sales person. When demonstration on the use of the product is important, the role of personal selling becomes essential.

Selling technical products such as an enterprise-level software package or a wholesale computer component or a high technology business-to-business service product that only engineers or computer programmers fully understand may require team selling where the team consists of sales people and technology experts. Sales managers in high technology industry often must choose between establishing permanent sales and technology teams that always go on sales calls together or placing the technology people in a pool of professionals who are on-call for different visits. A combination is often the result of experimentation with these diverse approaches. How the teams are formed is often a matter of trial and error. Some organizations use consulting firms initially as a pool of technical experts but once the organization has identified a good combination of sales professionals and high technology expertise, a more permanent team is formed.

While moving technically trained people into the marketing function may work well, reluctant technical experts should not be pushed into the sales role. Conversely, as a general rule marketing people are best served by learning the technical language and concepts they need to know on the job, rather than by trying to match their technical colleagues by obtaining a formal scientific training.

For such interdisciplinary marketing teams to function many companies agree that the sales or marketing person should be in charge of the sales effort. Doing so helps keep the lines of authority clear and communications with customers and prospects uncomplicated. Furthermore, even a well-briefed interdisciplinary team is unlikely to be successful if the technical experts are not enthusiastic about selling. Technically trained people sometimes have personalities which are not so resilient whereas the ability to deal with rejection sets successful sales people apart.

The key to successful technical selling is through consultation, communication and interaction – the ability to listen to customers and the ability to communicate technical information in a way that non-technical people understand. While technical people may discover that joining the marketing team means acquiring an entirely new set of skills, marketing people should acknowledge that they cannot easily develop a technical competence.

Process of selling

Similar to direct marketing, selling involves many stages, prospecting for new qualified customers, understanding the customer decision-making process and developing the sales approach including sales literature, contacting the customer and making a personal sales call, presenting the product or service to the customer, negotiating the sale and managing and supporting the account (Figure 11.8).

Prospecting is an important endeavour in the overall selling process which can be rewarding in terms of ultimate selling success. Successful prospecting for new customers or clients requires the company to reduce the difficulty of 'cold calling' potential customers by first reaching them with a public relations or direct marketing effort. In this way it is easier to obtain an appointment to discuss the possible sale.

During the presentation it is important to emphasize needs and problems facing the potential buyer. The organization's products must be presented

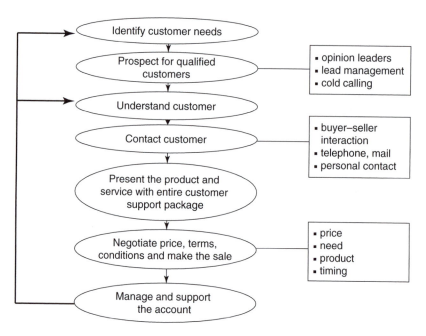

Figure [11.8] Sequential process of effective selling

as solutions to customers' problems. The organization normally presents a number of possible options at different price levels, not a take-it-or-leave-it package.

Sales prospecting is the search for sales leads to identify potential customers. Prospecting is not only in the sales person's domain: it is a team responsibility requiring techniques designed to give each sales person year-round support. Jolson and Wotrulea (1992, p. 59) note that 'nothing can happen until the selling firm finds a "prospect" for its products. Without a prospect there can be no meaningful sales presentation ... and surely no sale.' Efficient prospecting means:

- Minimizing sales time spent with people that are not potential customers.

- Saving travel time/expenses through better planning of sales calls.

- Providing optimum background information on prospects to help make smoother calls and easier sales.

- Creating meticulous customer or prospect databanks for efficient use.

Sales conferences

Sales conferences are very cost effective since client groups may be targeted accurately. Sales conferences are appropriate for organizations that can identify a relatively small number of people inside and outside the organization whose attitude and motivation towards the organization's well-being are likely to have the greatest effect. Included are organizations with large sales forces or dealer networks or companies which sell to a relatively small number of customers. Car manufacturing is a good example of a situation where, relatively speaking, the number of dealers in each region would be small with perhaps five or six key people in each outlet so that the total audience for a sales conference could be of the order of 100 to 200 which would be very manageable. A new product launch or presentation of the five-year marketing plan to dealers in such an environment can be very effective. Real success derives from combining the information giving and motivation process with the normal above-the-line activity, especially advertising, which is intended to encourage potential customers to visit the dealer.

Sales conferences have a number of distinct advantages. They are cost effective, they permit accurate targeting of the audience, and they are very flexible. Flexibility surrounds the duration of the event, the number of delegates, the location of the conference and the purpose of the conference. The principal purpose of a sales conference is usually to provide motivation for staff or the sales force, training programmes and dealer or retailer communications. Financial institutions are significant users of sales conferences as are retail organizations and industrial groups.

Organization of the sales force

The sales force may be structured according to territory, product or customer or a combination of these (Figure 11.9). The most common form of industrial sales organization is geographical. Here, each sales person sells all of the firm's products in a defined area. By reducing travel distance and time between customers, this method usually minimizes costs. Likewise, sales people know clearly the customers and prospects that fall within their area of responsibility. However, each sales person must be able to perform all of the selling tasks for all customers in that territory. A product-oriented sales organization is one in which each sales person specializes in relatively narrow components of the total product line and, hence, becomes more adept at communicating

Figure [11.9] Ways of organizing the salesforce

with members of buying centres. By learning the specific requirements of a particular industry, the sales person is more prepared to identify and respond to buying influences.

Sales force with marketing autonomy

There is a trend in many large successful companies to convert some regional or local sales forces into autonomous marketing staff under the strict guidance of the marketing department. Giving the sales force more autonomy is an attractive option for some companies. It means shifting from calling on distributors, retailers and other customers to spending more time meeting advertising agency creative directors and media buyers to create local advertising campaigns. More specifically, it allows for the possibility of better category management and more direct communication with large retail accounts, as discussed elsewhere in this book.

References

Bauer, Connie L. and Miglautsch, John (1992), 'A conceptual definition of direct marketing', *Journal of Direct Marketing*, **6** (2), 7–17.

Hutt, M. D. and Speh, T. W. (1985), *Industrial Marketing Management: A Strategic View of Business Markets* (2nd edn). Chicago: CBS College Publishing (Dryden).

Jolson, Marvin A. and Wotrulea, Thomas R. (1992), 'Selling and sales management in action: prospecting: a new look at an old challenge', *Journal of Personal Selling and Sales Management*, **12** (4, Fall), 59–66.

Reeder, R. R., Brierty, E. G. and Reeder, B. H. (1987), *Industrial Marketing: Analysis, Planning and Control*. Englewood Cliffs, NJ: Prentice Hall.

Roberts, Lou R. and Berger, Paul D. (1989), *Direct Marketing Management*. Englewood Cliffs, NJ: Prentice Hall.

Roberts, Mary Lou (1992), 'Expanding the role of the direct marketing database', *Journal of Marketing*, **6** (2), 51–60.

Schmid, Jack (1992), 'Growth and profit strategies in a maturing industry', *Direct Marketing*, **55** (8), 39–41.

Shapiro, B. P. and Posner, R. S. (1976), 'Making the major sale', *Harvard Business Review*, **54** (2), 68–78.

PART IV
Delivering the Value

Chapter 12

Pricing strategies and tactics

Price is a measure of expressed value, or wanting, usually expressed in monetary terms, which is agreed in some fashion between a buyer and seller in an exchange. Price is the element of the marketing mix that serves to generate revenue, hence, the setting of price is a crucial decision for the organization. Organizations adopt different approaches to pricing. Perhaps the most popular approach is to add a margin to costs and arrive at the price charged. Numerous versions of cost pricing exist; their principal attraction is their simplicity. Organizations also have regard for the competition in setting prices but this approach too has its limitations; it is difficult to know whether the price charged will generate sufficient profits. Customer-oriented pricing attempts to understand the needs of customers while also accounting for the cost conditions in the organization itself.

Pricing has a number of strategic dimensions that relate to the nature of the product and the sensitivity of the market. Organizations sometimes price to penetrate markets, to skim them or to achieve early cash recovery from the market. Different pricing strategies are required in each instance. There are also tactical aspects of pricing that relate to the psychology of pricing, discounts and calibrating price levels in relation to the other elements of the marketing mix.

Nature and significance of price

Prices reflect values, the value sellers believe their product possesses and, if sold at that price, the value to the buyer also. Prices reflect corporate objectives and policies and are important in the marketing mix. Price is often used by firms to offset weaknesses in other elements in the marketing mix, e.g. discounting. Price changes can be made more quickly than changes in the product, channels of distribution, advertising and personal selling. A price change is relatively unambiguous and easily understood so it is easy to communicate it to buyers. In general there are six major influences on the pricing decision:

- organization's marketing objectives
- customer perceptions

Figure [12.1]   Role of pricing in strategic marketing

- channels of distribution

- costs

- competition

- laws/regulations/directives.

Pricing has a strategic aspect which gives it a longer-term focus and it has a tactical focus in the short term. In forming pricing strategy the company must first determine or adopt a set of marketing objectives relevant to pricing. It must also be concerned with environmental and company constraints and with market-specific factors (Figure 12.1). These latter are concerned with customers, suppliers and competitors. Environmental and company constraints involve consideration of society and culture, legal factors, the interaction with other elements of the marketing mix and the impact of price decisions on general business functions in the company. Pricing strategy is concerned with how customers respond, how demand and cost are interrelated and how competitors respond. Tactical factors are concerned with the psychological aspects of pricing and the value and effectiveness of price discounting, Pricing strategy and tactics are determined by agreed marketing objectives regarding market shares and sales and profit growth.

Prices, costs and values

In spite of the importance of managing price decisions many firms do not charge the most appropriate price for their product. The most common mistakes include: pricing on the basis of costs only so that firms fail to take sufficient account of demand intensity and customer psychology, price is not revised (down as well as up) often enough to capitalize on changed market conditions, price is too often set independently of the other elements in the marketing mix. The pricing objectives of most organizations usually fall into one of three categories:

- Maintenance objectives

  - price stabilization

  - match the competition

- Sales objectives

  - increase sales volumes

  - increase market share

- Profit objectives

  - return on sales or investment

  - maximize profits

Customers expect markets to be price competitive so that products and services that deliver the same benefits are similarly priced. Differentiated products and services are, however, likely to be priced at different levels. Price differences among similar products may reflect a lack of competition, a different level of service or different product version or quality level. When comparing prices in different countries it is also important to make allowance for different taxation regimes and currency differentials.

In general, however, different price levels for similar products indicate different levels of competition. By comparing the prices of the same products in different markets it may be possible to make a judgement concerning the relationship between price and competition.

Customers experience great difficulty in comparing products for value. While the prices may be the same for competing products, other aspects may differentiate the products. In the US colour printer market in 2002 three popular brands retailed for $99 each but varied greatly in other dimensions. To some extent, the colour printer business is like the razor business – the razor is cheap, but the expensive part is buying the blades, or in the present case the ink cartridges. *The Wall Street Journal* (7 August 2002, p. D5) tested the three printers listed in Table 12.1. The test discovered that the Epson printer was best for quality photos on photographic paper costing $15 for 20 sheets, the reason being that the Epson was based on six ink colours which gave photos more definition and shades of colour whereas the other two printers had only four colours. When photos were printed on regular paper, however,

Table [12.1]   Comparing prices and other features of colour printers

Printer brand	Price	Dimensions*	Cartridge prices	Print speed
Epson Stylus Photo 820	$99	46.48 × 24.13 × 26.67	$21.95 colour $26.95 b&w	12 ppm
HP DeskJet 3820	$99	44.20 × 25.65 × 19.81	$34.99 colour $29.99 b&w	12 ppm
Canon S330 Bubble Jet	$99	39.12 × 24.89 × 18.54	$18.50 colour $ 7.00 b&w	14 ppm

*Dimensions (W × D × H) in centimetres.
Source: Based on data supplied in *Wall Street Journal*, 7 August 2002, p. D5.

the result was washed out and line-ridden using the Epson machine while the HP machine produced bright and colourful prints. The Canon machine came last on both the glossy and the regular paper because its colours looked garish and unnatural.

On the text document test the results were more mixed. The text colours seemed truer on the Epson machine but the text appeared crisper on the HP; again, the Canon was weakest. The Epson took up most desk space. Both the HP and Canon had smaller footprints, though the Canon paper trays did not fold up like those of the HP. In terms of print speed the Canon was best of the three printers but there was little to separate them including an easy-to-understand demonstration video to help installation. Replacement cartridges were cheapest from Canon but the test did not consider how long the cartridges lasted.

In summary, according to the *Wall Street Journal*, if the customer wanted a $99 printer that focused on extraordinary photo quality, on photo paper, but took up more space on a desk, the choice would be the Epson Stylus 820. If the customer wanted a printer that yielded a mix of good photos and sharp text, with a smaller footprint and more nice features, the choice would be the HP DeskJet 3820.

Approaches to pricing

Organizations use three sets of methods in establishing prices – the 3Cs of pricing – a cost-plus pricing approach; competition-oriented pricing; and customer-oriented pricing:

- Cost-plus pricing

  - break-even analysis

  - target rate of return

  - return on investment

  - payback period

- Competition-oriented pricing
  - going rate prices
  - sealed bid
  - competitive reaction
- Customer-oriented pricing
  - identifying customer value
  - matching buyer and seller benefits
  - perceived values
  - demand differentiation.

Influence of cost on price

The cost of manufacturing a product or producing a service may be variable or fixed. If fixed costs make up a large proportion of total cost, pricing to get maximum plant utilization is the dominant consideration. Until the company covers fixed costs, it loses money. After fixed costs have been met, each incremental sale contributes a proportionally large amount to profits. If variable costs are a relatively large proportion of total costs, pricing to maximize the difference between the variable cost of each unit produced and price, or unit contribution, is the key consideration for profits. Here the manufacturer attempts to maximize unit prices while reducing variable costs.

In the first situation the objective is to produce sufficient revenue to cover its fixed costs and above that to achieve maximum plant utilization to make profits. In the second case the organization prices to cover the relatively high variable costs on each unit and gain sufficient contribution to make a profit, having amortized the fixed costs.

Organizations when experiencing under-utilization of plant and equipment, will sometimes price below full cost. Firms with high fixed costs are known to accept business at prices which cover variable costs but make a contribution to overheads. Their ambition is to struggle through bad times, maintain staff and other key resources. A second situation arises when firms sometimes price below full costs to win a large order. By taking such business the company expects its unit costs to fall. Later the company attempts to raise price again. Attempting to offset short-term losses with longer-term profits may be a foolhardy strategy since there are no guarantees that the losses will be offset.

Of greater significance is the strategy of penetration pricing. Pricing near or below cost to gain a large market share is based on the assumption that unit costs will fall rapidly as volume increases which is thought to occur through gains in manufacturing experience. The 'experience curve' is used to calculate the effect of volume growth on unit costs. The learning curve experience reduces the variable cost component of unit costs. More efficient labour and better and larger purchases of materials and components result in process improvements and cost savings. Fixed costs may also be affected.

Larger plants may be more cost efficient. Larger-scale selling and advertising may also be more cost efficient. In circumstances where the product is sensitive to heavy advertising or requires widespread distribution or extensive field sales and service support, fixed marketing budgets may be relatively high. If, therefore, significant scale economies exist, some firms may be willing to price low enough to gain volume thus preventing competitors going down the learning curve. The objective would be to establish themselves as low-cost manufacturers with dominant market shares.

The cost of a product is not, therefore, a single indisputable number. Price–cost planning is needed in a number of circumstances, especially when the situation changes in the organization or the competitive environment (Figure 12.2). The calculation of relevant cost depends on the judgement and objectives of managers. Relevant product cost depends on the company's marketing objectives. Six steps may be identified in evaluating the cost–price structure in a company:

- Define the existing price structure.

- Identify the prices of competing products for each item in the product line.

- Decide the product items in need of attention.

- Calculate the profitability of the current product mix.

- Identify the products for prices changes.

- Define the new price structure in the organization.

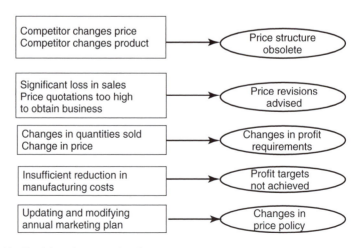

Figure [12.2]   Need for price–cost planning

Customer-oriented pricing

Customer-oriented pricing, as the name suggests, is an approach to pricing that examines the intensity of demand expressed by customers for a given product. The objective is to set price at a level which reflects the intensity of demand; a high price might be charged where there is a high degree of interest in the product and a low price charged when demand is weak even though unit costs may be the same in both instances. Frequently, these approaches are referred to under the heading 'price according to what the market will bear'.

It is difficult, however, to price according to the value to the customer since it is difficult to determine that value. The perceived value of the product may be different for different market segments. Different market segments may place different values on the different attributes that constitute the product or service. In industrial markets technical services may be more important for the small under-resourced company than the large technically competent enterprise.

The level of competition in the market helps to determine the level of perceived value. If a buyer faces a number of options and can purchase a product at a lower price from one supplier than another, the lower price sets the upper band of the perceived value range. In such circumstances the ability of the buyer to substitute one competitive offering for another helps to determine the effective upper band to perceived value. In many circumstances the buyer may be able to avoid purchasing altogether or to postpone the purchase.

The price set by the selling firm is often taken by the customer as a measure of value of the product. The price quoted is taken by buyers as the seller's estimate of the product's worth. The company may wish to avoid pricing a product significantly below what the buyer might pay for its functional equivalents. Buyers often infer that value is reflected in price; for these people higher prices mean higher value.

In many situations prices reflect values and quality in items purchased. Price also reflects the newness of technology and the degree of finish and styling in industrial equipment and consumer durables. Price–quality relationships are an important feature of many markets. In the market for consumer electronics quality and price are important discriminating variables (Figure 12.3). In this case suppliers of electronics were evaluated by store buyers to determine similarities and preferences. Using multidimensional scaling the two most important underlying evaluative criteria were price and quality. These two variables serve to discriminate simultaneously among suppliers and buyers and a number of groups or segments are identified. ABC Durables was perceived to be a high quality supplier with price on the high side. Two department stores, A and B, also positioned themselves in this segment. The two discount stores were clearly seen as low price but medium level of quality. The three general merchandisers were seen at a slightly higher price–quality level.

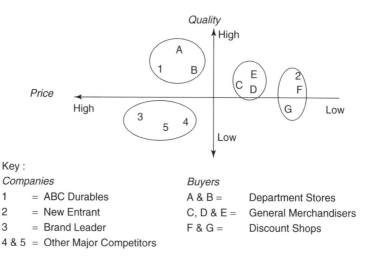

Key :
Companies
1   = ABC Durables
2   = New Entrant
3   = Brand Leader
4 & 5 = Other Major Competitors

Buyers
A & B =   Department Stores
C, D & E = General Merchandisers
F & G =   Discount Shops

Figure [12.3]   Identifying supplier and customer positions in the consumer electronics market

The brand leader and two other major competitors were judged to supply high priced products at a relatively low level of quality. This would give considerable concern to each of these suppliers particularly the brand leader who may have been living on past investment in a brand now in need of renewal.

In some circumstances it may be possible for the firm to base its pricing decision on the product's perceived value. Here the buyer's perception of value and not the seller's level of cost is taken as the key to pricing. The firm develops a product for a particular target market with a particular market positioning in mind with respect to price, quality and service. The firm thus makes an initial decision on the value of the product to the customer and the acceptable price level. The next step for the firm is to estimate the volume it can sell at this price and cost. If the result is positive, the product is selected for development; if negative the idea is dropped.

The R. & A. Bailey and Company Limited followed such a pricing strategy for Baileys Original Irish Cream Liqueur. The firm decided to position the new brand in the exclusive end of the liqueur market and accordingly charged a relatively high price. Imitators, economy products and other substitutes have come and many have gone but the successful high price quality image has stood this now universally known brand in good stead. The key to perceived-value pricing is to make an accurate determination of the market's perception of the value of the total offer, i.e. product and accompanying services.

Multidimensional pricing

Perceived value pricing or charging a price that the market will bear is a version of price customization whereby every customer is charged the price he or she is willing to pay based on the value placed on the product. Usually it is very difficult to identify that value for each customer. As discussed elsewhere the Internet may assist in this price customization in the way it provides an auction environment for a number of products, airline tickets especially. It is necessary, however, to segment the market in a water-tight fashion to prevent trades between customers with high value perceptions and customers whose value perceptions are lower. One of the most effective and practical ways of price customization is to use a multidimensional approach to pricing which involves using a multiple price parameter, multiperson pricing or price bundling (Simon and Butscher 2001).

In the first approach the organization uses a multiple price parameter such as a unit price and a rental element. Mobile telephone companies make effective use of this approach to customize price for various user segments. In multiperson pricing different prices are charged to different customer groups whereby the first person pays the 'full price' while all others in the group receive a discount, e.g. the first person to register for a conference pays the full fee while additional colleagues receive a discount. The third and very popular approach is to price bundle, e.g. two or more products sold together at a price that is less than the sum of their individual prices. Bundling is used extensively in fast food – 'value meals'; cars – option packages; vacations – air travel and accommodation; and information technology – Microsoft Office.

Fixed price lists, haggling and auctions

Most of us buy products and services based on best price and occasionally we benefit from seasonal sales and discounts. Additionally, some of us become involved in price haggling, especially when we change our cars, though many car dealers try to avoid this method of reaching an acceptable price. Furthermore, in recent years the combination of industry deregulation, especially in the airline industry, and access to timely and accurate information on the Internet has given a new impetus to the widespread use of auctions.

The fixed price list is the most commonly used way to 'clear the market' or to establish equilibrium in supply and demand. In this approach providers announce a price at which they are willing to sell and potential customers either accept it or reject it. Customers examine the products or services offered and decide when and from whom to buy. Selling organizations adjust price lists and customers buy over a period until the market clears.

Haggling is common in some markets, cars especially, but it is also found in country markets, stalls and throughout the developing world. In this case a customer and a provider, both with some knowledge of the market, enter a rather unstructured negotiation to discover a mutually acceptable price. The marketing transaction occurs if the negotiation succeeds; otherwise both try again with different parties. The market is cleared as a result of a series of negotiations.

Auctions offer a simple but powerful way of discovering market-clearing prices. Suppose there is a single seller and a group of potential buyers. The organization has an idea of a minimum acceptable price – the reserve price. At the same time each buyer has an idea of a maximum price to pay. The key point is, however, that nobody knows the price threshold of the others. Additionally, as buyers and sellers are self-interested they will reveal private information only if it is to their benefit.

Suppose, for example, Buyer A is the one who is willing to pay the most for a Ryanair ticket and Buyer B the one who is willing to pay the next lower amount and so on. The market clears at any price between that which Buyer B and Buyer A are willing to pay, provided that it is higher than the seller's reserve. At any price between these two Buyer A is the only one willing to buy this airline ticket. There is one buyer and one seller, and supply equals demand and the market clears.

Auctions provide an effective means of discovering Buyer A. This may be done as an ascending price auction where a low price is announced and potential customers are given the opportunity to accept. The price is increased until only Buyer A remains. The resulting price clears the market. A descending price, or Dutch auction, works in reverse. A high price is announced and then decreased, as occurs, for example, in the Aalsmeer and Naaldwijk flower markets in the Netherlands. The first buyer to accept the price becomes the owner of the item being auctioned. Again, a price is discovered at which the seller is matched with the buyer willing to pay most – Buyer A.

The Internet allows the traditional price discovery mechanisms to work in new ways. While auctions are simple and effective, they require simultaneous participation by all buyers and sellers. The Internet must provide product information to buyers, prices must be announced, customer responses collected and new prices disseminated. The Internet allows these functions to be carried out remotely whereas previously such co-ordination required the presence of all participants in the same locations, except for a few highly publicized specialist art auctions where bids by telephone under restricted conditions have occurred.

Strategic pricing

Marketing strategies tend to dictate the pricing strategy to use in particular circumstances. To be useful, pricing strategies must be specific and practical to assist the company in pricing for different marketing circumstances. Strategic pricing is an issue in four situations, when:

- a firm sets a price for the first time;

- circumstances force the company to consider a price change;

- the competition initiates a price change; or

- the firm produces several products that are interrelated on the demand side or on the cost side.

Pricing for market segments

For most companies the market is a series of segments, each warranting a distinct marketing mix package which means separate pricing treatment. Pricing for different market segments means considering the possibility of price skimming, using penetration pricing or combining these two to recover cash early. It is also necessary to determine the appropriate level for the company, given customer and competitive circumstances (Figure 12.4).

Companies sometimes face the opportunity in the introductory stage of the product life cycle of skimming the market by pricing high to maximize short-run unit contribution or penetrating the market by pricing low to maximize unit volume and thereby pre-empt competition. Sometimes the decision is to combine both approaches over time in a sequenced way as the life cycle evolves.

Each of these three pricing strategies is used by firms when introducing new products to a market. The choice of strategy depends on the firm's objectives and the circumstances in the market. Penetration pricing and price skimming are distinct strategies whereas early cash recovery pricing may refer to a high or a low price depending on market circumstances.

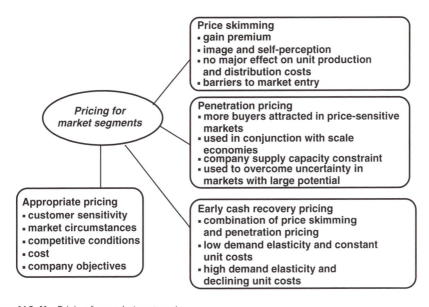

Figure [12.4] Pricing for market segments

Price skimming

There are many marketing circumstances where it is possible for a firm to take advantage of the tendency of some buyers to pay more for a product than other buyers because the product, for one reason or another, has a high present value to them. A price-skimming strategy is designed to gain a premium from these buyers. After a period, for some product categories the premium segment becomes saturated so the firm gradually reduces price to draw in the more price-sensitive segments of the market. A price-skimming strategy makes good marketing sense when one of the following conditions exist:

- The segment of the market prepared to pay the premium price is such that the revenues forgone from charging a low initial price would be significant.

- The company's unit production and distribution cost function is relatively flat over the entire range of output, i.e. there are no benefits from learning or experience so that costs fall with increases in output.

- The premium charged is not so large that it entices competitors into the market.

The implication of the second condition is that the unit costs of producing and distributing a smaller amount should not be so high that they cancel the advantage of charging the premium price. The last point refers to the issue of exclusivity which appeals to the top end of the market.

On the cost side a price-skimming strategy works well where there are significant entry barriers such a patents, high development costs, raw material control or high and sustained promotional costs. For example, Sony introduced its mini-disk and hi-fi sound system at a high price. It initially did not have to worry about competition due to the long lead-time needed in developing a mini-disk system. As a result, it could afford to focus on the high price market segment first. Eventually, it moved down to a low price and started mass producing the mini music system. For a price-skimming strategy to work the quality produced must be relevant to customers in the premium segment. A distinct advantage of this strategy is that it leaves room for a price reduction subject to costs if a market miscalculation had been made. It is always easier to reduce price than to raise it once a product has been established on the market.

A skimming strategy by an innovator may encourage others to enter the market at lower prices. This often occurs in fast-moving consumer products and in fashion where innovative products are relatively easy to imitate. In such circumstances the imitators often capture the mass market leaving the exclusive segments to innovators.

A form of price skimming may be used in commodity pricing if certain conditions prevail. Customers frequently are willing to pay a premium to the supplier that understands and reduces their risks. This willingness may help even the commodity provider to segment the market on the basis of aversion to risk whereas the lack of differentiation in the product itself offers few possibilities for obtaining a premium. A restaurant may pay a premium for consistently prepared chicken breasts because eliminating variations in portion size reduces the risk of customer dissatisfaction. Organizations selling commodities should evaluate each customer's perception of risk and its true exposure. Because customers may not articulate this information, and indeed, may not be fully aware of the consequences, it is nevertheless important for the organization to recognize that 'the greater the loss a customer stands to incur, and the less its ability to withstand that loss, the more a supplier can add value by reducing that customer's risk. And, of course, the more the customer may be willing to pay' (Lurie and Kohli 2002, p. 26).

Penetration pricing

One way of achieving a large share of the market for a new product is to set a relatively low price initially to stimulate demand. There are a number of conditions, any one of which might favour such a price strategy. If the market appears to be highly price sensitive, setting a low price may bring additional buyers into the market. Existing market prices are undercut so much as to make it impossible for competitors to follow. If the firm succeeds it will experience a large increase in sales volume. Penetration pricing can unlock markets that may not have even been anticipated, as has occurred in the low-cost air travel market. Alternatively, the organization may initially develop the commercial and industrial markets but as prices begin to fall rapidly, the much larger personal market may become more important.

When a product is being produced under conditions which give rise to scale economies, i.e. when unit production and distribution costs fall with increased output, a low initial price permits the firm to move to a lower position on its cost curve. Costs fall as the firm learns how better to produce the product. The more experience the firm has in producing the product, the lower its costs.

A danger with a market penetration strategy is that it may encourage demand far in excess of the firm's capacity to supply. To succeed, a strategy of penetration pricing must be based on the recognition that the company will attract a very large number of new customers and that a large new market will develop. The key to this strategy is that the competition must be unable to compete with the company on price. This means that penetration prices must be significantly below existing or going-market prices otherwise the competition will match or better the low price. Should this happen the penetration price strategy would be in danger of turning into a price war based on promotional prices. To follow a price penetration strategy, therefore, the company's technology and cost structure must be such to allow it to separate itself significantly from competitors on price.

Price wars frequently break out at the low end of the market especially when large organizations, traditionally associated with the premium and higher priced market segments, attempt to compete on price with low-cost organizations for market share. In the autumn of 2002 airline travellers between Los Angeles and Las Vegas were offered flights by Southwest Airlines at $19 each way. Apart from a signal that the market was weak Southwest was forcefully reminding customers that while other airlines were trying to position themselves as low-price carriers too, that it, Southwest, was the low-price airline. Its pricing actions on the West Coast coupled with its $79 to $129 round-trip fares on routes in the East, South and Midwest sent a clear message to competitors and customers alike – Southwest was laying claim to the cheap fares position.

Penetration pricing is appropriate for defect-free products for which there is a very large potential market. Penetration pricing in the early stages of the life cycle is unlikely to benefit products which require explanation. In such circumstances, low prices are unlikely to overcome market uncertainty. Furthermore, the company needs to have sufficient production capacity and have ready access to distribution channels to respond quickly to market demand. Successful penetration pricing depends on an element of surprise to constrain competitors' ability to respond.

Early cash recovery pricing

Organizations sometimes do not believe that the market for their product will exist for a long period, or they experience a shortage of cash or survival may be the overriding objective facing them. In such circumstances the future is too uncertain to justify patient market cultivation and the firm tends to set a price which brings in cash at an earlier stage rather than in the longer term.

Early cash recovery pricing is a combination of the previous two pricing strategies played out at different time periods (Figure 12.5). Whereas price skimming refers primarily to markets which are small, exclusive and therefore not highly price sensitive, it is conceivable that for some products the organization might wish to charge a high price now and when capacity is fully operational to lower prices to attract the much larger mass market. It may be possible to use the two pricing strategies in tandem over a period of time. The circumstances under which this strategy works are limited. Market conditions again dictate whether the price should be high to permit price skimming, or low where penetration pricing would be advisable. Two sets of conditions are identified:

■ The presence of a low demand elasticity and constant unit costs of production and distribution means that the organization can maximize immediate cash flow through a high price strategy.

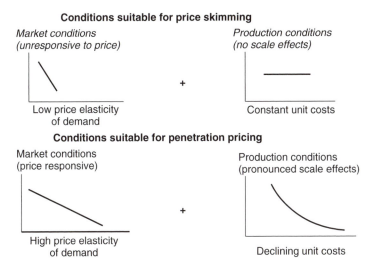

Figure [12.5] Early cash recovery pricing

■ The presence of a high demand elasticity and declining unit costs means that the firm can maximize immediate cash flow through a low price strategy.

The choice of strategy depends on the company's objectives and its view of market conditions. Market conditions should dictate the appropriate price to charge. Low demand elasticity and constant unit costs favour a high price, whereas a high demand elasticity and declining unit costs favour a low price (Figure 12.5). The choice of strategy depends on the firm's objectives and its view of market conditions. The first set of conditions outlined above is typically found when a new product is first introduced to the market and for a short period thereafter while the second set of conditions is found later when the product becomes well known and everybody or almost everybody in the market wants it and its costs of production have declined significantly. By following this price variation over time, the company recognizes the life cycle implications for pricing strategies.

Product line pricing

Most companies sell a variety of products which are interrelated on the demand side, i.e. possible substitutes in the minds of customers and on the cost side, i.e. the cost of producing one product in the line is affected by the production of other items, which has repercussions for pricing strategy. An effective pricing strategy should consider the relationship between the firm's products rather than view them each in isolation. On the demand side product line pricing means the marketing of products at a limited number of prices.

Product line pricing requires the manager to identify the market segment or segments to which the firm is appealing. The firm must then decide how to line its prices. Effective price lining can produce additional profits for the company and benefits to different customer segments. Price lining, the practice of offering two, three or four brands or qualities of the same product at different prices, is a well-accepted strategic device used to establish a value concept in the customer's mind. In a simple demonstration of this principle Max Brunk of Cornell University ran a test in 12 supermarkets over a three-week period in which he and his graduate students offered identical apples side by side with one lot priced two pounds for 19 cents and the other two pounds for 23 cents. As (Brunk 1963) later recalled:

> I shall never forget my experience in putting up the first display. A graduate student and I were stacking two pound bags of apples on the counter working out of the same shipping container on the floor. I was filling the 23 cent display and he was filling the 19 cent side. A shopper came in, looked at both displays and at the common shipping container from which we were working. She then asked 'Well, what's the difference?' Without a pause the graduate student simply replied, 'These are two for 19 cents and those are two for 23 cents.' The shopper picked up two bags of the 23 cents apples and put them in her cart. Over a three-week period in 12 supermarkets over 40 percent of the apples sold were from the 23 cent side of the display.

Price lining not only simplifies the administration of the pricing structure but it also alleviates the confusion of a situation where all products are priced separately. A major problem confronting a price line decision is, however, that once it is made, retailers and manufacturers have difficulty in adjusting it. Changes in the cost side of the equation place the seller in the position of:

- changing the price lines with the resulting confusion in the minds of customers; or

- reducing costs by modifying the product or service.

Demand interrelationships

Two products are interrelated on the demand side when the price of one affects the demand for the other. The expression, cross-elasticity of demand, is often used to express this relationship. A positive cross-elasticity of demand means that two products are substitutes. In most instances the product items in a manufacturer's line of products are substitutes for each other but not perfect substitutes. For example, a prospective automobile buyer can obtain higher quality, better styling or extra features by paying more money; the seller is able to attract a wider range of buyer types and perhaps induce buyers to trade up to the more expensive versions when the manufacturer offers a multiple line of products.

The manufacturer's problem is how to price these versions to obtain the greatest overall revenue. If a vehicle manufacturer lowered the price of the luxury cars in the line, this would decrease the demand for the lower priced cars, increase the demand for items such as expensive seat covering, and stereo sound equipment, and probably would not affect the demand for the manufacturer's range of farm tractors and trucks. Before changing the price of any single item in the line, the manufacturer should consider the various cross-elasticities of demand to determine the overall impact on profitability.

Cost interrelationships

Two products are interrelated on the cost side when a change in the level of production of one affects the cost of the other. By-products and joint products are related in this sense. A reduction in the level of output of one product thus related will result in higher unit costs of the second because the overhead is spread over fewer units. For this reason the marketing manager must consider the cost interactions before changing the price of a single product in the line.

Various products in an organization's line are exposed to different degrees of competition. Sellers may have little latitude in pricing products in their line where existing or potential competition is keen and they will have varying degrees of price discretion in the other cases. The structure of the prices for the products in the line should not, therefore, simply be proportional to costs but should reflect the profit opportunities inherent in the different degrees of competition in the market.

The pricing trap

The decision to lower prices is a difficult one for the company since it can easily fall into a classical pricing trap. The price trap arises when a market becomes price sensitive and competitors begin to discount. If the company decides to maintain price levels a series of events may occur which will leave it worse off than before (Figure 12.6). Since the company holds prices firm and assuming product substitutability in the market, the company sales will begin to fall and market share is lost. In evaluating its position the company may be well advised to recognize the danger of too much confidence in the value of product differentiation to protect it from price competition. Product differentiation which existed may have vanished with time and improvements in competing products.

In such circumstances the company may be forced to reduce prices to protect its market share. In some instances companies faced with these circumstances raise prices in an attempt to recover lost overheads. Normally, however, revenue is lost. As the situation becomes more serious the company begins to reduce excess capacity and plants may be closed. Faced with rising unit costs, declining sales volumes and low profitability the company may finally decide to regain lost ground by following a discounting strategy which, because it is forced upon it, is often indiscriminate.

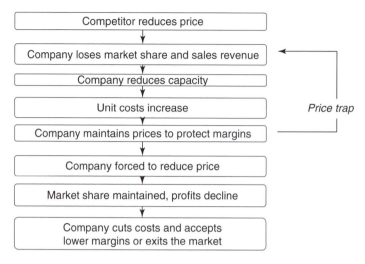

Figure [12.6]   The price trap

When the company decides to discount to maintain or rebuild market share it must be confident that it possesses a cost advantage over competitors and that the products in question have quality parity with those of market leaders. Market share may be maintained but with lower profits. Losses are, of course, possible. The company may also be forced into reducing costs and accepting lower margins. Sometimes organizations faced with such a situation leave the market altogether.

Limits of pricing discretion

There are many business situations in which the organization has little or no discretion in setting the price for its products or services. The organization has little discretion in the pricing of a product for which there are numerous substitutes and well-established markets. Unprocessed food and fibre products fall into this category. Typically, manufacturers of these products are also numerous and relatively small. In contrast, a firm in a market where there are only a few competitors also has little discretion in product pricing since the behaviour of one firm has an immediate effect on the behaviour of other firms in the industry.

Pricing discretion remains very much with organizations that operate in markets with a competitive structure that places them somewhere between these two extremes. Organizations possess pricing discretion if they produce products which for some reason or other are perceived as differentiated from others.

For many consumer products, buyers are not very aware of the prevailing prices. Products in the luxury classes and items not purchased on a frequent basis fall into this category. Consumers are usually very aware of the prices of staples and regularly purchased items. Buyers of industrial goods such as capital equipment, plant and raw materials tend to be very price aware for the general range of items bought. However, in terms of the magnitudes involved it is not certain that industrial buyers are any more aware of prevailing prices than are final consumers.

If price awareness is low, the firm is less inhibited in raising prices. It is dangerous to assume, however, that prices can be changed with impunity in such situations. Where price awareness is low, companies intent on lowering price sometimes attempt to increase the level of price awareness in the market so that they can oust rivals. Information on price awareness may be a useful guide to marketing activity, by indicating those products for which a policy involving a strong emphasis on price is most, or least, appropriate. Price awareness for services as distinct from products tends to be very uneven since it is difficult to quantify something intangible such as a service, the dimensions of which change frequently. Companies frequently display low price awareness for many services such as transportation which has marketing implications worth noting.

In situations and markets where the level of price awareness is high, the firm must take great care to ensure that its prices are not out of line with competitive products. Should the firm wish to charge a different set of prices it would be well advised to ensure that its products are well differentiated in the eyes of its customers.

The value of a product or service to the best prospective customer fixes the ceiling for pricing while cost sets the floor. Between the cost floor and the appropriate value ceiling is a gap. This gap varies depending upon the type of product and customer involved. Setting the price within this gap depends upon the firm's analysis of such factors as the nature and type of competition, the overall marketing programme used and various public policy considerations.

References

Brunk, Max E. (1963), 'Principles of product pricing', paper presented at 58th Annual Meeting of the American Meat Institute, Palmer House, Chicago.

Lurie, Robert and Kohli, Ajay (2002), 'A smarter way to sell commodities', *Harvard Business Review*, **80** (4), 24–6.

Simon, Hermann and Butscher, Stephan A. (2001), 'Individualized pricing: boosting profitability with the higher art of power pricing', *European Management Journal*, **19** (2), 109–14.

Chapter 13

Marketing channels of distribution

A concern for marketing channels of distribution refers to the institutional and logistical arrangements for delivering value to the customer. More precisely, marketing channels deal with the issue of the arrangements the organization makes to physically deliver its products to the customer. Marketing channels perform the function of accumulating products into assortments required by customers and ensuring that this assortment is delivered to the location desired at the time required and in the quantities demanded. Wholesalers and retailers play a key role in this process.

In developing a marketing channel strategy the company decides the most appropriate way to reach its customers. This may be through intense, selective or exclusive distribution depending on objectives and the nature of the product, the service and the market. In managing the marketing channel the company must select, motivate and evaluate distributors. Because marketing channels comprise a set of interdependent organizations, conflict can arise among channel partners. Power is used to manage this conflict so that the marketing channel develops and grows. From time to time channel members at one or more levels dominate this power relationship. In the market for consumer products and food, large retailers, especially supermarkets, currently dominate and lead the marketing channel.

Nature and function of channels of distribution

A channel is a set of intermediary companies, people or agents who manage the movement of products and services from the manufacturer to the final user. All firms which take title to the product, or assist in transferring title as it moves from manufacturer to consumer form part of the distribution channel. A marketing channel is a set of interdependent agencies that by the exchange of products provides time, place and possession utilities to make that product available for final consumption. These three utility factors are required in addition to the form utility provided by the manufacturer. A product is complete when all four dimensions have been included. Channels

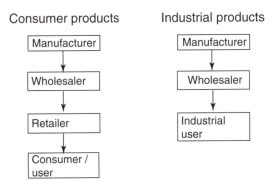

Figure [13.1]   Typical marketing channels

may be short or long depending on circumstances. Typical channels used in the marketing of consumer and industrial products are shown in Figure 13.1. Variations of these forms are found in practice.

The value of marketing intermediaries may be judged by their superior efficiency in making products widely available and accessible to target markets. Marketing intermediaries, at all positions in the marketing channel, on account of their experience, their specialization, their contacts and their scale, offer the manufacturing company more than it can usually achieve on its own. The entire channel helps to deliver customer value.

In this context it is necessary to distinguish clearly between the concept 'channels' and the concept 'physical distribution'. Channels are defined as the vertical marketing system of forces, conditions and institutions associated with the sequential passage of a product through two or more markets or sets of contractual relationships through which the exchange of goods is consummated (Bucklin and Stasch 1970). Marketing channels have also been viewed as 'sets of interdependent organizations involved in the process of making a product or service available for use or consumption' (Coughlan *et al.* 2000, p. 3). Physical distribution on the other hand is viewed as the functional areas of marketing associated with inventory and transportation or the temporal and spatial inputs to the logistic system within the channel (Heskett 1966).

Multiple channels

In designing a channel system it is necessary to recognize that many firms are multichannel business units, i.e. they offer identical products to customers in the same market through a variety of different outlets. Beer sales through public houses and supermarkets and increasingly through private clubs is a good example of the use of multiple channels. Likewise, Michelin tyres are sold directly to Citroën where they serve as a fabricated part of new Citroën cars.

They are also found in car accessory shops and some garages. Each channel enables the manufacturer to serve a different market; they complement each other. There are circumstances, however, where conflict can easily arise. The onset of the Internet in direct distribution has often created unnecessary conflict between manufacturers and their more traditional distributors.

Attempting to bypass traditional distributors by using the Internet is fraught with difficulties as the car industry in the US has experienced. Originally announced as a revolutionary way of purchasing a car whereby the customer could buy the desired model on-line with a click of the mouse, the reality has proved to be much less appealing to customers and dealers. At first, General Motors Corporation and the Ford Motor Co. attempted to completely bypass their distributors and create a new direct relationship with customers on the Internet. Resistance from dealers and lack of enthusiasm from customers have forced these companies to restrict their efforts to encouraging customers to visit showrooms by removing the price haggling process so pervasive in this market but hated by customers. In contrast, Toyota merely refers customers to dealers after they have selected all the features of their cars.

It seems that such experimentation will continue for some time until an appropriate on-line marketing paradigm emerges. Car manufacturers believe the on-line approach provides them with an opportunity of getting to know their customers better – a relationship that is now dependent on their dealers – and ultimately allow customers to buy customized cars which are then delivered in a fraction of the time it now takes. While such unfiltered relationships with customers may appear attractive to manufacturers, there is still the need to measure the performance of the Internet in regard to customer behaviour, including sales.

Complex industrial products favour direct distribution through the company's own sales force. Standard components, on the other hand, can be distributed efficiently through third-party distributors. In some cases industrial products are distributed by specializing by customer which usually means taking account of product applications. Organizing distribution by product application is a way for smaller firms to use their limited resources effectively and for larger firms to protect against such niche strategies by offering applications expertise across a range of product uses (Corey *et al.* 1989, p. 113).

A common alternative way to organize distribution, in industrial markets particularly, is by size of account. Company sales teams may serve large customers directly whereas independent distributors may be used to reach the smaller users.

Functions of marketing channels

Channels of distribution provide three major benefits. The first benefit is a time benefit which means having the product available when the user wants it. Fashion fairs take place months before the relevant season. Ladies fashion shoes for the summer season, for example, are produced during the previous winter. Long lead times such as these are required to produce the necessary quantities and to transport the finished product to retail outlets.

Location is the second benefit. Since few customers are willing to devote the time and energy to seek out the manufacturer, retailers provide a supply of products in locations convenient to the user. Retail shops, vending machines and mail-order catalogues provide the means of conveniently supplying products to the user. It was said of the Coca-Cola brand that it should always be available within arm's reach!

The channels of distribution also function in reverse. In industries from computers to washing machines reverse supply chains or the series of activities required to retrieve a used product from a customer and either dispose of it or reuse it are becoming an essential part of business. Starting in 2003 the European Union implemented legislation that requires tyre manufacturers operating in Europe to recycle one used tyre for every new tyre sold. Whether a company is establishing a reverse supply chain by choice or necessity it will face a number of challenges among which are the need to educate customers and establish new points of contact with them (Guide Jr. and Van Wassenhove 2002, p. 25).

Marketing channels also provide a means of conveyancing title to the product from the manufacturer to the buyer. The purchaser obtains physical possession of the product, and the title to ownership of the product at the retail outlet. The importance of the distribution channel in transferring title to products is much more apparent for industrial products, in situations where a financial institution is involved in facilitating the sale, and where products are exported or imported.

These three benefits, time, location and conveyancing, are inseparable from the product itself; there can be no complete product without incorporating all three into the product or service.

Role of wholesalers and retailers

The major function of a wholesaler is to break bulk and send small orders to the retailer thereby realizing substantial savings on physical distribution costs. Functions performed by wholesalers today have emerged as a result of:

- large-scale mass production in distant factories

- product volumes manufactured on a speculative basis

- need for product adaptation to suit intermediaries and final users

- increases in the quantities and varieties of products.

The sorting process performed by wholesalers is the key to their economic viability. It frequently happens that the quantities in which products are manufactured or the characteristics with which they are endowed by nature do not match either the quantities in which they are demanded or the characteristics desired by those who consume them. Hundreds of pairs of Tommy Hilfiger jeans are produced in a single cutting, but they are ultimately sold one pair at a time in myriad retail stores all over the world.

Wholesaling has been under increasing pressure from manufacturers who have expanded the scale of their factories, broadened their product lines and integrated forward into distribution. A more serious threat from the other end of the channel comes from the chain stores, especially supermarkets. These outlets, in their endeavours to obtain large volumes of supplies at low cost, have in recent years bypassed wholesalers and gone directly to manufacturers. This has caused great friction in the channel of distribution.

Glen Dimplex, manufacturer of smaller electrical appliances including electric heaters, with a turnover of €1.3 billion and employing 8,500 people world-wide announced in May 2002 the acquisition of the two largest Irish distributors of its products. Glen Dimplex bought Dimpco and Brownbrook because, with consolidation in the European retail and wholesale industries, it was deemed essential for the group to have direct trading relationships with its key customers. According to Sean O'Driscoll, the chief executive of Glen Dimplex, 'Dimpco and Brownbrook have been the Glen Dimplex Group's long-term distributors in the South and North of Ireland. Both companies have been tremendously successful and we plan to further expand their product range as part of the Glen Dimplex Group' (*The Irish Times*, 25 May 2002, p. 17).

Retailing includes sales through shops, the mail, door-to-door selling and automatic vending machines. It also includes all outlets that seek to serve ultimate consumers: hotels, hospitals, schools, banks and other financial institutions.

Frequently, the same products are found in different types of retail outlet thus showing how the manufacturer, by co-operating with different types of retailer, can reach different market segments. The different types of retail outlet attempt to maintain an assortment of products and services to cater for specific market segments. Thus it is possible to think of price-conscious shoppers who might frequent discount stores more often than they would department stores.

Within the channel from provider to wholesaler to retailer to customer there are a number of functions by which products and services are made available for consumption referred to by Coughlan *et al.* (2000) as channel flows: three are forward flows only, two are reverse flows only and three are bi-directional (Figure 13.2). Physical possession, ownership and promotion are forward flows from producers to consumers. Negotiation, financing and risking flows move in both directions, ordering and payments are backward

Source: Adapted from Anne T. Coughlan *et al.* (2000) *Marketing Channels*,
6th edition, Englewood Cliffs, NJ: Prentice Hall

Figure [13.2]   Marketing flows in distribution channels

flows. A ninth flow could be added which is a backward flow, that of market intelligence.

In developing the ideal channel it is necessary to achieve a subtle blending of the objectives of all parties in the system – provider, customer and intermediaries. The ultimate criteria for evaluating the pay-off of alternative channel systems for the manufacturer or intermediary is profit flows over time, related to the resource commitments involved in each alternative and the associated risks.

Channels consist of interdependent institutions and agencies which implies that within a channel some agreement concerning the domain of each member is required regarding the population to be served, the segment and territory to be covered and the functions to be performed by each member of the channel.

Formulating a distribution strategy

Intensity of market coverage

Some products require intensive distribution, others may be distributed through selective outlets while others may require exclusive distribution. Manufacturers of convenience products, such as toothpaste, who attempt to provide a saturation coverage of their potential markets are the prime users of intensive distribution. Soft drinks, cigarettes, sweets, newspapers and magazines are made available in convenient locations to enable the buyer to obtain the desired article with a minimum of effort. Consequently, for products that people wish to buy anywhere, the company must consider intensive distribution. Mass coverage and low unit prices make the use of widespread distribution almost mandatory.

Not all products benefit from intensive distribution. A policy of selective distribution means selecting a small number of retailers to handle the firm's product line. Motor manufacturers follow a policy of selective distribution. Very few car dealers handle Ford, Nissan, Fiat, Renault, Citroën, Volvo and Toyota cars at the same time. Usually a number of dealers are appointed for a given area. A large city might be served by five to six dealers. By limiting the number of retailers, the firm may reduce its total marketing costs while establishing better working relationships within the channel. Co-operative advertising can be used for mutual benefit. Marginal retailers are avoided. Where service is important, dealer training and assistance are usually provided by the manufacturer. Price cutting is less likely since fewer dealers are involved.

Manufacturers sometimes grant exclusive rights to a distributor to sell in a geographic region. Imported durable consumer goods, expensive cars and industrial equipment are frequently handled on an exclusive basis. Exclusive dealerships are also found in the distribution of some major electrical appliances and fashion apparel. Some market coverage may be sacrificed through a policy of exclusive distribution, but it is often offset through the development and maintenance of an image of quality and prestige for the products and the reduced marketing costs associated with a small number of accounts. Both manufacturer and retailer co-operate closely in making decisions concerning advertising and promotion, the inventory to be carried by the retailer, and pricing.

In 2002 the Ford Motor Co. embarked on a rationalization of the distribution of its luxury cars in Europe with the objective of obtaining synergies among the brands. In 2001 Jaguar had about 270 dealerships in continental Europe, 69 linked with Volvo or Land Rover and 12 joined with both these brands. By 2004 these figures are expected to increase to a total of 400 Jaguar dealerships with 110 linked to either Land Rover or Volvo and 66 linked to both. There are a number of advantages of combining dealership as Ford has done: reduce back-office costs such as accounting, personnel and information systems; reduce repair shop costs and there is the opportunity of cross-selling brands. Within the new dealerships each luxury brand is treated separately, e.g. separate entrances to the showrooms.

There are a number of advantages and disadvantages of exclusive distribution and by implication intensive distribution. Among the more important are:

Advantages

1 Shorter distance and lapsed time between manufacturer and outlet improves organization's control of outlet – can respond more quickly to sales fluctuations at retail level.

2 Guarantees more retailer effort due to exclusive rights; increases manufacturer control.

3 Larger margins for retailers.

4 Lower distribution costs for manufacturer.

5 Sales people (on commission) concentrate on fast-moving brands within multi-dealers.

Disadvantages

1 Easy to lose potential customers, competing brands; difficulty finding the product quickly in shops.

2 Provokes additional competition; retailers carry competing brands.

3 Smaller market share; choosing among retailers in areas may result in a loss of sales.

4 Reduces advertising effectiveness; advertising must include dealer costs to avoid customer loss through selection of wrong outlets.

Strategic goals for distribution

The organization has five strategic distribution goals (Cateora and Graham 2002, pp. 459–61): cost, management control, coverage, character and continuity; commonly referred to as the five Cs (Figure 13.3).

In regard to cost, companies must consider the capital or investment cost of developing a marketing channel and also the cost of maintaining it. The maintenance costs cover the direct expenditure of a sales force or the margins and commissions of distributors. Marketing channel costs, including the costs of physically distributing the product, discussed in detail below, refer to the entire difference between the factor price of the products and the price the customer in the market ultimately pays for them.

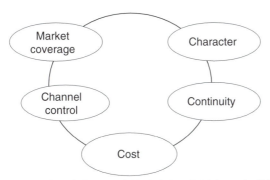

Source: Based on Philip R. Cateora and John L. Graham (2002) *International Marketing*, 11th edition, New York: McGraw-Hill, pp. 400–38.

Figure [13.3]   The five Cs in distribution

Using its own sales force will give the organization maximum control though it imposes additional cost burdens. In longer channels, however, the ability of the manufacturer to control price, sales volume, promotional methods and type of outlet used is diminished. Many firms do not attempt to control the final destiny of their products and are satisfied merely to use the services of a distributor who in turn passes them to others for further distribution. Such an organization can hardly be expected to know where its product is going, what volume of sales can be expected and so on.

The third major goal for the marketing channel is target market coverage. This means gaining the optimum volume of sales obtainable in each segment, securing a reasonable market share and attaining satisfactory market penetration. Coverage also includes the concept of full representation of all the organization's product lines. Sometimes distributors are willing to take the high margin products in the manufacturer's line and neglect or refuse to handle other products which the provider might wish to emphasize. Indeed, broadened product lines may make it possible to have a dedicated sales force in the market that could not be supported by single products or a limited range of products.

The fourth goal is to ensure that the marketing channel must fit the character of both the firm and the markets in which it is doing business. Sometimes fitting or matching the two characters is impossible. In such circumstances some firms leave a market rather than compromise on company standards. In other instances company standards are adhered to and local channel characteristics ignored with resulting distribution disasters. Such conflicts are common especially in longer channels and in intermediate markets.

Finally, if a channel is to perform consistently, it must have continuity. This reason by itself encourages many companies to set up their own sales force and distribution organization. Channels of distribution often pose longevity problems. Many distributors have little loyalty to their suppliers. They handle brands in good times when the line is making money but quickly reject such products within a season or year if they fail to perform during that period. Less well-known brands are particularly vulnerable to this type of threat among larger retailers. Supplier allegiance is easily tempted by larger margins, better promotional allowances and other types of inducements. These are the issues which give rise to the greatest difficulty between manufacturers and retailers.

In building and managing the overall marketing channel strategy the five Cs must by matched, balanced and harmonized with one another to build a service-oriented and cost-effective distribution organization. The company's entire distribution strategy should be one of balancing the desirable goals of minimizing distribution cost and maximizing the advantages of the other four Cs.

Selecting and motivating intermediaries

Channel partners are frequently criticized by manufacturers because they do not stress a given brand or because their salesman's knowledge of the product is not adequate or because they neglect certain customers. Shortcomings from the manufacturer's point of view may be understandable from the intermediary's viewpoint, since distributors:

- are independent companies
- serve their own customers
- control market information
- focus on product assortments.

Consequently, there is no point in manufacturers developing a mismatch of hastily improvised trade deals, uninspired dealer contests and unjustifiable discount structures. A more sophisticated approach is to forge a long-term partnership with distributors. This means that manufacturers should have a clear idea of what they expect from their distributors and what the distributors can expect from manufacturers in terms of:

- market coverage
- product availability
- market development
- technical advice
- service and marketing information.

By cultivating a sense of partnership in the distribution channel it may be possible to convince intermediaries, retailers in particular, that they make profits through being part of a marketing system linking manufacturer, distributor and buyer and that it is not always necessary to seek profits primarily on the buying side through an adversarial relation with the supplier.

In the short term, there are a number of things the organization can do to improve the motivation of its distributors:

- More frequent and timely deliveries.
- Stricter sales quotas for each product line for various channels.
- Creating better profit opportunities for distributors – easier terms, more advertising and promotion support, etc.
- More powerful incentive systems for sales people.
- Problem-solving sessions where manufacturers and distributors forge joint plans to eliminate weaknesses in the system.
- Sanction poor performers.

Evaluating distributors

It may be possible to manage the marketing channel by occasionally evaluating distributor performance against standards. Much argument can be avoided if standards of performance and sanctions for not complying with these standards are agreed between the manufacturer and channel partner at the outset. The areas requiring explicit agreement are:

- sales intensity and coverage
- average inventory levels
- customer delivery time
- treatment of damaged or lost products
- co-operation on promotional and training programmes
- distributor services to be provided to the customer.

Manufacturers frequently use sales quotas to define performance expectations. Car and appliance manufacturers are common users of quotas. In some cases these quotas are treated only as guidelines; in others they represent performance standards. One of the better ways of evaluating distributors is to set quotas and to compare each distributor's sales performance for a period against performance in the preceding period. The average percentage of improvement or decline for a group of distributors can be used as a norm. In this way underachievement can be identified and the underlying reasons sought with a view to a possible solution.

Cost and efficiency in distribution

Substantial costs arise in the physical delivery of value to customers. Physical distribution deals with all the move–store activities in the channel of distribution as products move from the point of manufacture to the point of consumption or use. Often referred to as market logistics or physical distribution, the actual delivery of products emphasizes service to customers. The delivery system, physical distribution, market logistics, the terms are interchangeable, comprises a transportation system and a storage system. The total cost concept applied to delivery activities attempts to minimize the total distribution system cost subject to delivering a desired level of customer service while making a profit for the company. There are cost and revenue factors to be considered.

Physical distribution has been defined by Pope (1974, p. 154) as 'a part of the science of business logistics, whereby the right amount of product is made available at the place where demand for it exists at the time it exists'. There are five tasks associated with physical distribution:

- Determining the places where stocks have to be held and designing a storage system.

- Introducing a materials handling system.

- Maintaining a stock control system.

- Devising procedures for processing orders.

- Selecting a transportation system.

Total distribution cost analysis

The objective from the perspective of the distribution channel as a whole is to minimize the cost of handling for the total channel. This often means minimizing the number of levels in the process and increasing productivity. A second principle is to reduce the volume of the product held anywhere in the channel compatible with supplying expected demand at each stage in the distribution process. A third principle, often referred to as the principle of postponement, refers to the guideline of delaying as much as possible the breaking of bulk loads into heterogeneous assortments. These principles raise the need to consider trade-offs among the attributes and characteristics of the logistics system to achieve the objectives specified.

Total cost analysis is a decision methodology which allows the company to design an appropriate physical distribution system. Storage facilities may be used in physical distribution as long as their costs, including local delivery, are equal to or less than the total cost of direct shipments to customers. The total transportation cost declines as storage facilities are added to the logistics network. The reduction in transportation costs arises from consolidated volume shipments to storage facilities combined with short-haul small local shipments from warehouse locations to customers. The optimum number of storage facilities to produce the lowest total transportation cost may be identified this way.

Low-cost high-quality customer service

From the customer's view, customer service means several things.

- The speed of filling and delivering normal orders.

- The supplier's willingness to meet emergency needs of the customer.

- The care with which goods are delivered.

- The supplier's readiness to take back defective goods and resupply quickly.

- The availability of installation and repair services and parts from the supplier.

- The supplier's willingness to carry inventory.

In some organizations, too much emphasis in total distribution planning has been placed on approaches and techniques that produce the lowest possible physical distribution system cost. Cost minimization does not necessarily mean profit maximization. Conversely, a policy of service maximization is unlikely to lead to an optimal profit situation either. There is a trade-off between the level of service offered and the other system costs that results in an optimal profit situation. The distribution manager should seek to maximize the logistics contribution. Distribution is an element in the marketing mix, an activity that can contribute to the organization's profits if managed properly.

The linkages in the delivery system demonstrate the trade-offs which may arise when considering elements of cost and service (Figure 13.4). In Quadrant 1 a total systems cost curve is shown which has been derived from a total cost analysis in which costs are expressed as a function of the level of service offered. Quadrant 2 postulates the familiar S-shaped response curve with areas of diminishing returns at low and high levels of service. Quadrant 3 incorporates several sets of cost data and suggests that sales revenue, net of direct manufacturing costs, is an increasing function of sales, i.e. economies of scale are reflected in the cost of manufacture. Quadrant 4 merely serves to project total costs onto the net revenue axis and this provides an estimate of the market logistics contribution to the fixed costs of the operation and profits.

It is apparent from the solid lines in Figure 13.4 that contribution is not being maximized where system costs are at minimum since the market is highly sensitive to the distribution service offered, represented by the shape of the response function in Quadrant 2. The lowest system cost does not

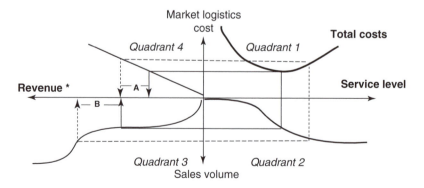

* revenue net of manufacturing cost
A = revenue contribution based on minimizing market logistics costs
B = revenue contribution based on improving customer service

Source: Christopher, M. (1971) *Total Distribution*. Aldershot: Gower, p. 101.

Figure [13.4] Market logistics revenue and cost linkages permit a sufficiently high level of service to be offered to take advantage of the increasing returns to service.

The objective of physical distribution management is to develop logistics systems which minimize total costs while providing a level of service consonant with customer satisfaction. For this to happen it is necessary to have a correct identification of the form of the cost–service–revenue relationships in the system.

Power conflict and co-operation

The ability of channel leaders to exercise power and control in the distribution channel stems from their access to economic, social and psychological resources. Power also accrues to the leader as a result of experience, the history of the organization, thus the management of the organization or power may reflect characteristics of the environment facing organizations.

The power of channel leaders may, therefore, reflect both the organization itself and the characteristics of the market environment. In this context channel objectives change throughout the product life cycle. During the introductory stage little or no control is necessary because the market is beginning to open. In contrast at the maturity stage deeper penetration is desired so the need to ensure delivery, develop and maintain loyalty is greater and there is a greater need for more control. Channel partners often seek a channel leader to impose this discipline and harness the efforts of the entire channel.

The Levi Strauss Company, attempting to assert leadership position, objected to Tesco, the UK retailer, regarding its imports of Levi jeans from outside the European Union with the objective of selling them at heavily discounted prices. Part of Levi's case prepared for the European Court of Justice was that its jeans should not be sold in supermarkets because sales staff need special training to explain the different styles to customers. According to Mark Elliot of Levi Strauss, 'Customers need advice on what's on offer and the difference between loose and baggy, straight and slim' (*The Irish Times*, 16 January 2001, p. 18). Tesco and Levi dispute the position of leader in the channel, each making a claim for their own reasons. Levi believe that style and advice on style provided in specialist clothing stores differentiate their brand which would be debased if sold in a supermarket as a virtual commodity.

Managing channel conflict

Channel conflict arises when one channel member perceives another to be impeding the achievement of its goals. The frustration arises from a restriction of role performance. For example, large retailers, especially large supermarkets, frequently have objectives which are incompatible with those of small manufacturers.

Domain conflict may also exist when manufacturers compete with some of their own wholesalers. Price competition for an identical product sold through different channels may give rise to this form of channel conflict. An example would be an article of clothing sold through a department store, sold in a traditional drapery store in the suburbs, or sold in a boutique. Such price competition can be damaging to any carefully cultivated image the manufacturer may have created.

Frequently an adversarial relationship develops between the organization and its distributors. Instead of viewing the distribution task as a necessary element in delivering value to customers, suppliers and distributors – a partnership in the marketing system – they both see the opportunity of taking a larger share in the overall marketing system margin. These divergent interests may be summarized as shown in Table 13.1.

There is, therefore, often considerable friction in the distribution channel, much of which occurs because intermediaries, for whatever reason:

- are exclusively tied to competitors

- do not wish to expand their range of products

- do not accept the terms of sale they are offered

- are not suitable but there is no alternative available

- have large turnover and hence exert power regarding price and discounts

- wish to promote their own brands and not those of the manufacturer.

Sometimes power can be used to manage conflict and turn it to good effect; low levels of conflict are associated with high performance in the

Table [13.1] Divergent interests

Supplier's perspective	Distributor's perspective
We need you to concentrate on our products.	We need exclusive territories.
You must carry a full line of all the products we make – no cherry picking!	We can try but we cannot sell weak products – we should concentrate on our strengths.
We need your entire involvement in selling new products and developing new markets.	That is very costly – how will you compensate us for the effort?
We need to know about our final customers in greater detail.	We do not keep such records.
You must improve your effort.	You need to improve your sales promotion.
Your channel margins are too high.	Your prices are too high.

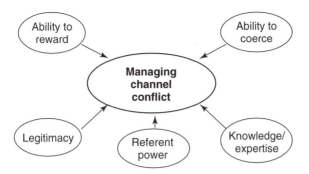

Figure [13.5] Use of power to manage channel conflict

channel. In such circumstances the successful exchange of assets in a marketing channel requires the specification of a role relationship for each channel member. The ensuing interdependency gives rise to conflict and the subsequent use of power to resolve the conflict. In such circumstances it is necessary to recognize that there is an interrelation among the specification of roles for channel members, conflict in the channel, the use of power to specify these roles and ensure conformity which thereby resolves conflict.

Role prescriptions are determined by the norms channel members set for each other or are dictated by the channel leader. Role consensus enables channel members to anticipate the behaviour of others and to operate collectively in a unified manner.

Using channel power to manage conflict

A constructive use of power can also ensure that conflict is a positive force in the distribution channel. Power is the ability of one channel member to get another to do what the latter would not otherwise have done. There are five sources of power in the channel (Figure 13.5). Rewards are beliefs by one organization that a second organization has the ability to mediate rewards for it, e.g. provide wider margins, promotional allowances. Coercion refers to the belief that some form of sanction will ensue if the firm fails to conform, e.g. margin reduction, slowing down of shipments, reduced territory rights and other such restrictions. Expertise refers to the organization's perception that another possesses special knowledge, e.g. manufacturers providing managerial training for marketing intermediaries. Referent power refers to the identification of one organization with another and reflects the attraction of being associated with the other. The power arising from legitimacy stems from values internalized by one organization giving it the feeling that the other has a right to exert influence and that the first has an obligation to accept it.

The ability of one organization to exert power indicates that a dependent relationship exists in the channel. Other organizations in some way depend on the more powerful company. Dependence of buyers on sellers and the power of the former over the latter may be viewed from the perspective of the buyer and seller. From the buyer's perspective dependence represents the seller's ability to contribute needed resources to the success of the buyer's operations, e.g. merchandising equipment and training programmes, and is the basis of the seller's power. From the seller's perspective the basis for buyer dependence represents the seller's ability to create distinct buyer advantages unattainable from alternative suppliers.

Block exemption allows the car industry to restrict distribution of its products whereby dealers are tied to manufacturers who operate closed sales and repair networks. This anti-competitive practice has been allowed by the EU on the basis that the car is a dangerous product that needs to be controlled. Under new rules introduced in September 2002 dealers are allowed to sell cars anywhere within the EU and manufacturers can no longer prevent authorized mechanics who meet the company's criteria from offering after-sales services. Dealers and repair companies have greater freedom to set their own prices.

Under the new rules car manufacturers must choose whether they want a selective or exclusive dealer network. Under a selective network, car manufacturers set up a fixed number limit on the dealers in a particular area, generally accepted to be the national boundaries. The exclusive option limits dealers to one car brand (marque). Such dealers may sell to resellers. To date virtually all car manufacturers have chosen the selective option in order to prevent the large supermarkets and hyperstores from entering the market.

Furthermore, under the selective option a car manufacturer can decide how many dealers it will have in Holland, for instance, and until 2005 they can indicate the locations for those dealers, keeping them spread across the country and not all located in Amsterdam or Rotterdam, for example. After 2005 dealers will be able to open further dealerships anywhere else in the EU provided they can meet certain standards. The block exemption has merely been adjusted as car manufacturers can still choose their dealers under the selective option. This is the EU Commission's second attempt to control the dealership position but due to loopholes it has failed again.

In markets for industrial products the supplier of an original brand may increase the distributor's switching costs by calling directly on user-customers to encourage their shifting to another distributor as a source of supply (Corey *et al.* 1989, p. 143). Seller activities contributing to buyer efficiency also help to motivate buyers to remain loyal and committed to the relationship. The reverse may also be true; that the seller depends on the buyer for an outlet for the product and an efficient way of reaching the final user. In some situations dependence is mutual. In retail food markets, manufacturers are very dependent on a handful of large buyers in any national country market.

Controlling the marketing channel

Smaller firms have particular problems in regard to channel control and often discover that they must trade off control with the cost of that control. Channel control is affected by whom the company sees as the customer, the intermediary or the final customer and user, and whether the company takes a passive or an active interest in the market.

If there is too much control, one party may perceive a loss of autonomy which introduces conflict. The use of economic performance measures can introduce a feeling of conflict between suppliers and retailers whereas non-economic incentives such as providing expert advice or reliable market-related information can increase dependence and create the opportunity for control while reducing the feeling of conflict (Brown *et al.* 1983, p. 77).

Category management and distribution

Close relationships between manufacturers and retailers arising in the channel partnership agreements, whereby two organizations at different levels in the distribution channel co-manage the overlapping parts of their supply chain as in a vertically integrated company, have given rise to the concept 'category management'. Category management calls on retailers to plan marketing strategy for an entire group of products rather than brand by brand. Eventually retailers farmed out category management to their suppliers. Mass-market advertising began to give way to in-store merchandising. The first proponents of category management were Procter & Gamble and Wal-Mart. Category management has implications for other aspects of the organization's activities besides branding. In 1993 Kraft Foods in the US began offering category management. By 1995 it had reorganized its sales force by centralizing it, then it divided it into groups focused on customers, not brands. By 2002 Kraft, similar to Procter & Gamble and Unilever has one customer manager for each major chain in a city or region.

The dominant brand in a category is often appointed category captain by retailers in the belief that the manufacturer has the greatest resources and the will to exert them to drive sales across the category. The major objective for the category captain in that role is to make money for the retailers. That is having the means to learn everything about the category – sales volume, shelf-space allocations, placement, pricing, retailer costs. Retailer costs include the price paid for competitor products, information which may be obtained from third parties for the category captain's sales people. With such information the category captain is able to analyse the category data and create a management plan. The plan tells the retailer which products to move to eye level, for example, where to position house brands and how much to charge for each brand. These relationships, driven by the move toward category management, have allowed these strong manufacturers to re-assert themselves as they began to lose the battle of the brands.

References

Brown, James R., Lusch, F. Robert and Muehling, D. Darrel (1983), 'Conflict and power dependence relations in retailer–supplier channels', *Journal of Retailing*, **59** (4), 53–81.

Bucklin, L. P. and Stasch, Stanley F. (1970), 'Problems in the study of vertical marketing systems', in *Vertical Marketing Systems*, Louis P. Bucklin, ed., Glenview, IL: Scott Foresman.

Cateora, Philip R. and Graham, John L. (2002), *International Marketing* (11th edn). New York: McGraw-Hill, pp. 400–38.

Christopher, M. (1971), *Total Distribution*. Aldershot: Gower.

Corey, E. Raymond, Cespedes, Frank V. and Rangan, V. Kasturi (1989), *Going to Market*. Boston: Harvard Business School Press.

Coughlan, Anne T., Anderson, Erin, Stern, Louis W. and El-Ansary, Adel I. (2000), *Marketing Channels* (6th edn). New Jersey: Prentice Hall.

Guide Jr., V. Daniel R. and Van Wassenhove, Luk (2002), 'The reverse supply chain', *Harvard Business Review*, **80** (2), 25–6.

Heskett, J. L. (1966), 'A missing link in physical distribution design', *Journal of Marketing*, October, 37–41.

Chapter 14

Aligning performance with marketing strategy

Aligning marketing performance with marketing strategy involves deciding on appropriate ways of organizing the company's endeavours and deciding the appropriate performance criteria. It involves the entire organization in a multifunctional boundary-spanning effort with a focus on the conditions that improve performance not just the profile of the leadership of the organization. Aligning performance with strategy means changing the behaviour of people in the organization so that there is a close fit between their actions and performance outcomes. Crucial to an organization alignment is the design of the core value provision, communication and delivery processes used by the organization and aligning them with supporting processes such as human resources and modern communications technologies.

Consultation with customers often indicates that change somewhere in the organization is required. Successful organizations constantly change their behaviour and activities. Eventually such changes filter into a new corporate culture or mind-set. Change occurs by altering behaviour and anything that alters behaviour positively drives performance. The need for change in an organization derives from an understanding of customers. Everybody in the organization should have direct contact with customers including operations, manufacturing, services, not just marketing and sales.

Organizing for marketing

The organizational framework of a company provides a structure for the alignment of implementation with marketing strategy. An organizational structure creates authority and responsibility within the firm to guide and promote desired relationships among people. In earlier chapters it was seen that new technologies and the changing marketing environment facilitate new forms of organizational structure among the providers of customer value.

When it is cheaper to internalize transactions, organizations grow larger but when it is cheaper to do it externally, with independent organizations in the open market, organizations stay small or shrink. The co-ordination technologies of the industrial era made internal transactions not only possible but also advantageous. Firms were able to manage large companies centrally which provided them with economies of scale in manufacturing, marketing, distribution and other activities.

Nowadays, however, because information can be shared instantly and inexpensively among many people in many locations, the value of centralized decision making and expensive bureaucracies decreases (Malone and Laubacher 1998). Individuals and small companies can manage themselves, co-ordinating their efforts through electronic links with other independent parties who are partners in the process of providing customer value.

Electronic networks enable smaller businesses to access the global reservoirs of information, expertise and financing that used to be available only to large companies. Smaller firms enjoy many of the benefits of the large ones without sacrificing the leanness, flexibility and creativity of the small.

Aligning organization with marketing strategy

There are a number of factors to consider when aligning marketing operations with marketing strategy. The primary driver in designing the organization should be the customer. There are myriad organizational forms that result in a mismatch of success as perceived by the customer and writers on the subject (Ambler and Kokkinaki 1997). The question becomes one of identifying the organization structure that best serves the customer. At the same time successful organizations maintain a form of matrix structure as there are distinct benefits for the customer. The organization must, however, avoid anything that distracts from a customer focus. Misapplied technology, for example, can be a distraction. During the dot.com craze the banks particularly, and other organizations, emphasized more the technology than the customer's true needs. Many firms established separate Internet marketing units. Such a narcissistic approach to products is clearly another form of marketing myopia. While technology may be needed, it should be used in an integrated way around customers. It may be expensive but organizations today can install systems that can unify a diverse organization. A tool as basic as e-mail can be a step in the right direction.

Companies organize themselves for marketing in different ways. The focus of the organization, in general terms, may be products, customers or market, either global or regional, based on country-language groupings (Figure 14.1). Sometimes, however, organizing along functional lines is best suited to the company's needs, particularly if the company is small or produces few products. Such companies are often organized around functions such as customer care, promotions or marketing research. Organizing by product and brand focuses attention on the marketing strategy implementation needs of the company's products. Organizing by product or brand is probably the most fundamental form whether it is for a personal care product or an industrial

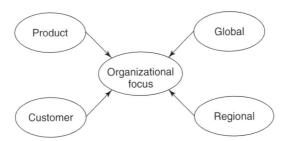

Figure [14.1] Focus of the organization

compressor. Brand marketing is most popular, note how Intel bases its marketing operations around the brand. Increasingly, however, many successful companies organize with a focus on customers. Many large companies selling to the retail trade organize around customers. For example, Procter & Gamble in the US have a marketing unit just for Wal-Mart while in the UK Unilever operate a similar unit to serve Tesco. Some organizations set up units to serve particular markets. Canon has established a separate unit to deal with the small business market. Many organizations establish separate specialist marketing departments to deal with international markets. Some organizations have corporate marketing groups and subsidiary marketing groups.

Customer-focused organization

An organizational focus on customers requires the company to develop a unique structure. A customer-oriented structure reflects differentiation in the market. A customer structure may be appropriate when there are different customer groups, each with different needs and each buying sufficiently large quantities of the company's products to warrant a separate organizational response. Companies organized along customer lines can develop separate marketing mixes for each customer segment. This structure may take several forms such as consumer and industrial markets, domestic and export markets or by industry as would occur if the company were selling to various industries. Increasingly companies attempt to focus their organizations on customers which means designing a flatter organization with fewer levels of command in which the customer holds a central position. Increasingly, the trend toward category management has meant that manufacturers must focus closely on the needs of their customers, especially if those customers are large retailers, e.g. supermarket chains.

The organizational focus on the customer attempts to satisfy two objectives simultaneously. The first is the need for integration of segments and the second is the need to create higher value in relationships with customers. The central feature of such an organizational form is the separation of the front-end or demand side from the back-end or supply side of the organization. The structure of the customer-oriented front-end varies according to circumstances but typically it is separated first into relevant customer segments with specific needs within that segment and then individual customers are treated separately.

As an example when Carly Fiorina became chief executive of Hewlett-Packard in 2000 she established a customer-focused structure resulting in two back-end units devoted to developing computers and printers and two front-end units focused on corporate sales and consumer sales. This approach has, however, received a mixed welcome. The focus may require further development to make it more relevant to Hewlett-Packard customers.

In recent years ABB, once famous for its country business matrix, has shifted from four industrial divisions to four customer segments – utilities, process industries, manufacturing and petrochemicals – and two product segments – power technology products and automation technology products. According to Jorgan Centreman, ABB's chief executive, the company aims 'to provide increased transparency to customers by providing a single full service point of entry into ABB through which we offer our full range of solutions, products and services' (*The Financial Times*, 7 August 2002, p. 9).

There are problems, however, in separating front-end businesses from back-end businesses. Back-end businesses in the regimes just described are no longer connected to customers and are often asked to accept lower margins on their products which are often sold as part of a bundled offering. Front-end businesses often complain that they do not obtain the level of customization and attention they require from the back-end units and that they spend too much time attempting to resolve the transfer pricing issue between the front-end and back-end businesses.

These issues may be resolved by using market-based transfer pricing that allows front-end units to source from third parties if necessary. IBM has adopted such an approach by selling whatever combination of products the customer requests whether that means sourcing the products from within IBM or selling competitors' machines. In such an organizational structure a strong centre is required to mediate disputes.

This may mean working with new partners in very different industries as well as sourcing competitors' products. This poses a problem for the back-end unit of the company, particularly if it depends for its success on a stream of innovative technologies. Unless the front-end and back-end work effectively together, the company faces various difficulties.

Assessing marketing performance

As discussed in Chapter 1 the objective of the organization is to maximize shareholder value. In practice such a goal rarely dominates the strategic thinking of managers. Managers display additional objectives usually involving a combination of sales, measured as turnover, and profits, measured as return on investment. Sales are important because they are a source of profit growth in the company and reflect management rewards such as bonuses and promotion. Profits are important because they are used to satisfy shareholders and are required in raising new capital.

These two objectives are in potential conflict since sales can be increased by lowering prices which would have the adverse effect of lowering profits. Increasing marketing expenditures like advertising should result in increased sales but this would raise costs and thus reduce profits. A particular problem facing the company is that the conflict between sales and profits 'becomes much more acute when the time dimension is added. Specifically, while positive marketing actions (lowering prices, boosting advertising) have these positive effects on market performance and negative effects on profitability, the positive effects come slowly and the bad effects come quickly' (Doyle and Hooley 1992, p. 60). The management objective becomes one of balancing short-term profits with long-term market performance.

Integrated marketing performance

Measuring marketing performance means deciding appropriate measurement criteria. Criteria used include marketing and financial measures. Marketing measures deal with causes and include factors such as customer satisfaction, loyalty, new product introductions, market share and sales growth. Financial measures deal with effects and include profit, cash flow and return on investment. Both sets of measures are necessary and their use should be integrated (Clark 1999). An integrated control of marketing activities requires the organization to first establish performance standards to allow an evaluation of marketing performance derived from an analysis of sales performance (Figure 14.2). The sales performance analysis depends on the outcome of a cost analysis and a marketing performance analysis. The outcome may encourage the organization to take corrective action by calibrating or changing some of its marketing activities.

Major firms now almost universally accept that the primary task of management is to maximize shareholder returns (Black *et al*. 1998). Shareholders possess property rights, that combined with capital market requirements, increase the pressure to remove managers who do not deliver competitive returns (Doyle 2000, p. 234).

Over the years organizations have discovered that there are three generic ways of increasing profits (Figure 14.3). The organization may attempt to increase unit sales volume which means increasing primary demand by developing new products and serving new segments, for example. It can also manage brand switching by maintaining loyalty among existing customers or recruiting new customers from competitors. Sales increases may also be

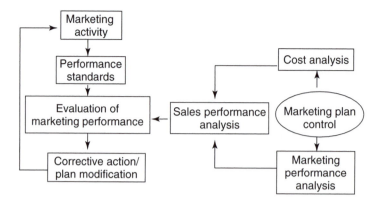

Figure [14.2] Marketing plan evaluation and control

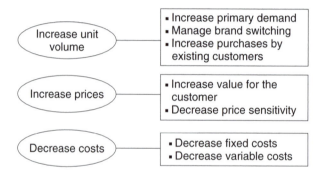

Figure [14.3] Frequently used strategies to increase profits

obtained by encouraging existing customers to buy more, for example, by increasing usage rates, promoting trade-ups and encouraging complementary purchases within the product line. Second, it may be possible to increase prices which may be done by increasing value for the customer, for example, by providing higher benefits or lowering transaction and usage costs. Finally, the organization may attempt to decrease costs. Decreasing fixed costs by 'milking' the brand, reducing marketing and research and development expenditure may be feasible. Variable costs may be reduced by improving deals with suppliers and resellers.

While increasing unit sales is a common criterion for measuring marketing performance, the consequent growth may as easily decrease, as increase, profits. Sales growth increases profits only if the operating margin on the additional sales covers the higher costs of any investment incurred to achieve the growth.

Other criteria for justifying expenditure on marketing strategies include brand awareness, customer attitudes, repeat purchasing and customer satisfaction ratings. None of these criteria, however, have much relationship to profit even if their relationship to sales is weak. Noting this lack of correlation led Doyle (2000, p. 234) to conclude that 'Marketing's lack of credibility in the boardroom is much to do with its failure to quantify the contribution of marketing strategy to corporate performance.'

Choosing performance criteria

The company must develop a set of performance criteria to measure its marketing activities and its financial position as a result of its endeavours. Profit measures, cash flow, return on investment measures are all financial criteria which show the effects of marketing activities. Financial evaluations do not identify the key success factors in the business nor do they focus on what the company is doing well or badly. Marketing performance criteria, on the other hand, deal with causes not effects. It is much more useful from a management point of view to discover the contribution of product innovation, customer satisfaction, product and service quality or on-time delivery to the reasons for success.

There is still a strong tradition in the use of financial criteria which leads companies to ignore the less tangible non-financial measures but these are the real drivers of corporate success over the medium to long term. In choosing performance criteria the company recognizes that the choice must be:

- customer/user driven

- supporting value provision strategy in the company

- capable of change

- simple and easy to understand

- including financial and marketing criteria

- providing positive reinforcement in the company.

Measuring marketing performance

In evaluating and controlling marketing activities the organization should establish a set of performance standards by which these marketing activities can be evaluated. Performance standards should be appropriate in determining whether objectives have been achieved.

During the next stage the company audits its marketing activity in order to evaluate marketing performance. This is a detailed assessment of marketing implementation and an evaluation of performance against budget. One very popular measure of marketing performance is the extent to which actual sales are more or less than budgeted sales for a given period. Marketing control takes the form of a cost analysis and marketing performance analysis in relation to sales in the company. The cost analysis addresses the issue of improving efficiency without jeopardizing present or future sales volume or profit targets. Marketing performance focuses on the cause and effect relationships between marketing inputs and outputs to decide how much money should be spent in the various marketing activities. In this regard marketing expenditure adds value when it creates assets that generate future cash flows with a positive net present value (Srivastava *et al.* 1999).

If targets are not met the company may need to take corrective action of some form. It may be sufficient to modify the plan or manage expectations so that the appropriate performance signal can be used to influence marketing activities. In this fashion the marketing plan is evaluated and controlled. Measures of marketing performance that can be used include:

- new product introductions each year

- product modification introduced each year

- customer orders processed on day received (order response time)

- on-time delivery

- order cancellations or changes

- customer satisfaction score

- number of customer complaints

- number of product defects

- health and safety standards met

- customer loyalty index.

Financial performance criteria

While non-financial criteria such as market share or sales growth may be used in determining the value of a market investment, many firms employ a version of return on investment as the means of measuring the long-run profit performance of their operations. It is generally essential that both approaches are used in an integrated way. While full integration of the two approaches still eludes management thinking, we discuss a practical approach to integration in a later section of this chapter.

Where return on investment is used, a number of comparisons are possible: comparisons with similar companies in the market, or with the company's operations in different markets, or with targets established before entering the market. Unless historical measures such as the above indicate the relative returns to be expected from future investments, there is no point in using any of the above measures. The most important comparison that can be made is between actual results and ex-ante budgeted figures since a post-investment audit can help a firm to learn from its mistakes as well as its successes.

The choice of appropriate measures to use in evaluating and controlling operations depends on the nature of the business. For marketing-oriented companies, market share, sales growth or the costs associated with generating a unit of sales revenue may be the most relevant measures. These measures would seem appropriate for industrial, consumer and services companies.

The important point is to use those measures which experience has shown are the key indicators of performance in the business. An important objective in deciding on the approach to performance evaluation is to ensure that managers and other staff are motivated to attain corporate objectives. A well-designed marketing strategy which does not capture the imagination and support of managers at all levels is likely to fail. It is thus necessary, in selecting the performance criteria, to anticipate managerial reaction. Ultimately, all performance measures are subjective since the choice of which measure to stress in particular circumstances is a matter of judgement for the individual (Shapiro 1985, p. 231).

Benchmarking the marketing contribution

By evaluating its performance against competitors and predetermined stand-ards, the organization normally uses external independent benchmarks. Competitive benchmarking information may be obtained from a variety of sources: customers, suppliers, machinery manufacturers, technical journals and the trade press. Financial benchmarks such as inventory turnover and operating profit may be found in business publications and from marketing intelligence.

In Chapter 1 it was emphasized that the key organizational performance measure is profitability since profitability is the best measure of value created in the marketing system – value created for all participants. For accounting purposes most organizations calculate revenues and costs by product, factory overhead and business expenses. Customers are, however, the organization's most important asset and its only significant source of cashflow. The objective of the Guinness organization is not to sell Guinness stout but rather to attract, satisfy and retain target customers in a way that produces the profits of the business. These are the customer acquisition and customer retention objectives discussed in Chapter 6.

A focus on market-based value measures means that the appropriate accounting unit is not products, but customers. As discussed in Chapter 3 groups of customers with common needs form market segments. The organ-ization's profits are an aggregate of the profitability of the markets in which the organization competes less operating and overhead expenses which can-not be allocated. A worked example of product-based and customer-based accounting is shown in Figure 14.4.

Product-based		Market segment-based	
Market demand – units	45,000	Market demand – customers	11,500
Market share – units	12%	Market share – customers	12%
Unit volume	5,400	Customer volume	1,380
	€		€
Price/unit	1,500	Revenue/customer	5,869.6
Variable cost/unit	1,000	Variable cost/customer	3,934.8
Margin/unit	500	Margin/customer	1,935.6
Total revenue	8.10m	Total revenue	8.10m
Total variable costs	5.43m	Total variable costs	5.43m
Total contribution	2.67m	Total contribution	2.67m
Marketing expenses	1.08m	Marketing expenses	1.08m
Net marketing contribution	1.59m	Net marketing contribution	1.59m
Operating expenses	0.81m	Operating expenses	0.81m
Overhead expenses	0.27m	Overhead expenses	0.27m
Net profit	0.51m	Net profit	0.51m

Figure [14.4] Customer-based and product-based performance

Net marketing contribution represents the organization's profitability, at the level of the market. This is driven by the organization's marketing strategy and is a measure of the revenues derived from that market segment less direct expenses associated with marketing to and servicing them. Net marketing contribution specifically excludes overhead and operating expenses that are fixed, indirect or allocated expenses with little relation to performance in individual markets, e.g. corporate overhead. The profitability of a division within the organization is the profitability of individual market segments less operating and overhead expenses. The concept of net marketing contribution is important not only because it directly links customers to profitability, but also because it provides powerful leverage for the development of a more market-oriented organization.

There are a number of clear benefits of using the net marketing contribution approach. First, it integrates internal and external information that is not dependent on complicated and costly marketing research. It can be targeted at key strategic areas of the business, e.g. customer groups, and may be used in variance analysis – actual compared to plan. In the previous analysis the number of existing customers is taken as a benchmark, customer retention, which is then calibrated by the number of new customers acquired. Distinguishing between the customers lost and the new customers acquired during the period is important since the profit impact of customer retention strategies is markedly different from the profit impact of new customer acquisition. Greatest care should be given to customer retention as the cost of acquiring new ones is relatively higher, resulting in a higher overall cost of marketing.

Customer acquisition strategies require a narrow focus on the key product attributes that create the most value for customers and generate customer satisfaction. Each organization should measure the value it creates for customers relative to the competition in the recognition that there is no unique leading indicator of customer value that is optimum in all situations or can be accommodated within every budget. Similarly, as most markets are limited in size, the organization attempts to increase customer margins or profits for each customer. This may mean resorting to an analysis of customers based on the framework discussed in Chapter 2 to derive categories based on core, star and marginal customers. Another component of the net marketing contribution framework is that marketing expenses are treated explicitly – advertising, customer service, market research – which do not vary with volume in the short term. By measuring these expenses by market segment it is possible to calculate a return on marketing investment:

$$\text{return on marketing investment} = \frac{\text{net marketing contribution}}{\text{marketing expense}}$$

By ignoring the return on marketing investment, marketing is taken as an expense rather than an investment. The purpose of expenditure on marketing is surely as an investment that generates profits! In this way the productivity of marketing may be determined and compared to other investments in the organization. A marketing orientation in the organization is essential to ensure that marketing is treated as an investment and exposed to the same critical analysis as other elements of the organization's investments.

Aligning operations with marketing strategy

Marketing operations may be aligned with marketing strategy in a variety of ways. The most popular are sales quotas, financial controls and cash flow management techniques. It is necessary to maintain both a long-term and a short-term view in deciding the appropriate method.

Using sales quotas

Sometimes organizations monitor sales from one year to the next to judge performance, good or poor, depending on the trend. Other organizations adopt a more formal sales control approach, where sales are classified by country or region of a foreign market, by customer, or by product group. The next step is to select appropriate criteria to decide the sales level which should fall into each category. The organizations might develop an index to measure the importance of each of the categories used. An analysis of previous sales might be used to establish quotas which, over time, are adjusted to accommodate changes in the market. Usually, effective sales control systems require a variable standard, as implied here. If economic activity in a particular market is very high and developing rapidly, sales in that market might also be expected to grow. Similarly, a decline in the market should also be reflected in a downward adjustment of the quota. The assumption behind such a sales control system is that factors causing an expansion or contraction in the market beyond the influence of the company should not be used in evaluating sales performance.

Using financial controls

Having decided to expand, the company should ensure that the strategy to be followed is costed properly. It must also decide how to finance the strategy, from internal resources or from selected external sources. Finally, good financial management dictates that the expansion strategy should not jeopardize the survival and growth of the company.

The costs of entering and expanding in slow-growth markets are particularly high. Expansion for the company, even in industries which are not capital intensive, requires large cash outlays, the postponement of income, and skilful marketing and financial management. It is necessary to co-ordinate marketing strategies and financial planning if the company is to avoid the possibility of decline or even collapse.

The costing and financial control of marketing strategies are difficult tasks for most companies and can be very complicated. Marketing strategies are difficult to quantify; they refer to the longer term and consist of numerous steps with varying impacts. In regard to cost strategies it is difficult to separate costs into fixed costs, variable costs, and then to prepare cash flow projections. To overcome these difficulties, successful companies attempt to ensure that control rests with financial, marketing and general management people since such a team effort is likely to better understand the cost implications of marketing strategy.

Cash flow management

The significance of cash flow may be gleaned by observing the difference between profits and cash flow. Profit is the difference between the prices customers pay; and the total of prices the firm agrees to pay for all the inputs used in preparing the product or service for sale. Profit is the difference between agreed prices.

Cash flow is the difference between money lodged in the bank and the money withdrawn from the bank. The size of the cash flow and its direction, positive or negative, depend every bit as much upon when the money is lodged or withdrawn as upon how much is deposited or withdrawn. Profit is therefore very different from cash flow. It is possible to have a very profitable business but still fail due to poor cash flow performance.

The significance arises most dramatically as the company expands. A major benefit of examining the company's cash flow requirements related to a new marketing strategy is that the amount of financing required to carry out the anticipated expansion programme is determined. An instinctive urge to expand has led many organizations into the growth trap. In general a faster growth in sales should produce an attractive increase in profits. There may, however, be an adverse impact on cash flow. This in fact is often the situation. The company may experience impressive growth in many of its markets with an equally impressive growth in earnings and at the same time face a severe financial constraint. Sales growth in most businesses consumes cash. Consequently, during periods of rapid growth the cash flow is characteristically negative. It is perfectly normal to find that a business is growing profitably while bank balances are negative. Initial success brings with it rapid sales growth which requires considerable amounts of cash to service it.

Current earnings and profits

The managers of marketing operations evaluated on the basis of current earnings are likely to emphasize short-run profits and neglect long-run profits. This is particularly true if managers are frequently moved from brand to brand or product to product, which would allow them to avoid the longer-term consequences of their actions. These actions could involve reducing advertising and general marketing expenditures, reducing research and development work under their control, and not spending sufficient sums on staff training and development.

Too great an emphasis on sales promotion, for example, may be symptomatic of longer-term marketing myopia. Because circumstances can be different in different markets and outside the control of management, performance measures based on sales, profits or return on investment can be misleading at best and inaccurate at worst. For this reason companies frequently compare actual results with budgeted estimates. Variances in costs and revenues can then be examined to determine whether these are affected by outside events or caused mainly by management intervention.

Commitment to the customer

As a final note people generally behave the way they are measured so the organizational structure and performance measures used should be reinforced through compensation and performance. This means rewarding performance that serves the overall customer relationship. People are the key collaborators in the successful organization. While technology helps, success depends on people who understand the customer's point of view. This means that the organization should hire people who are better at managing connections than managing things.

Marketing success means focusing the entire organization on customers. Focusing on customers for many organizations means changing the way chief executives view their role, the way people are hired and trained and the way they are motivated and paid (Figure 14.5). It is necessary to inspire top down in most organizations. This means that managers must frequently visit customers and be involved with the sales team in actual selling and in training sessions. It is also important that everybody in the company from product designers to section managers and finance people be involved in marketing and selling. No longer is it acceptable that the sales person acts in splendid isolation. It is everybody's task to serve customers.

To be effective, managers must become advocates for the customer's needs. High pressure selling techniques do not have a place in customer-oriented companies interested in delivering value. It may be necessary that the organization changes its motivation system. The successful marketing organization builds into the remuneration package for managers measures of long-term customer satisfaction.

Above all, successful organizations speak to their customers and increasingly have established electronic contact with them. Indeed, most organizations usually find that it is necessary to maintain regular communications with customers and, if feasible, appoint an account executive responsible for

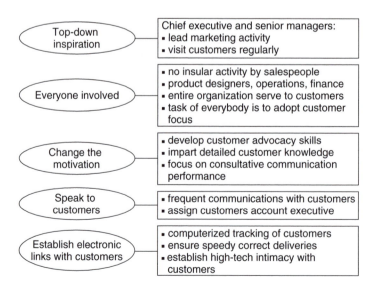

Figure [14.5]   Keys to better customer focus

the customer's business with the organization. Customer loyalty is built on attention, communication and organizational commitment.

References

Ambler, Tim and Kokkinaki, Flora (1997), 'Measures of marketing success', *Journal of Marketing Management*, **13**, 665–78.

Black, A., Wright, P. and Bachman, J. E. (1998), *In Search of Shareholder Value*. London: Pitman.

Clark, Bruce H. (1999), 'Marketing performance measures: history and interrelationships', *Journal of Marketing Management*, **15**, 711–32.

Doyle, Peter (2000), 'Valuing marketing's contribution', *European Management Journal*, **18** (3), 233–45.

Doyle, Peter and Hooley, Graham J. (1992), 'Strategic orientation and corporate performance', *International Journal of Research in Marketing*, **9** (1, March), 59–73.

Malone, Thomas W. and Laubacher, Robert J. (1998), 'The dawn of the e-lance economy', *Harvard Business Review* (September–October), 145–52.

Shapiro, Alan C. (1985), 'Evaluation and control of foreign operations', in *Strategic Management of Multinational Corporations: The Essentials*, Heidi Wortzel Vernon and Lawrence C. Wortzel, eds, New York: Wiley.

Srivastava, R. K., Shervani, T. A. and Fahey, L. (1999), 'Market based assets and shareholder value: a framework for analysis', *Journal of Marketing*, **62**, 2–18.

Index of authors

Index of firms

Index of subjects

Note: Page references in *italics* refer to Figures.